Translated Texts for Historians

This series is designed to meet the needs of students of ancient and medieval history and others who wish to broaden their study by reading source material, but whose knowledge of Latin or Greek is not sufficient to allow them to do so in the original language. Many important Late Imperial and Dark Age texts are currently unavailable in translation and it is hoped that TTH will help to fill this gap and to complement the secondary literature in English which already exists. The series relates principally to the period 300-800 AD and includes Late Imperial, Greek, Byzantine and Syriac texts as well as source books illustrating a particular period or theme. Each volume is a self-contained scholarly translation with an introductory essay on the text and its author and notes on the text indicating major problems of interpretation, including textual difficulties.

Front cover drawing: A group of bishops as depicted in the *códice Emilanense*, Biblioteca de El Escorial, Madrid (drawn by Gail Heather)

A full list of published titles in the Translated Texts for Historians series is available on request. The most recently published are shown below.

Caesarius of Arles: Life, Testament, Letters
Translated with notes and introduction by WILLIAM E. KLINGSHIRN
Volume 19: 176pp. 1994, ISBN 0-85323 368-3

The Lives of the Ninth-Century Popes (*Liber Pontificalis*)
Translated with an introduction and commentary by RAYMOND DAVIS
Volume 20: 360pp., 1995, ISBN 0-85323-479-5

Bede: On the Temple
Translated with notes by SEÁN CONNOLLY,
introduction by JENNIFER O'REILLY
Volume 21: 192pp., 1995, ISBN 0-85323-049-8

Pseudo-Dionysius of Tel-Mahre: *Chronicle*, Part III
Translated with notes and introduction by WITOLD WITAKOWSKI
Volume 22: 192pp., 1995, ISBN 0-85323-760-3

Venantius Fortunatus: Personal and Political Poems
Translated with notes and introduction by JUDITH GEORGE
Volume 23: 192pp., 1995, ISBN 0-85323-179-6

Donatist Martyr Stories: The Church in Conflict in Roman North Africa
Translated with notes and introduction by MAUREEN A. TILLEY
Volume 24: 144pp., 1996, ISBN 0 85323 931 2

Hilary of Poitiers: Conflicts of Conscience and Law in the Fourth-Century Church
Translated with Introduction and notes by LIONEL R. WICKHAM
Volume 25: 176pp., 1997, ISBN 0-85323-572-4

Lives of the Visigothic Fathers
Translated and edited by A. T. FEAR
Volume 26: 208pp., 1997, ISBN 0-85323-582-1

Optatus: Against the Donatists
Translated with Notes and Introduction by MARK J. EDWARDS
Volume 27: 220pp., 1997, ISBN 085323-752-2

For full details of Translated Texts for Historians, including prices and ordering information, please write to the following:
All countries, except the USA and Canada: Liverpool University Press, Senate House, Abercromby Square, Liverpool, L69 3BX, UK (*Tel* 0151-794 2233, *Fax* 0151-794 2235).
USA and Canada: University of Pennsylvania Press, 4200 Pine Street, Philadelphia, PA 19104-4011, USA (*Tel* (215) 898-6264, *Fax* (215) 898-0404).

Translated Texts for Historians
Volume 26

Lives of the Visigothic Fathers

Translated and edited by A. T. FEAR

Liverpool
University
Press

First published 1997 by
Liverpool University Press
Senate House, Abercromby Square
Liverpool, L69 3BX

British Library Cataloguing-in-Publication Data
A British Library CIP Record is available
ISBN 0-85323-582-1

Printed in the European Community by
Bell & Bain Limited, Glasgow

Contents

Acknowledgements

I would like to thank the participants of the Mediber internet group, members of the Department of Classics at the University of Keele, Gillian Clark and Roger Wright of the University of Liverpool, Peter Heather of University College, London, and Georgina Olivetto of the University of Buenos Aires for their generous help in the creation of this book. The errors which remain are, of course, entirely my own responsibility.

Abbreviations

AB	Analecta Bollandiana
AeA	Archivo español de Arqueología
BRAH	Boletín de la Real Academia de la Historia
Dial	Dialogues
DVI	The Lives of Famous Men
GC	The Glory of the Confessors
GM	The Glory of the Martyrs
HF	History of the Franks
HG	History of the Goths
ICERV	Inscripciones cristianas de la España romana y visigoda (ed J Vives, Barcelona 1942)
IHE	Inscripciones hebraicas de España (eds F Cantera Burgos & JM Millas Vallicrosa, Madrid 1956)
LV	Leges Visigothorum (ed K Zeumer, Hannover 1902)
PL	Patrologia Latina
PLS	Patrologia Latina Supplementum
REE	Revista de Estudios extremeños
Settimane	Settimane di studio del Centro Italiano di studi sull' Alto Medioevo
VP	Life of the Fathers
VPE	Life of the Meridan Fathers
VSA	Life of St Aemilian
VSF	Life of St Fructuosus
VSM	Life of St Martin

Church councils and their numbers have been italicised with any canons referred to left in Roman type thus: *3 Toledo* 4

INTRODUCTION

An Arab chronicler tells us that when Musa ibn-Nusayr, the conqueror of Visigothic Spain, returned to Damascus and was asked by the Caliph what had struck him most about the country he had subjugated he replied, 'The effeminacy of the princes'. This picture of the Visigothic domination of the Iberian peninsula as a period of barbarism and decadence intervening between the glories of Roman Spain and Caliphate of Cordoba has long coloured the histories of the period.[1] Recently however there has been a greater appreciation of the achievements of the Visigoths. These were considerable not only in terms of the intellectual achievements of the period, but also the creation of a political system whose stability is all the more apparent if it is contrasted with the kingdom's northern neighbour, Merovingian Gaul.

The architect of Visigothic Spain as it was known in the times the texts translated here were written was King Leovigild. Leovigild was made joint ruler of the Visigothic kingdom by his brother Liuva in AD 568 and became sole ruler in AD 572. He did not come to the throne in a prosperous hour. His realm had been racked by a civil war between Liuva's predecessor, Athanagild, and the king from whom he had seized the throne, Agila. Athanagild when launching his rebellion in Seville had called on Byzantine assistance and the emperor Justinian seeing an opportunity to further his dream of re-establishing the Roman Empire despatched troops to aid him. With this East Roman help Athanagild was able to beat off initial attempts to crush his rebellion and drive Agila back north to Merida. However he was unable to deliver a decisive blow against his king and in the ensuing stand-off Athanagild's Byzantine 'allies' busily set about re-establishing a province of *Mauretania II* centred on Cartagena. This may in fact have consisted of a group of key cities rather than a continuous strip of occupied territory. It was probably the obvious threat posed by the Byzantines to continued Visigothic supremacy in Spain which led the supporters of Agila to murder him and declare for Athanagild. Athanagild then turned on his 'allies' but while retaking some towns was unable to expel the

---

[1] Shaw [1906] is particularly notorious however this opinion is not dead - see Glick [1979].

Byzantines from the peninsula:[2] *Mauretania II* was to remain a feature of the Iberian political landscape until its final reconquest by Suinthila in AD 624. Other areas of the peninsula were also outside Gothic control. The largest of these was the Kingdom of the Sueves centred in the North West of Spain. However Cantabria and parts of La Rioja were ruled by an independent senate, Sabaria (probably located in Zamora) was also in rebellion and a further statelet existed in the North West centred around Orense run by the 'leading man of the place,' a certain Aspidius. To the south Cordoba had used the war between Athanagild and Agila to establish its independence and a similar situation obtained in the Orospeda mountains in the Andalusian Corderillo. Disintegration in Spain was not Athanagild's only legacy to the politics of western Europe. His daughter Brunhilda was married to the Frankish King Sigibert and henceforth played an active and colourful part in Frankish politics until her death in AD 613.[3]

Leovigild's main aim as king was to weld together his disintegrating realm and this he pursued with vigour. AD 570 and 571 saw the king campaigning against the Byzantines in the south and the liberation of Medina Sidonia from East Roman rule. The following year the rebel town of Cordoba and its possessions were brought inside the kingdom once more. These southern campaigns may well have been to arrest further Byzantine attempts at expansion. By AD 573 Leovigild thought his southern borders secure enough to march north. He first successfully turned his attention to the re-incorporation of Sabaria into the kingdom,[4] in AD 574 most of Cantabria was reconquered, and the rule of Aspidius was brought to an end in AD 575. The northern campaigns ended with advantageous peace made with the Sueves in AD 576. Leovigild then moved south again and re-established his rule in the Orospeda Mountains in AD 577. These years saw the Gothic kingdom re-established with a degree of authority that it had rarely enjoyed in the past. Leovigild celebrated his achievement by the foundation of a new town, named Reccopolis after his son Reccared. John of Biclarum states that by this time Leovigild had suppressed all the usurpers to be found

---

[2] Gregory of Tours, *HF* 4.8.
[3] See *VSD* below.
[4] Probably located in the modern Tras Os Montes e Alto Duero province of Portugal.

in the peninsula and overcome its invaders.[5] These invaders were of course the Byzantines and Leovigild's conflict with the East Roman Empire led to a remarkable degree of self-assertion on the Gothic king's part. Leovigild broke with the polite political fiction of the day which assumed the notional supremacy of the Byzantine Emperor. The foundation of Reccopolis was one aspect of this, the striking of coins in his own name another. He was also the first Gothic king to adopt full royal regalia, including possibly a crown.[6] Toledo became the *urbs regia* or the permanent royal capital of the Kingdom[7] and the metropolitan of Toledo began his gradual rise to de facto supremacy over the Visigothic church in the same way as the Patriarch of Constantinople came to head the Eastern Orthodox church.[8] In short Leovigild saw himself as building a parallel and fully independent 'Byzantium' in the West.[9]

A major setback came when Leovigild's son, Hermenegild, who had been appointed governor of Baetica, rebelled against his father. If we are to believe John of Biclarum's chronology of the rebellion, it is likely that at its outset Hermenegild declared himself a convert to Trinitarian Christianity. This was of considerable significance. It allowed Hermenegild to appeal, like Athanagild before him, for Byzantine support which he received albeit in a half-hearted fashion.[10] Moreover, it created potential support for the rebellion among the majority Hispano-Roman population. The Sueves were also Trinitarian (their previous conversion from Arianism may have been undertaken through a wish to establish a distinct identity from the Goths) and hence further potential allies. The rebellion spread over Andalusia and Extremadura as far as Merida; but there was to be no repeat of Athanagild's success. The initial gains of the rebellion may have been due to Leovigild campaigning in the North once more where we are told he captured part of the Basque country and founded the town of Victoriacum in AD 581.

The following year Leovigild raised an army against his son and retook Merida. He went on to besiege Seville, beating off an attempt to

---

[5] Jo Biclar., *Chron.* 51.
[6] Isidore, *HG* 51. For the possibility of a crown see Milne [1952] 48.
[7] Ewig [1963] 31-36.
[8] See Rivera Recio [1955].
[9] For Visigothic rivalry with Byzantium see Hillgarth [1970].
[10] See Gregory of Tours *HF* 5.38 & 6.43 and Goffart [1957].

lift the siege by the Suevic King Miro who had marched south to aid Hermenegild only to lose his life. Leovigild then refortified the old Roman town of Italica to mount a permanent blockade of Seville. In AD 584 the town was recaptured and the rebellion brought to a close. Hermenegild was sent into exile first to Valencia and then Tarragona, where he met his end at the hands of an assassin in AD 585. The Sueves paid dearly for their support of Hermenegild; in the same year as he was assassinated, Leovigild put an end to the Suevic kingdom's independent life and Arianism was re-imposed as the area's official creed.

Prior to raising the army to suppress the rebellion, Leovigild tried a religious solution to undercut his son. Previously unconcerned over the confessions of his subjects, he now initiated a policy of religious unity.[11] There was no attempt to impose the religion of the Goths, often referred to as Arianism,[12] on the population at large; rather Leovigild sought to impose a compromise creed in the form of Macedonianism (i.e. the acceptance of the parity of the Father and the Son, but the subordination of the Holy Ghost).[13] The king prayed ostentatiously at Trinitarian

---

[11] See Orlandis [1956].

[12] The Goths were converted to Christianity by bishop Ulfila in the late fourth century. Their version of Christianity was opposed to the conclusions of the Council of Nicaea held in AD 325 and hence became referred to as Arianism. Arianism, named after its first exponent, Arius, a leading *presbyter* in the church of Alexandria, was the main concern at Nicaea. It was a form of subordinationism which held that Christ, although not a mere man, was nonetheless created by God the Father and hence subordinate, not co-equal to him. Similar beliefs are held today by the Jehovah's Witnesses. There is, however, no evidence that Ulfila or the Goths were followers of Arius, see Heather and Matthews [1991] ch.5. 'Arianism' had simply become a term of ecclesiastical invective. For a parallel phenomenon see Cronin's [1985] discussion of 'Pelagianism'. This presents several problems with terminology, as the Goths referred to their brand of Christianity as the 'Catholic' faith as opposed to the 'Roman' faith of the Trinitarians, see Gregory of Tours, *GC* 24 and Jo.Biclar. *Chron* 58. Throughout this book 'Arianism' is used to denote the beliefs of Gothic Christianity prior to the Visigoths' conversion to Trinitarianism under Reccared, whereas 'Catholic' and 'Orthodox' are used in their modern Trinitarian sense.

[13] See Jo.Biclar., *Chron* 58. This passage where John refers to Leovigild's 'alteration of an old heresy by a new error' shows that it was not Arianism the King wished to encourage. The heresy takes its name from its chief early exponent Bishop Macedonius of Constantinople who was deposed in AD 360. Its supporters were sometimes known as *pneumatomachi*, 'those who fight against the spirit'.

shrines, probably as a way to claim them for the new creed.[14] In fact Leovigild appears to have made it as easy as he could for those who wished to change their faith; at an Arian synod called at Toledo in AD 580 he overcame one major difficulty for potential converts by establishing the principle that a second baptism would not be required to profess his new doctrine.[15] Nevertheless, there was also a darker side to his strategy: there seems no reason to think that Gregory of Tours' statement that those who did not go along with Leovigild's policy were persecuted with vigour is false.[16] Indeed, given that the king showed little mercy to Gothic political dissidents,[17] it would have been out of character for him to have shown less determination here. Leovigild's aim was surely the same as that of Justinian at the abortive 5th Ecumenical Council held at Constantinople in AD 553:[18] namely to construct a form of Christian belief upon which all his subjects could agree.

Leovigild notoriously failed in his attempt. His failure was in part due to the strong opposition of leading Trinitarian churchmen such as Leander of Seville, John of Biclarum, and Masona of Merida. Nevertheless, it would be unwise to attribute the king's defeat solely to their resistance.[19] Nor was Leovigild without his successes, at least one

---

[14] See Gregory of Tours, *HF* 6.18. He certainly seems to have wanted to appropriate prize Trinitarian relics for this purpose.

[15] Jo.Biclar., *Chron.* 55.

[16] *HF* 5.38, where it is said that in AD 580 the Catholic population of Spain suffered persecution which included confiscation of property, exile, corporal and capital punishment. Despite her formidable character, Gregory's statement that the chief instigator of this persecution was his wife Goiswintha is less credible and is surely simply a rhetorical denigration of Leovigild.

[17] Isidore, *HG* 51.

[18] The Emperor decided that Christ was 'incarnate and made man and crucified and is one of the Holy and Consubstantial Trinity.' (Theopaschism), *CJ* 1.1.6. This was acceptable to neither Chalcedonians nor the Monphysites, the two warring factions he wished to reconcile. The Emperor Heraclius' compromise of 'Monotheletism' (the doctrine that Christ had two natures, but only one will) was to fall on equally stony ground in the next century.

[19] The exile of at least two of these men, Leander and Masona, may well have been punishment for their support of Leovigild. It is easy to see how if Hermenegild had made Trinitarianism a rallying call a spiral of persecution could have evolved in this period.

xiv   LIVES OF THE VISIGOTHIC FATHERS

Bishop, Vincent of Saragossa, converted to his new creed.[20] Gregory of Tours remarks that there were few Catholics left in Spain as a result of the king's actions and though his statement may be provoked by a wish to show the faithlessness of the Goths, a race he despised, John of Biclarum also states that many Catholics converted to the new doctrine.[21] *VPE* also shows that there were Orthodox clergymen willing to go along with Leovigild, quite possibly for patriotic reasons. The dangers to the kingdom posed by rebellion were all too obvious and even staunchly Trinitarian contemporaries such as John of Biclarum had little praise for Hermenegild.[22] The early death of the king in AD 586 may well have been the most important factor for the failure of the Macedonianist policy.

Leovigild's son, Reccared, succeeded him, converted to Trinitarianism, and announced the conversion of the entire Gothic nation at *3 Toledo* in AD 589. Unsurprisingly this act provoked resistance in some quarters and the Burgundians saw fit to invade Septimania to exploit the situation. Although they were resoundingly defeated by Duke Claudius outside Carcassone, the victory was probably only bought with aid from Austrasia the price of which was the loss of at least two towns in Septimania.[23] Thereafter king and church marched together, albeit frequently out of step. National church councils were often used to promulgate legislation well beyond the ambit of normal ecclesiastical matters, but it would be wrong to see the kingdom as a theocracy or an absolute monarchy. The king always had the upper hand and would have been regarded as a poor monarch if he had not used his power to correct his flock;[24] however there was always the psychological restraint of the notion that a king's rule was ultimately granted by divine sanction and that as God's representative on earth the king *ought* to behave in certain ways and not in others.[25] This view, best summarised

---

[20] Isidore, *DVI* 43, *HG* 50.

[21] Gregory of Tours, *HF* 6.18, Jo. Biclar., *Chron* 58.

[22] John of Biclarum, *Chron* 55 notes that Hermenegild's rebellion did more harm to Spain than any foreign invader had managed to do.

[23] See Bulgar, *Ep* 3 = *PL* 80 112.

[24] Isidore *Etymologiae* 9.3, 'Indeed a man who does not set things to rights is not a king.'

[25] See *8 Toledo Tomus*, where Reccesvinth states 'all kings on earth serve and obey God'. Similarly his father Chindasvinth had declared to Braulio, 'Do not believe that I would be able to do anything that is displeasing to God', *Ep*.32.

by Isidore's dictum, 'You shall be king if you act rightly; if you do not you shall not be king', was, of course, frequently honoured in the breach.[26]

After Reccared's rule there were no attempts by outside powers to encroach on the Kingdom and the size of the Byzantine enclave was slowly whittled away until it was finally reconquered in its entirety by Suinthila in AD 624. Nevertheless dangers from abroad did remain in the form of *refugae* or refugees who had left the kingdom and then attempted to make a come back often with overt or covert foreign assistance. The danger posed by such individuals can be seen in the frequent laws enacted to control travel abroad. *4 Toledo* 30 (AD 633) forbade clergy who lived close to the frontier to communicate with foreign powers without express royal permission. King Chindasvinth passed a law on treason in AD 642 condemning *refugae,* or even those who wished to flee abroad, to death.[27] If the king decided to show mercy, the guilty would still be blinded and in all events their property was forfeit to the crown. *7 Toledo* 1 (AD 646) continues the theme, denouncing the damage caused by *refugae.* The canon decrees that any cleric of any rank who goes abroad is to be instantly deprived of his rank and anyone found aiding a rebel or foreign power is to be excommunicated. Nor was such legislation without foundation. Suinthila was overthrown in AD 631 by Sisenand who relied on aid from the Franks, Reccesvinth took four years to put down Froia's rebellion which had the support of Basques from outside the Kingdom, and in AD 672 Count Paul's rebellion against Wamba in Septimania again relied on Frankish assistance. Visigothic Kings therefore had good empirical precedents to make them suspicious of nobles or clerics who cultivated links with foreigners. Nor were such rebellions the only danger faced by a King, internal intrigue was also ever present. Usurpation was

---

[26] *Etymologiae* 9.3.4, '*rex eris, si recte facias: si non facias, non eris*', based on Horace, *Epistles* 1.1.59. Isidore's relationship with Suinthila warns of the reality underlying such sentiments. While he was fulsome in his praise of Suinthila in his *History of the Goths* which was published in the king's lifetime, Isidore is the first name in the list of bishops denouncing him at *4 Toledo* (AD 633) which was held two years after Suinthila's death. The *History of the Goths* commends Suinthila for acting as a father to the poor, but *4 Toledo* 75 denounces his avarice at the poor's expense. For a full discussion of the Visigothic ideology of Kingship see King [1972] ch.2.

[27] *LV* 2.1.8.

anathematised by *4 Toledo* 75. The following Council at Toledo decided that this canon should be read out at the end of every subsequent National Council and that conspirators against the king were to be excommunicated.[28] *6 Toledo* 18 (AD 638) called on a new king to avenge the murderers of his predecessor as if they were the murderers of his own father and anathemas were pronounced on conspirators. Chindasvinth's treason law dealt with internal rebels in the same terms as *refugae*. Again this plethora of legislation is symptomatic of a continual problem. Few Visigothic monarchs can safely be said to have died a peaceful death. Reccared's son Liuva II, was deposed, mutilated, and murdered by Witteric, who was murdered in his turn seven years later. Some have seen the cause of Sisebut's demise as due to poison rather than hypochondria. The young king Tulga was deposed by Chindasvinth, who promptly made him a monk, thus disqualifying him from further involvement in politics. In two and a half centuries of rule the Visigoths had thirty kings - therefore it is small wonder no one of them felt easy on his throne.

This lack of longevity among the Gothic Kings along with Gregory of Tours' remark on the 'Gothic Disease' of killing unpopular kings[29] has fuelled the conception of Visigothic Spain as a profoundly unstable state. However it must be remembered that Gregory, never an impartial witness at the best of times, was no friend of the Goths and that turmoil at the top of a society need not cause extensive disturbance to its essential structures and stability. A good example is Early Imperial Rome. Here again the Imperial mortality rate was alarmingly high, but few would describe the Principate as a chronically unstable period. It would be wrong therefore to use the admittedly lurid personal careers of many Visigothic Kings to infer that their realm led an equally precarious existence.

For a modern historian the lack of contemporary historical accounts of the kingdom comes as a great disappointment. While we have in the Visigothic Lawcode and the decrees of a multitude of church councils a detailed account of how life ought to have been lived in Gothic Spain,

---

[28] *5 Toledo* 7 (the reading of *4 Toledo* 75) and 4 (excommunication of conspirators). The council took place in AD 636.

[29] Gregory of Tours, *HF* 3.30. A phrase picked up by Pseudo-Fredegar, *Chron.* 4.82 when speaking of Chindasvinth's successful usurpation against Tulga.

we have less idea of how this law operated or did not operate.[30] There was no Gothic equivalent of Gregory of Tours; instead we have only Isidore of Seville's *History of the Goths* and the *Chronicle* of John of Biclarum, both of which provide only the barest account of events. Of Isidore's efforts EA Thompson has unkindly remarked, 'He could hardly have told us less, except by not writing at all.'[31] It is necessary therefore to turn to other texts to penetrate the opaque nature of the period and place flesh on the skeleton provided by our historical sources. Needless to say caution is needed in such a task. Given that writing, if not literacy, was mainly the preserve of churchmen, it is inevitable that the overwhelming majority of the texts available for study will be religious ones.[32] The most controversial of these are hagiographies. Hagiography was not, of course, written as a subgenre of social history, but for the spiritual edification of its readers. Nor is it satisfactory to approach hagiographic texts in the spirit of a historiographic gold prospector hoping that by panning the material it will be possible to extract historical nuggets while discarding the rest as dross and pious fiction. However, this does not make these texts unusable. While the modern mind approaches such documents with more prejudice than the works of the classical historians, in fact the claims that both sets of writings make are remarkably similar. History too in antiquity was written not in the spirit of Ranke as an impartial record of what 'really happened', but with an edifying purpose in mind, as can be seen from the comments of Tacitus and Livy.[33] There is an equal insistence on veracity in both cases and on the use of eye-witness accounts.

Why then are hagiographic texts regarded with suspicion? Two main sources for concern can be identified. The first is the seemingly stereotyped nature of many saints' lives. But need such 'stereotypes' be simply pious forgery? It is important to remember the power of rhetorical training on ancient writers. Tacitus' and Suetonius' 'good' and 'tyrannical' emperors exhibit many similar features, yet the general veracity of their accounts is rarely doubted. The use of literary convention need not in anyway rule out the truth of what is being

---

[30] For a masterly, though highly positivist synthesis of this evidence see King [1972].
[31] Thompson [1969] 7.
[32] For an optimistic view of the levels of literacy in Visigothic Spain see Collins [1990].
[33] Tacitus, *Annals* 3.65, Livy, *Praef.*

reported. On many occasions it is a way of enlivening the text and making it more understandable to its readers. The use of biblical parallels in our texts deserves special mention here. These parallels can be seen as playing two roles. The first is to show what kind of incident is being described by reference to a parallel incident which is well-known to the audience (it must be remembered that while the somewhat brutal world of the Old Testament in particular seems distant to modern readers, a Visigothic audience would have no such sense of distance). The historical incident therefore helps to elucidate the Bible. At the same time the Bible can be seen as revealing the underlying purpose in recent events and thus demonstrating to the reader that Biblical teaching was not a mere record of things in times gone by, but dealt with and explained events known from his own time. This secondary effect would have been of great importance to our hagiographers who are at pains to emphasise how God is at work as much in their own day as in the past.

Apart from such theoretical points, practical considerations also need to be taken into account. We must bear in mind that hagiography was meant to inspire emulation: the lives of early saints provided models for their successors who might well have tried to conform to these paragons of virtue. If life imitated art, as was clearly the intention, we ought not to be surprised that broad patterns of similar behaviour emerge in accounts of saints' lives. The refusal to become a bishop had a time-honoured pedigree which might easily have altered the perception of the desirability of this office in the eyes of later hermits. The spurning of an episcopal see, often followed by a reluctant acceptance may well have been regarded as *de rigeur* by those in pursuit of the religious life.

The single-minded purpose of hagiography also increases its seemingly artificial nature. For the hagiographer, unlike the biographer, the mere personal aspects of his subject would be of no interest whatsoever - we learn nothing for example of the appearance of Aemilian or Fructuosus, and the description of the Meridan Fathers is given to reflect their sanctity not for its own intrinsic interest. The stereotyped nature of the accounts is produced at least in part by this concentration on what are seen as the salient aspects rather than the entirety of the subject's life. All forms of professional life are stereotyped to some degree. A collection of the lives of famous footballers, for example, if stripped of incidental detail would show widespread correlation as would a less plausible collection of the lives of famous university lecturers.

The second and greater objection is hagiography's insistence on the miracles performed by the saints. Miracles were, and indeed are, not an optional part of a saint's life but integral to it.[34] At the end of St Mark's gospel Christ promises that those who believe in Him will perform miracles,[35] and earlier in His Earthly life He sends out His apostles with the power to heal and raise the dead.[36] Canonisation at the period we are considering was not a regularised procedure. Nevertheless, miracles provided a test of the holy man's true worth. However debatable a man's style of life might be, the performance of miracles marked him out as special. The nature of a man's life could then be used to check whether such supernatural acts were a product of divine intervention or black magic. Thus the combination of miracles and an approved way of life could bar the path to canonisation to both the sanctimonious and the sorcerer. The ability to perform miracles therefore was regarded as a necessary, though not sufficient, condition of sanctity.[37] Quite apart from this consideration, miracles were regarded as proof that Christianity was a living faith. The acts performed by the saints showed that God was still in the world and cared for His creation. This insistence on contemporary miracles can be seen in *VPE* here and in earlier martyrologies such as the *Passio* of Saints Perpetua and Felicity.[38]

The centrality of the miraculous presents a major problem in our own age which is only just learning to discard the claims of scientific positivism. Normal approaches include the dismissal of such material as simply embedded folklore, happy coincidence, or misunderstood forms of psychosomatic healing. Running alongside such methodology is frequently the view, either stated overtly or implied covertly, that the acceptance or fabrication of such stories on the part of the author means

---

[34] The modern Roman Catholic church demands one miracle for beatification and two for canonisation.

[35] *Mark* 16.17-18.

[36] *Matthew* 10.8.

[37] See the comments of Pope Innocent III to Hubert Walter over the canonisation of Gilbert of Sempringham: 'To be accepted for a saint among men in the church militant, two things are essential: holiness of life and mighty signs... separately [they] are not fully sufficient to establish sainthood here on earth' in Cheney [1955] 27-28.

[38] *Passion of St Perpetua and St Felicity* 1.

that he cannot be relied upon in the rest of his narrative. Quite apart from the fact that the blanket *a priori* dismissal of the possibility of miracles is a position equally irrational as an uncritical acceptance of all miracle stories, it would simply be wrong to regard either the authors of these pieces or their intended audiences as credulous fools in the way that the people of the early Middle Ages are frequently caricatured. Our authors are more than aware of the scepticism that some of their tales may engender, hence their continual insistence on their use of reliable and eyewitness accounts of the events they record. Indeed *VPE*'s ostensible reason for composition is to prove the veracity of the miracle stories in Gregory the Great's *Dialogues* by setting down parallel and irrefutable local examples of similar occurrences. This is a tradition which can be traced back to the New Testament where there is a frequent insistence on the contemporaneity and verifiability of the narrative[39] and continues in Christian writing - Papias, for example, remarks that eyewitnesses are more reliable than sources derived from book-learning.[40]

Nor can the fact that most miracles fall into stereotyped patterns be regarded a proof of the 'fictional' nature of these accounts. The gospels outlined the signs which accompany belief and therefore clearly it is these in which a hagiographer would take especial interest. Centring on such signs from the hagiographer's point of view is not recounting tired literary *topoi*, but sticking to the point at issue. Even therefore if a modern reader is predisposed to reject miracles, such an inclination must not lead him to the view that the author he is reading is necessarily uncritical in his work or that he is likely to fictionalise his narrative for ulterior motives.

While these considerations may seem to save hagiography from certain forms of criticism, unfortunately they only highlight other problems. The single-mindedness of the texts means that their context can sometimes be very distorted. If we are to look for a hagiographer's crimes, they are more often to be found in omission rather than fabrication. There is no mention in *VPE*, for example, of the civil war

---

[39] See *John* 19.35, 21.24; *Acts* 10.39,41; *1 Corinthians* 15; *1 John* 1.1-3; *1 Peter* 5.1; *2 Peter* 1.16.

[40] As quoted by Eusebius, *HE* 3.39. Papias was Bishop of Hieropolis in the early second century AD.

fought between Leovigild and his son Hermenegild, despite the fact that Merida was occupied by Hermenegild. These events occurred in the same period which occupies the longest narrative in *VPE*, the rule of Bishop Masona. To most historians they might be thought to have an important bearing on Leovigild's treatment of Masona, yet such secular considerations are of no interest to *VPE*'s author and hence omitted. Similarly we only incidentally hear of Leovigild's campaigns in the North of Spain in *VSA* because they serve to underline Aemilian's sanctity. The geography of Merida is described in *VPE* in ecclesiastical terms. This might be seen as an indication that a major alteration in the perception of the antique town had occurred by the Visigothic period with a civic geography being superseded by a sacred one, until we remember that the author is a cleric who would naturally be inclined use such landmarks. This would not necessarily have been the case with his fellow townsmen (the story of the two Oxford dons, one of whom knew his way around Oxford by pubs, the other by churches springs to mind) and to Merida's Arab conquerors the town's Christian buildings were insignificant compared to the surviving remains of the Roman period.[41] Similarly, although the activities of the Trinitarian church may have been of great importance in Merida, we must remember that they are recorded by a *parti pris* and may have been magnified accordingly. We learn nothing of the Trinitarians' Arian rivals nor of civil authority in the town, though both were certainly present. Masona indeed had cause to thank the latter when he was rescued by Duke Claudius. Moreover, as *VPE* is a history of individuals rather than a community, some other important individuals appear to have dropped out of the record. In John of Biclarum's *Chronicle* the priest John of Merida, is said to have been 'held in high esteem' in AD 578, but we learn nothing of this in *VPE*.[42] Similarly we are not told of the monk Tarra's problems at the monastery of Cauliana which we only know of because his appeal to

---

[41] al-Idrisi, for example, singles out the town's aqueduct, the 'arch of Trajan', and a mysterious mirror on the town walls. For a translation see Dozy & De Goeje [1969]. A similar view is taken by al-Himyari (translation by Maestro González [1963]) Only the walls (minus the mirror) are mentioned in *VPE*. The aqueducts and arch, substantial structures even today, are omitted entirely.

[42] Jo Biclar., *Chron.* 52.

king Reccared has survived.[43] Yet both these incidents fall in the timespan covered by the narrative dealing with Masona. Even Masona's own acts in AD 573 which earned praise from John of Biclarum are omitted from *VPE* presumably because they did not add to the hagiographer's overall purpose.[44]

Another hazard in dealing with the history of Visigothic Spain is the linguistic illusion of unity produced by the anachronistic use of the singular term 'Spain'. Although the Iberian peninsula appears at first sight to be a natural unit, in reality it is an extremely diverse area with many different regions. Similarly 'Christianity' too often creates a false monolithic impression to the mind. The texts selected here aim to cover the variations both in the geography and religious experience to be found in the Iberian peninsula in the Visigothic period. The scene of the events described, their protagonists, and authors differ strongly. Both the North and South of the peninsula are represented and the authors vary in rank from a King to the deacon of a church school. Their subjects are also diverse, ranging from the reclusive hermit St Aemilian to the metropolitan bishops of Toledo who were very much immersed in the world around them.

The earliest text is Sisebut's *Life of St Desiderius* (St Didier) of Vienne. Sisebut (AD 612-621) is perhaps the Visigothic King about whom we know most and yet his character remains enigmatic (though as questions multiply with knowledge, perhaps this is no surprise).[45] Described as the 'Maecenas of his age',[46] Sisebut took a keen interest in scholarship, being a predecessor in this respect of Alfonso X 'el Sabio' of Castile or al-Hakam II of Cordoba. Another parallel which springs readily to the English reader's mind is that of Alfred the Great of Wessex (AD 871-899). Sisebut was a friend and correspondent of Isidore of Seville who described the king as 'eloquent in speech, informed in his opinions, and imbued with some knowledge of letters.'[47] The bishop dedicated his treatise on Natural History, the *De Natura*

---

[43] *PL* 80 19-22.
[44] Jo Biclar, *Chron.* 30.
[45] For a general account of Sisebut see Orlandis [1992] ch.7.
[46] A reference to Gaius Maecenas, the close associate of the Emperor Augustus and literary patron of Virgil, Horace, and Propertius.
[47] Isidore, *HG* 60.

Rerum,[48] and the first draft of the *Etymologiae* to Sisebut. It is possible that Isidore's *History of the Goths* was commissioned by the king, though this was not completed until after Sisebut's death. Sisebut, however, was more than a mere patron of learning: he wrote a 61-line poem on the eclipses of the Sun and Moon in good Latin hexameter verse.[49] A collection of seven of the king's letters to a variety of correspondents has also survived,[50] along with the text translated here: the Life of St Desiderius. A further poem, *On the Ordering of Time*, has been occasionally, though incorrectly, attributed to him.[51] Sisebut's Latinity, particularly his prose, described by Fontaine as 'un galimatias grandiloquent et prétentieux',[52] is tortuous and highly variable in its quality which probably explains Isidore's qualified praise of his king. The variation in quality is so marked that some commentators have rejected Sisebut's authorship of the *Life* altogether and others have postulated a ghost writer. Certainly the King's poem is of much better quality than the *Life*, but this may reflect the nature of Sisebut's education in his second language and is more a warning that different registers of linguistic ability can be present in the same individual than a reason to deny authorship of the *Life* to Sisebut.[53]

Sisebut was deeply religious. Among his correspondence is a letter of encouragement to his illegitimate son, Theudila, who had announced to his father his wish to become a monk.[54] Another feature of the King's piety was his attempt to convert his Jewish subjects forcibly to Christianity. This policy drew a rebuke from Isidore[55] and was abandoned after the king's death.[56] Sisebut's actions left a powerful

---

[48] The preface begins 'Isidore to his Lord and son Sisebut', *PL* 83 963-1018; for a modern edition see Fontaine [1960].

[49] = *PL* 83 1112. For a modern edition see Fontaine [1960].

[50] *PL* 80 303-378.

[51] = *PL* 94 605.

[52] Fontaine [1960a].

[53] See, for example, Jiménez Duque [1977] 109 'Is the work his? From its subject and style apparently not.'

[54] Sisebut *Ep.*7 = *PL* 80 370-372. It could be suggested cynically that Theudila's decision to become a monk would solve a potential problem of royal succession for Sisebut and that was the reason for the king's enthusiasm.

[55] Isidore, *HG* 60.

[56] It was renounced by the church after the king's death by *4 Toledo* 57 (AD 633).

impression on the Jewish community in Spain which is recorded for us by the fifteenth century historian Saloman ibn Verga.[57]

It would be very wrong however to see Sisebut as a monkish *roi fainéant* interested only in the cloister and scriptorium. He was prepared to intervene actively in church politics - one of his surviving letters rebukes Eusebius, bishop of Tarragona, for failing to appoint the king's favoured candidate to the bishopric of Barcelona.[58] His reign also saw extensive military activity in the Asturias, possibly campaigns against the Franks in Cantabria,[59] and against the Byzantines whose power in Spain was broken by the King's vigorous action. By the end of Sisebut's reign the Byzantine province was reduced to a rump and was finally reconquered in its entirety by Sisebut's successor, Suinthila. Yet competent general that he was, Sisebut took little delight in battle. Pseudo-Fredegar records that after a victory over the Byzantines he lamented that his reign had seen such bloodshed.[60]

Perhaps these two aspects of Sisebut's character can be seen as combined in *VSD*. Given his piety, it comes as little surprise to find Sisebut writing a saint's life. Nor should his pious protestations that his work is for spiritual edification be simply dismissed out of hand; there can be little doubt that Sisebut did indeed wish to educate his readership in this way. His choice of saint, however, is much more striking. There was no cult of St Desiderius in Spain[61] and it might have seemed more natural for the King to write a life of a popular Hispanic saint such as St Vincent, Sta Eulalia, or Sta Leocadia, the patron saint of Toledo, whose cult he is known to have sponsored. The subject of the life has also been used along with its style to cast doubt on Sisebut's authorship. A variety of reasons suggest themselves to explain Sisebut's choice. It could be argued that Sisebut is writing an account which sets out the ideology of kingship championed by his friend Isidore of Seville and the consequences for royalty of failing to live up to this ideal.[62] Clearly it

---

[57] See his *Staff of Judah*.
[58] Sisebut, *Ep* 6 = *PL* 80 370.
[59] See Larrañaga Elorza [1993].
[60] Pseudo-Fredegar, *Chron.*, 4.33.
[61] He is entirely absent from the Mozarabic liturgical works we possess.
[62] Isidore expresses his views that kingship has a moral content in his *Etymologiae* 1.29 and *Sententiae* 3.48. See King [1972] ch.2 for a full discussion of Visigothic kingship.

would be best to tell such a cautionary tale of neighbou
than of one's own predecessors. Such a strategy wo
prestige and authority of the Visigothic monarchs
continued survival implied their adherence to such values, while at the
same time questioning the legitimacy of neighbouring kings. An attack
on the Franks would also appeal widely to Gothic prejudice and hence
increase the King's popularity. Moreover the Franks involved, Brunhilda
and Theuderic, appear to have used the instability in Spain at the time
of the Kingdom's conversion to Orthodoxy in AD 589 to extort territory
in Visigothic Septimania[63] - an event which would have only occurred
some twenty years before the writing of the *Life* and as such would
have been within the living memory of many of Sisebut's audience. A
reminder to his audience, especially those living in Septimania, of the
horrors of Frankish tyranny now that Merovingian Gaul was reunited for
the first time for two generations and so potentially posed a much
greater threat to Sisebut's Gallic possessions may have seemed no bad
thing to the king. Fontaine has suggested plausibly that the work could
also have been aimed at preserving good relations with the new unitary
state created in Gaul by Clothar II after his defeat of Brunhilda in AD
613.[64] Clothar is depicted by Sisebut as the innocent victim of
Brunhilda's ambitions, whereas in fact he appears to have been heavily
implicated in Austrasian conspiracies to remove her. If this is the case,
Sisebut can be seen as neatly killing two birds with one stone, both
creating hostility to further Frankish expansion in Septimania and at the
same time presenting an account of recent events in Burgundy which
could not be faulted by its current ruler.

As an attack on Brunhilda Sisebut's work must be seen as a striking
success spawning as it did a 'leyenda negra' of Brunhilda the wicked
queen which persisted virtually unchallenged until late in the nineteenth
century.[65] Sisebut draws a much more black and white picture of what
took place at the saint's martyrdom than our other accounts.[66] Desiderius
is portrayed as steadfast in his righteousness and enjoying absolute

---

[63] See Bulgar, *Ep.*3 = *PL* 80 112.

[64] Fontaine [1980].

[65] The first major revisionist work casting doubt on Sisebut's account of Brunhilda was
that of Kurth [1891].

[66] See in particular the anonymous *Passio Sancti Desiderii*, printed in *AB* 9 (1890).

popular support, neither of which seems entirely certain when compared with our other, admittedly later, sources, and Brunhilda is set up as the evil genius of Burgundy, in contrast to Pseudo-Fredegar's account which attributes the demise of Desiderius as much to Bishop Aridius of Lyons as to Brunhilda.[67] The success of Sisebut's strategy could not have been immediately predictable. Pope Gregory the Great was a correspondent and apparently a friend of Brunhilda[68] and Gregory of Tours also has good things to say of her.[69] Nonetheless, presumably because it fitted the plans of the rulers in both Spain and Gaul, the black legend of Brunhilda set up by Sisebut was to become the norm. One example of its success in Spain is that the author of *VPE* draws heavily upon Sisebut's work to depict paragons of good and evil. Sisebut died in AD 621 in confused circumstances. Isidore is unclear whether natural causes were to blame or whether the king took an overdose of a medicine.[70]

The second text, St Braulio of Saragossa's *Life of St Aemilian* (San Millán de la Cogolla) may also exhibit rivalry with the Franks. Born in c.AD 585, Braulio was a pupil of Isidore of Seville. He appears to have returned to his home town of Saragossa in c.AD 619 and in AD 631 became bishop there succeeding his elder brother John. He was to hold this post until his death in AD 651. In the preface to *VSA* we are told that Braulio intends to involve his great friend Eugene in writing the *Life* a task which the priest Fronimian has asked him to undertake. As Eugene was appointed bishop of Toledo in AD 645, *VSA* must have been written between AD 631-645, probably towards the end of this period if Braulio did indeed lose his initial draft of the work as he claims. Apart from *VSA*, we possess a collection of 44 letters from Braulio's correspondence,[71] and a poem in praise of St Aemilian, though this is rejected as spurious by some commentators.[72] A sermon on St Vincent of Saragossa has also been occasionally attributed to Braulio.[73]

---

[67] Pseudo-Fredegar, *Chron.* 4.32.
[68] See Gregory, *Reg. 6.5,* 6.50, 11.62 (thanking her for helping Augustine's mission to Britain) and 13.6 (praising her for building a *xenodocium* in Autun).
[69] e.g *HF* 4.27.
[70] Isidore, *HG* 61.
[71] For an English translation see Barlow [1969]. The text of the letters was recently edited by Riesco Terrero [1975].
[72] eg by Barlow [1969].
[73] *PL* 54 501-504 (collected with the works of Pope Leo the Great).

Many attempts have been made to give Braulio a more extensive family by extrapolation from his letters. The priest Fronimian, for example, is often claimed as his brother on the strength of Braulio's use of 'frater' at the beginning of *VSA*. However, given the context of one priest writing to another, this is to enter into the realms of unsustainable conjecture.[74] Braulio, like his master, was a learned man and a keen collector of books who acquired an extensive library.[75] He appears to have been familiar, at least in the form of excerpts from *florilegia*, with a substantial number of classical authors.[76] He was clearly highly respected by the Spanish church. His friend and former archdeacon, Bishop Eugene II of Toledo, turned to him for advice on the problem of an irregular ordination at Toledo and its consequences;[77] and the Spanish church as a whole mandated him at *6 Toledo* (AD 638) to write in its defence to Pope Honorius who had accused his Iberian brethren of laxity in their attitude towards the Jews.[78] Braulio's relations with the kings of his day were varied. He pleaded with Chindasvinth not to remove Eugene from Saragossa to Toledo, but failed to persuade him,[79] though it could be argued that Chindasvinth, who wished to create an intellectual centre in Toledo, paid Braulio a great, if perhaps unintentional, compliment in removing his favourite pupil to boost this project. Braulio was more successful when he wrote to Chindasvinth along with bishop Eutropius and Count Celsus urging him to share his throne with his son Reccesvinth.[80] The letter reveals a man very much involved in the secular as well as the ecclesiastical concerns of his day. Reccesvinth who became sole ruler on his father's death seems to have

---

[74] Lynch [1938] is a prime example of this flawed methodology.

[75] See especially Braulio, *Ep.* 42, where Braulio begs Taio to send him copies of the works of Gregory he had found in Rome, and *Ep.* 44, where St Fructuosus in his turn asks for various books from Braulio.

[76] See, for example, Braulio *Ep.* 11, where Braulio misquotes Horace, *Ars Poetica* 21f. and ascribes the quotation to Terence.

[77] Braulio, *Ep.*35-36.

[78] Braulio, *Ep.* 21.

[79] Braulio, *Ep.*31-33.

[80] Braulio, *Ep.* 37.

been on friendlier terms with Braulio than his father. He may well have employed him to draft his new law-code, the *Liber Iudicorum*.[81]

Braulio's choice of Aemilian as a subject for hagiography is much less surprising than Sisebut's choice of Desiderius. There is little reason to doubt that it was motivated by the request from his colleague Fronimian as a piece to be read out at a local mass in honour of the saint as mentioned at the beginning of the *Life*. The scope of Aemilian's cult at this time is difficult to ascertain. It appears that its appeal was increasing at the time Braulio wrote as *VSA* is one of the works that St Fructuosus requests from him.[82] Braulio may well have seen part of his task as firmly to entrench a source of popular veneration within the ambit of the Orthodox church. In the terminology of Benedict's or Isidore's monastic rules Aemilian, an uneducated shepherd, would have come close to being categorised as a *Sarabaite*, or self-inspired hermit who recognised no superior earthly authority.[83] Such behaviour was, wisely in an age when wonder workers were rife, heavily frowned upon by the church.[84] Braulio therefore labours the point that Aemilian in fact had a mentor for his spiritual development and that the cultivation of correct spirituality requires such a teacher. Similarly Braulio's audience is explicitly warned off imitating some of Aemilian's heterodox

---

[81] Braulio, *Ep*.38-41 refer to a manuscript sent by Reccesvinth to Braulio for correction. This is commonly held to be the draft law-code. Even if it is not, the incident shows the prestige of Braulio as a man of learning at the royal court in Toledo. See King [1980] for the possibility that this was a major enterprise.

[82] See *contra* Fernández Alonso [1955] who believes the cult was purely local when *VSA* was written. Aemilian's cult as San Millán de la Cogolla was to grow rapidly in the early Middle Ages. Count Fernán González adopted him as his personal saint and after St James he came to be regarded as the patron saint of Spain and of the Reconquista. He is normally depicted astride a horse holding a sword and Christian banner. He remains the patron saint of Aragon. Despite pious assertions that Aemilian himself was a monk and that a monastery was founded on the site of his cell on his death, there is no evidence for a monastery here until the early tenth century AD.

St Fructuosus' request and Braulio's reply can be found in the surviving collection of Braulio's letters. *Ep*.43-4. In *Ep*.44 Braulio states that Fructuosus is close to him 'in family ties'. This has been used to argue that the two men were related. Such arguments however ignore the metaphorical use of such terms among churchmen; see for example Jerome, *Ep*.103 to Augustine where there is no question of a family link.

[83] St Benedict, *Rule* ch.1, Isidore, *De Eccl.Off.* (= *PL* 83 537-826) 2.16.24.

[84] See *4 Toledo* 53 (AD 633) & *7 Toledo* 5 (AD 646) for attempts to suppress unauthorised hermits. For a modern treatment of this topic see Markus [1990].

practices as these according to the author will place their souls in danger. Such control might have been thought all the more necessary in Northern Spain which had a history of extreme ascetic spirituality, the most notable example being the Priscillianist movement.

Braulio's text was the basis for a lengthy poem in praise of the saint by Gonzalo de Berceo written in Romance in the thirteenth century AD. Gonzalo fleshes out much of Braulio's narrative, alters some to fit his own day, and includes additional material which may be drawn from earlier traditions not used by Braulio or simply be later legendary accretions to his account.[85]

Throughout *VSA* there are strong parallels with Sulpicius Severus' life of St Martin of Tours. These can be regarded in several ways. A naive view would be that these incidents are merely hagiographic *topoi*. However, given the prestige that St Martin came to enjoy in Gaul and the intense rivalry between the Franks and the Goths, the creation of a Gothic parallel to Martin, a parallel who on certain occasions goes one better than his Frankish model, could also be seen as an attempt by Braulio to demonstrate the superior spirituality of the Gothic church. This may have been of particular importance in the North of Spain as the conversion of the Sueves of Galicia to Orthodoxy in c.AD 550-560 is attributed to miracles performed by St Martin's relics by Gregory of Tours.[86] Braulio's lionisation of Aemilian could therefore have been an attempt to show that the Gothic church too had produced saints of unimpeachable Orthodoxy in the North of Spain in this early period. Such an assertion would legitimate the rule of the Gothic church in the region and also that God's representatives on earth, the Visigothic kings.

The third and most extensive text translated here is the *Lives of the Meridan Fathers*. The episodes described by it are all associated with the town of Merida in Extremadura. The town had a long history, being the former Roman city of Colonia Augusta Emerita which itself was built on the site of a previous Iberian village in 25 BC by Carisius for veterans (*emeriti*) of the *X Gemina* and *V Alaudae* legions, hence its name. The Roman city was founded as the capital of the Roman province of Lusitania and has often been thought to have been the capital of the diocese of the Spains in the Late Roman period (Étienne

---

[85] For a full account of Gonzalo's poem see Dutton [1967] & [1992].
[86] Sulpicius Severus, *De Virtutibus S Martini* 1.11.

[1982]), but recent archaeological finds at Cordoba now make this hypothesis unlikely. The town was occupied by the Alans in AD 409, fought over by the Vandals and Sueves in AD 429, and in AD 439 the Suevic capital was established here; the Suevic king Requila dying in the city in AD 448. A Gothic attempt to take the town in AD 457 under Theoderic failed and the city was finally captured by the Goths under Euric in AD 468. It was heavily involved in the civil wars between Athanagild and Agila (AD 551-555) and between Leovigild and Hermenegild (AD 579-584), being recaptured by Leovigild in AD 582. Leovigild celebrated his victory by striking coins and the legends 'Victoria' and 'Victor'.[87] It is not known when Christianity arrived in Merida; the first attested bishop is bishop Martial, mentioned by Cyprian, *Ep*.67. The town appears to have been a bastion of Orthodoxy. Bishop Hydatius led the attack on Priscillian who along with his supporters was driven out of the town when he attempted to take the fight to Hydatius there in AD 380.[88] It resisted the Arab invasion fiercely, falling on 1st June AD 713. It was liberated on 15th January, AD 1228 by Alfonso IX of León.

The author of the *Lives* is unknown and merely identifies himself as a deacon in the ecclesiastical school of Sta Eulalia at Merida. A weak tradition, beginning only in the fourteenth century, assigns the text to an otherwise unknown 'Paul the Deacon', but there is little substance for this belief. The name 'Paul' was probably generated by the *Lives'* reference to the *Dialogues* of Gregory the Great and the fact that a deacon named Paul wrote a life of Gregory.[89] The greatest interest of the text from the historian's point of view is the light that it throws on life in Merida in the seventh century, albeit from a very specific point of view. Unfortunately the date of the text is disputed. *VPE* draws on Gregory's *Dialogues* which provide a *terminus post quem* for the work in its present form. The date of the *Dialogues* has recently been challenged by Clark and if his hypothesis were correct the *Lives* would need substantially postdating, a view shared by some older commentators.[90] The shift of the date would make the account of the

---

[87] See Miles [1952] nos 38-41.
[88] Psuedo-Priscillian, *Tractate* 2 p.40 = *PLS* 2 1439.
[89] = *PL* 75 41-60.
[90] For example Menéndez Pelayo [1880] t.1 183.

town given much more suspect. However there are major problems with Clark's position, and at present there seems no reason to change the traditional date for the composition of the *Dialogues* (AD 593/4) or consequently assume that the *Lives* is other than a seventh century composition.[91] It is not known exactly when the *Dialogues* became known in Spain. Clearly some of the works of Gregory were not available in the peninsula in the bishopric of Eugene of Toledo (AD 646-657) as can be seen from a letter sent to the bishop by his envoy to Rome, Taio.[92] However other works were known and had a high reputation - Braulio asked Taio to send him manuscripts of the new works he had uncovered as quickly as possible.[93] Unfortunately there is no way of telling in which of these two groups we should place the *Dialogues*. Nevertheless, the fact that Isidore does not list the *Dialogues* in his *DVI* must create a suspicion that they were one of Taio's discoveries. Garvin attempting to rationalise the rough chronology given in the text itself, believes that *VPE* was composed during the episcopacy of the bishop who succeeded Bishop Renovatus, the last named bishop in the work. This is most likely to have been bishop Stephen (AD 633-638). But Garvin's date seems a little too early and *VPE* is probably a product of the mid rather than the early seventh century.[94]

At the beginning of the text we find that the stated purpose of the author is to justify the stories found in Gregory the Great's *Dialogues* and provide local parallels to them. The statement is of interest for two reasons. First, it might lead us to think that there was scepticism about some of Gregory's stories at the time *VPE* was written. It also suggests that Gregory's *Dialogues* were a popular work in Spain and that our anonymous author was attempting to exploit this popularity by producing a local version of such tales. It is also possible that given the rising pretensions of the see of Toledo at the time of writing that *VPE* was an attempt to assert the importance of the Meridan church and its bishops.[95]

---

[91] See Clark [1986] & [1987] and *contra* Meyvaert [1988] and Straw [1989].
[92] Taio, *Ep. ad Eugenium = PL* 80 725.
[93] Braulio, *Ep.*42.
[94] The view of Díaz y Díaz [1981].
[95] See the comments of Fontaine in Díaz y Díaz [1981].

If the author was attempting to cash in on the popularity of Gregory's *Dialogues*, he must have left his readers bitterly disappointed. Although the first episode in *VPE* does bear some resemblance to the *Dialogues*, the rest of the *Lives* is very pedestrian compared to Gregory's stories and contains very little in the way supernatural incidents. The work is a compilation of lives of various priests in Merida with little attempt to link the different episodes. The deacon first speaks of an incident which occurred in his own day, but then moves back into the past. The largest narrative concerns Bishops Paul, Fidel, and Masona and the struggle of the Trinitarian church in Merida to preserve itself and the relics of the town's patron saint, Sta Eulalia, under the last of the Arian kings of Spain, Leovigild. Throughout the account there is a strong element of selectivity, as discussed above. If a centre of unity is to be sought, the best candidate would be the devotion to Sta Eulalia, the patron saint of the town, which the author shows. Sta Eulalia was a young girl martyred in Merida in c.AD 304. An account of her martyrdom can be found in Prudentius, *Peristephanon Martyrorum* 3. Prudentius' account describes, with some exaggeration, a 'tumulus' or richly decorated church erected in her memory. Damaged by the Vandals in AD 429, it was soon repaired.[96] A larger church was built on the same site in the 5th Century which remained in use throughout the Visigothic Period. The building fell into disuse during the Arabic occupation of the town, but was rebuilt after the *reconquista* in the thirteenth century and remains in use today. Outside the church were trees said to flower on the cult day of the saint (December 10). Eulalia enjoyed more than local fame; the church in Berceo where St Aemilian served as a priest is said to have been dedicated to her (*VSA* 12) and Fructuosus of Braga visited her shrine on his pilgrimage to the south of Spain (*VSF* 11). Her cult is also found beyond the peninsula: she was the subject of a sermon by St Augustine;[97] is found listed with other saints on a mosaic in the church of St Martin in Ravenna;[98] mentioned by Venantius Fortunatus[99] and

---

[96] Hydatius, *Chron. Min.* 2.21.
[97] *Serm.Morin.* 2.
[98] *CIL* 11.281.
[99] 8.3.170 'De Virginitate'.

Gregory of Tours in Gaul;[100] and by Aldhelm in both his prose and verse works on virginity.[101]

According to Bishop Pelagius of Oviedo (AD 1101-1129) Eulalia's relics were rescued from the Arabs by King Silo of the Asturias (AD 774-783) and placed in Oviedo cathedral. A group of relics said to be Eulalia's remain there to this day. However, the metric martyrology of Wandelbert implies that saint's bones remained in Merida and have subsequently been lost.[102] There is no reason to assume that the saint is a syncretic version of the Celtiberian goddess Ataecina as is sometimes asserted.[103] The most prominent monuments of the saint to be seen in Merida today are the *Hornito de Santa Eulalia*, a small shrine built from reused blocks of classical and Visigothic masonry on the supposed site of Eulalia's martyrdom by the side of the Church of Santa Eulalia in AD 1617, and a crude statue of the saint (decried by Almagro [1957] as in 'lamentable bad taste') erected on a column consisting of reused classical column capitals which was originally erected in AD 1652 and moved to its present site in the Calle de Santa Eulalia near the church in the last century.

St Ildefonsus, bishop of Toledo AD 657-667, is the author who had the most impact in future years of all those translated here.[104] He is said to have entered the monastery of Agali as a youth against the wishes of his father who came and attempted to extract him forcibly.[105] Having survived this attempt to cut his religious life short, Ildefonsus went on to become abbot of the monastery and was present at *8* and *9 Toledo* while holding this office. No trace of Agali now remains. The *Deeds of Ildefonsus* attributed to Cixila (bishop of Toledo AD 744-753), but in fact written in the 10th century, speaks of Ildefonsus serving in a church

---

[100] *GM* 90.

[101] *PL* 89 146, 273.

[102] *PL* 121 621, written c.AD 842.

[103] For a modern account of the saint's cult see Recio Veganzones [1992].

[104] We possess two accounts of Ildefonsus' life - one by his successor Julian of Toledo the *Baeti Ildefonsi Eulogium* (*PL* 96 43-44) and another purportedly by Cixila, archbishop of Toledo AD 774-783, but in fact dating to the 10th century, one manuscript in fact attributes the work to a predecessor of Ildefonsus, Helladius...

[105] Julian of Toledo, *Beati Ildefonsi Elogium* = *PL* 96 43-44.

dedicated to Sts Cosmas and Damian located on the outskirts of Toledo and this is normally accepted as a reference to the monastery.[106] Pseudo-Cixila also asserts that Ildefonsus was a pupil of Isidore of Seville. However, as Ildefonsus himself makes no mention of this fact and speaks of his predecessor Eugene II as his master, it would be unwise to trust this statement, which was probably motivated by the author's wish to link together the two most famous churchmen of Visigothic Spain. In fact Ildefonsus seems poorly informed about Isidore's oeuvre. Braulio gives a much better catalogue of his books than does Ildefonsus in his *DVI*.[107]

Ildefonsus succeeded Eugene II as bishop of Toledo in AD 657. It was while bishop that he wrote his *On Famous Men*. Although it is purportedly a continuation of Jerome and Isidore's books of the same name, *DVI* is in fact much more narrowly focused than either of these two works. The 'famous men' described all have Spanish connections and Ildefonsus concentrates in particular on his predecessors at Toledo. In doing so he reveals much about the internal politics and divisions of the See; facts which, while fascinating for the modern historian, appear to have been less attractive to his immediate successors. *DVI* is omitted from the list of Ildefonsus' writings by his successor Julian of Toledo, probably because of the disreputable light it cast on the Toledan church. Throughout the work there is an insistence that many of those listed showed their holiness through their lives rather than by leaving writings. A certain defensive tone may be detected here. Perhaps the scholarly Ildefonsus sensed Isidore of Seville and his pupils overshadowing his own predecessors. Ildefonsus himself, however, could not be accused of academic sloth or worldly inaction. He both expanded his old monastery of Agali and built a convent for nuns near Toledo at Deibense.[108] He was also one of the few Spanish church fathers to engage in Theology. His *On the Perpetual Virginity of Mary against Three Unbelievers* which takes to extremes the fashion of the day for expressing ideas in

---

[106] Pseudo-Cixila, *Gesta Sancti Ildefonsi* ch.1 = *PL* 96 44 (here the work is named *Vita...*)
[107] The relationship between Braulio and Ildefonsus' accounts is explored by Vega [1961].
[108] Julian of Toledo, *Beati Ildefonsi Eulogium* = *PL* 96 43.

as many parallel forms as possible,[109] can be regarded as the foundation of the Cult of Mary in the Peninsula. The *Deeds of Ildefonsus* relates that Mary visited Ildefonsus and presented him with a gift.[110] This gift became fixed in tradition as a chasuble and the most frequent medieval depiction of Ildefonsus shows him receiving a chasuble from the hands of Mary. Ildefonsus' other works deal with a mixture of pastoral topics (e.g. *On Progress from the Spiritual Desert*, a treatise on how the recent convert should progress to achieve heaven, and theological themes such as *On the Persons of the Trinity* (now lost) and *On the recognition of one baptism*.[111] Other works attributed to Ildefonsus are several prayers to Mary found in the Visigothic Orational[112] and the mass 'Erigamus quaeso' for 18th of December held in honour of Mary.[113] A collection of sermons, mainly from Rheims, also became attached to his name in the Middle Ages.[114] Ildefonsus died on 23 January AD 667 and was buried at the feet of his predecessor Eugene II.

One absentee from Ildefonsus' list of Isidore's books in the chapter devoted to him in *DVI* is the *History of the Goths*. Some have seen this omission in a sinister light and as indicating that there was friction between the bishop and the king of the day, Reccesvinth. This, it is suggested, is why there was no national Church council while Ildefonsus was occupied the see of Toledo. However, Reccesvinth was not on bad terms with the church as a whole as has been seen from his friendly relations with Braulio of Saragossa and if he had been on poor terms with Ildefonsus, it seems unlikely that the bishop would have thought an apt way to gain his revenge was to attempt to conceal a minor work of Isidore's. It is more likely that Ildefonsus was trying to preserve Isidore's reputation by suppressing a book which had ended with an encomium of King Suinthila, and hence distance him from this king

---

[109] The so-called 'synonymous style'.

[110] Pseudo-Cixila, *The Deeds of St Ildefonsus* ch.7 = *PL* 96 48.

[111] Ildefonsus' surviving works can be found in *PL* 96 1-330. They are listed, along with his lost works, by Julian of Toledo, *Beati Ildefonsi Eulogium* = *PL* 96 44.

[112] n°s 202, 209, 222, & 223. The so-called *plegarias marianas*.

[113] Férotin [1912] 50-53.

[114] Maloy [1971].

who had been denounced by the church after his death at *4 Toledo* in AD 633.

The final text in this collection, *The Life of St Fructuosus,* is entirely anonymous. We are given no indication of the author or his rank in the text. Previously the work was assigned to Valerius of El Bierzo, but such an attribution is impossible and is based only on Valerius' undoubted devotion to the saint.[115] The date of composition must fall after the death of the saint in AD 665. As one source used by the author is *VPE,*[116] it must also postdate this work. However the author claims to have used sources who knew the saint so the work ought to have been written soon after Fructuosus' death. Díaz y Díaz plausibly places the date of its composition around AD 680.[117]

The manuscript tradition of *VSF* is complex and several large sections only occur in one codex, O. These have been left in the translation in brackets. In fact the whole document itself appears to be an awkward combination of two accounts of the saint, a biography and an earlier aretology, which are less than perfectly joined together at chapter 8.[118]

Like Ildefonsus, the author of *VSF* draws a contrast between writing on sacred topics and practicing the holy life. However, unlike in Ildefonsus' work, this time there is nothing defensive about the parallel. Isidore of Seville and Fructuosus are compared to the sun and moon, but it is Fructuosus who is the greater light and who reveals the inner secrets of the soul as opposed to Isidore, the lesser light, who merely catalogues the secrets of the world. The work, as we possess it, is a tract to promote monasticism. Fructuosus' journeys through the peninsula founding monasteries as he goes are presented in Pérez de Urbel's words as 'a holy Odyssey'.[119] We are told nothing of Fructuosus' life as bishop of Braga and indeed the very fact that he was, albeit probably briefly, bishop of Dumio is entirely omitted. Nor is there any mention

---

[115] For a linguistic analysis which casts grave doubt on the case for Valerius' authorship see Nock [1946].

[116] See Nock [1946] and Maya [1992] for a list of the passages drawn upon.

[117] Díaz y Díaz [1974] & [1981].

[118] See Díaz y Díaz [1953].

[119] Pérez de Urbel [1944] 392.

of Fructuosus' secular activities. The impression that the hagiographer wishes to give us is of an otherworldly founder of monasteries who was more or less indifferent to the secular world around him. Indeed at times, for example in the account of the foundation of the monastery of Nono in chapter 14, we are given a vision of Fructuosus creating a parallel world to the one around him. The impression our author wishes to give is that accepted by Jiménez Duque namely that Fructuosus was 'first and foremost an ascetic'. Certainly his rule for Compludo suggests that asceticism occupied an important place in his thought. Nevertheless we must be aware that our impression is conditioned by what the hagiographer wishes to tell us. Fructuosus was born of a noble family and his conversion to the religious life appears to have happened in his thirties. It is not beyond the bounds of possibility that he had been forced into monastic life by changes in the fortunes of his family.[120] Even so he was not uninterested in the world around him, as his petition to King Reccesvinth for the release of those imprisoned for conspiracy in the reign of Chintila (AD 636-639) shows.[121] Given Fructuosus' background, it is easy to see why Reccesvinth would have been alarmed by his plans to go abroad, even if the journey was as the hagiographer insists merely for the purposes of pilgrimage.

As can be seen, therefore, Spanish hagiography gives us a wide spectrum of viewpoints from which to look at the history of the Visigothic period. The nature of hagiography means that care has to be taken in the use of these texts; in particular we must always be aware that the vistas we are offered are presented to some purpose and often not quite what they seem. Nevertheless it is equally important not to over-emphasise the divergence between hagiography and history, nor to assume that the former has no regard for historical truth whatever and as such can provide material only for the history of ideas. The historical setting of their material was important for these authors, as their own writing makes clear. This should come as no surprise given that Christianity has always emphasised its historical context. There is no

---

[120] Relegation to a monastery was a useful way of marginalising an individual's influence on secular politics. See, for example, Chindasvinth's treatment of Tulga.
[121] *PLS* 4 2092-2093.

doubt that these texts do provide important information for the history of ideas, but a careful historian will also find in them a valuable aid to reconstruct the social and political history of this fascinating period.

Lives of the Visigothic Fathers

Translator's notes

Early versions of all these texts are to be found in Migné's *Patrologia Latina*. However, the following texts have been used as a basis for translation here.

Life of St Desiderius - J.Gil, *Vita Desiderii* in *Miscellanea Wisigothica* (2ed, Seville, 1991)

Life of St Aemilian - L.Váquez de Parga, *Vita S.Emiliani: edición crítica* (Madrid, 1943)

Lives of the Meridan Fathers - A.Maya Sánchez, *Vitas Sanctorum Patrum Emeretensium* (= *Corpus Christianorum* 116) (Turnholt, 1992)

On Famous Men - C.Codoñer Merino, *El <<De Viris Illustribus>> de Ildefonso de Toledo* (Salamanca, 1972)

Life of St Fructuosus - M.Díaz y Díaz, *La Vida de San Fructuoso de Braga* (Braga, 1974)

As these translations are intended for historians, very few notes on linguistic usage have been included.

Direct quotations from the Bible have been italicised and taken from the Authorised Version.

King Sisebut

LIFE AND MARTYRDOM OF SAINT DESIDERIUS

1 For imitation by the present generation, for the edification of men to come, and that Holy deeds may be done in future times, I have decided to write the life of the Holy martyr Desiderius. Whatever has been brought to our notice by reliable testimony, I have recorded in a bare style rather than in one loaded down with glistening words, begging that the Lord who gave, and not without reason, power to that man to perform miracles, might come and be present with us and, rousing my mind and tongue from sloth, grant me, unworthy though I am, the ability to tell of the passing of these deeds.

2 This man, born from a Roman family of noble stock, was dedicated to the Lord from his cradle, and certainly came from a glorious line. When he reached that age at which it is fitting to be educated, he was entrusted to the study of letters. In almost no time having surpassed his teachers as the power of his intellect grew and having fully learnt the art of grammar, he expounded the divine scriptures, committing them to memory with astonishing rapidity.[1] For he possessed great mental ability, a most prodigious memory, the sharpest of minds, great eloquence in speaking,[2] and, what is more important than all of these things, he was governed in all his deeds by his conscience. He brought food, as the gospels tell us to do, to the hungry, drink to the thirsty, gave solace to the weak and imprisoned, hospitality to the stranger, and clothes to the naked.[3] Pride, the enemy of all virtue, did not possess him, nor did he fall a victim to slothful drunkenness. He was not burdened with gluttony nor did insatiable lust corrupt him. Deceitful lies did not shake his resolve nor did the fatal love of money tempt him. When he grew strong in such virtues given by divine favour and, on leaving behind his boyhood, had not spent his youthful years lusting for

---

[1] cf the young Christ and the doctors of the Temple, *Luke* 2.42-47.
[2] The anonymous *Passio Desiderii* (= *PL* 124 435-442, also printed in *AB* 9, 1890) states that Desiderius possessed an extensive personal library. Desiderius' learning and love of secular writings can be seen from the fact that he began to teach secular grammar lessons and was rebuked by Gregory the Great for doing so. The Pope warned him that the praises of Christ and Jupiter were uneasy bedfellows, *Ep.* 10.54.
[3] cf *Matthew* 25.35-36.

earthly things,[4] he gained an ever increasing reputation as a good man and his works of light given by the true light shone forth in many regions.

3 Finally the people from many towns asked that he might become their bishop in order that they might receive his blessings. He, humble as he was, was unwilling to take up so great a ministry, saying that he was unworthy and would be unequal to the task. Finally the church at Vienne obtained their wish and made him, unwilling but persuaded by their many prayers, their bishop.[5] As bishop with his careful preaching he weaned the litigious from their anger, the false from their mendacity, the greedy from their rapacity, and the lustful from their sins. He tamed drunkenness through sobriety, overcame greed through abstinence, conquered discord through acts of charity, calmed pride by his sincere humility, and through his vigilance shook the worst doubter from his torpor. He taught them to be generous in the giving of alms, sincere in prayer, firm in friendship, just in legal matters, and surefooted in all their doings. All these things he taught more by example than by words, knowing that the Lord will come and judge not a man's eloquence, but his deeds.

4 While he was doing these things with Christ's aid, the enemy of the faithful and ally of the faithless, the devisor and friend of death, groaned and, having armed himself with every kind of weapon, came himself to fight the soldier of Christ. But in no way did the cunning of the enemy prevail: his dread wickedness harmed not the man of God whom the grace of the Redeemer armed with weapons of the Spirit. At last, the worthless spirit stung with his serpent's venom a man of evil

---

[4] cf 4 Toledo 25 (AD 633) 'All ages from adolescence incline towards wrong, and nothing is as unstable as the life of an adolescent'. As a result of this philosophy young novices were kept together under the charge of an elder monk 'in order that they might spend the years of this capricious age not in indulgence but in ecclesiastical discipline.'

[5] The unwillingness of holy men to take up ecclesiastical office is a common feature of hagiography, see VSA 12, VSF 18. Bede tells a similar story from seventh century England of St Cuthbert, Life of Saint Cuthbert 24 (= PL 94 763-765). For the importance of popular approval in the appointment of bishops see Gregory of Tours, VP 6.4.

mind,[6] and poured from itself allegations of crimes into his entrails like cups of poison so that spewing forth disgraceful slander which he made all the greater through his own malign nature, he defamed the athlete of God.[7] He won over some colleagues to his cause and, deceiver that he was, forged certain documents to incriminate the servant of the Saviour. At that time Theuderic,[8] a man of extreme stupidity, ruled with Brunhilda, a woman who enthused over the worst vices and was a great friend to the wicked.[9] Both of them made a pact with a certain lady who was of noble stock, but deformed in mind. Though called Justa, she was

---

[6] Though unnamed, this is likely to be Protadius, Brunhilda's lover. He received honours in the same year that Desiderius was exiled (Pseudo-Fredegar, *Chron.* 4.24) and became *Major Domus* of the palace two years later at Brunhilda's instigation (Psuedo-Fredegar, *Chron.*4.27).

[7] cf *1 Corinthians* 9.25, *2 Timothy* 2.5 and especially in this context *4 Maccabees* 6.10 where Eleazar endures torture like a noble athlete.

[8] i.e. Theuderic II of Burgundy (AD 596-613), son of Childebert II and grandson of Brunhilda.

[9] Brunhilda's political career would merit a book in itself. Born c.AD 545-550, a daughter of the Visigothic King Athanagild, she was married to Sigibert of Austrasia. (Unlike the Frankish princess Ingund who refused to abandon her Catholicism when married to the Goth Hermenegild, Brunhilda had no scruples about abandoning her Arianism for the Trinitarianism of the Franks.) After Sigibert's assassination in AD 575, she governed as regent for their son Childebert II. Rouche [1986], noting Brunhilda's philoRoman tendencies, sees her rule as a direct imitation of that of the Great Empress-mothers of the Byzantine Empire. Childebert reached his majority in AD 585 and on the death of King Guntrum in AD 592 acquired the Kingdom of Burgundy. However his sudden death in AD 596 led to the two kingdoms remaining separate entities. Both were ruled by sons of the dead King, Austrasia by Theudebert II (aged 9) and Burgundy by Theuderic II (aged 7). Brunhilda remained in Austrasia until at least AD 602 (Pseudo-Fredegar, *Chron.* 4.19 places her expulsion in AD 599; Gregory the Great however, *Register* 8.4, 9.213, was still urging the Queen to help reform the Austrasian Church in AD 602). The Austrasian nobility then finally forced her from the court and as a result she fled to Burgundy where she was well received (Kurth [1891] believes the account of the expulsion to be a fiction of Pseudo-Fredegar's). Here she exercised a dominant role in the Kingdom's politics until her death in AD 613. Sisebut's account of the Queen is extremely hostile as are all later accounts of her life (e.g. the anonymous *Passio Desiderii*), but earlier accounts such as those of Gregory of Tours are far more neutral in tone. Gregory the Great corresponded with the Queen in friendly tones, thanking her in particular for her help to the mission to England. For a revisionist account of the Queen's life which perhaps overstates its case see Kurth [1891]. A more balanced discussion of the Queen's policy is provided by Rouche [1986]. For the process of her demonisation see Nelson [1978].

in fact a wicked woman. She had a glorious name, but her acts were all the more inglorious for it. While lacking in goodness, she was possessed of an astounding number of vices, and, though a stranger to the truth, was never dissociated from crime. Summoned before the council, she made complaint that she had once been ravished by the most blessed Desiderius.[10] All were amazed that the servant of God should have been implicated in such things, but thought that the charges against him would be cast aside. Those presiding, however, in accordance with schemes they had devised beforehand, pronounced in their rash temerity a most unjust sentence against an innocent man. Straightaway men were sent to carry out his punishment. They stripped him of his office and banished him into exile to a monastery on an island.[11] His exile was the highest good fortune, these insults made his sanctity all the more obvious, and his degradation brought him that happiness which lasts for eternity.[12] In his place was appointed a false priest, Domnolus, a servant of the devil, who soiled himself by his disgraceful deeds to the same degree that the man of God flourished through his manifold virtues.

5 Indeed in that monastery, while the blessed martyr was leading his blessed life, a poor man came and made some gestures to ask for alms, for his mouth had been closed by dumbness since birth and an everlasting silence had shrouded his ability to speak. The almighty Father was not unheedful of the prayers of his soldier, granted a miracle, and made him speak. According to what we have heard, it was impossible to conceal the good deed that had occurred, and reports spreading everywhere brought it to the attention of the multitudes; whence it came about that a host cf the sick hastened to him in the hope of recovering their health nor did the works of the Lord fail to come forth to cure those for whom the servant of God had prayed to the Lord our Saviour.

---

[10] Pseudo-Fredegar, *Chron* 4.24, places this incident at the Council of Chalons-sur-Saône held in AD 603. There is no mention of Justa here or the rape allegation here; Desiderius' opponents are named as Brunhilda and Aridius the bishop of Lyons.

[11] This is named as Livisium by the *Passio* (ch.3). Its location is unknown.

[12] Sisebut's account is in stark contrast to that given by the anonymous *Life of Arigius of Vapin* (printed in *AB* 11) ch.11 where Desiderius is said to be on the verge of suicide because of the accusations made against him and is only consoled by the ministrations of Arigius.

6 It is sufficient, I think, to have given a general account about the cures he brought about; but lest elegant diction should open the door to those reading with a critical eye to complain that this is far too brief, I have made the point of recording in this work to the best of my ability some particular instances of his deeds. Some old men who lived always in darkness and dwelt in night having no sight, were called back through the grace of God to the longed-for bright light of day by the prayers of the Soldier of the Lord which cast aside their terrible veil of darkness.

[When three lepers were cured by the holy Desiderius]

7 After this, three lepers oppressed by the burden of their sickness came to him to be cured.[13] A disfiguring leucosis had entered their bodies and their wretched limbs were covered with scars. There was an unbearable stench and a vile, unspeakable yellowish flux was eating away the scabbed skin from their scalps and tearing out from its roots in a horrible fashion almost all their shorn hair[14] from the festering contagion.[15] The servant of God took their afflictions from the sufferers and restored them hale and hearty to their proper health.[16]

8 While the Lord was bringing such things to pass through the kindness that is his wont, the talk of the people brought to the attention of Theuderic and Brunhilda alike that the servant of God had been exalted through his magnificent miracles and that, through the grace of the power of the Almighty, he had been given power to heal which could

---

[13] It is highly likely that as Desiderius performed healing miracles one of them would involve lepers. However Sisebut's singling out of this incident may have other intentions. Leprosy was seen as a disease of the soul as well as of the body and as an allegory for heresy (Isidore, *Allegoriae* 221 = *PL* 83 127 & *Quaestiones in vetus testamentum, In Leviticum* 10-12 = *PL* 83 327-330) and sin - Isidore saw in the leper cured by Christ an allegory for the world polluted by sin cured by his incarnation (*Allegoriae* 150 = *PL* 83 118). The disease was also commonly connected with sexual licentiousness. The incident could therefore be seen as a demonstration of Desiderius' Orthodoxy and of his innocence of the charge brought against him. For a general discussion of leprosy see Brody [1974].

[14] Lepers' hair was often shorn to mark them as outcasts from the community, see *Lavaur* 21 (AD 1368).

[15] cf Julian of Toledo, *Hist.Wamb.* 19.

[16] A much shorter account is found in *Passio* 6.

not be denied. At once trembling and filled with the great dread, they looked into this great matter, seeking to know how they might return to the exile his rightful office or whether they should make the man they had condemned in vain an exile for ever. While they were carefully investigating the solution of this problem, divine vengeance justly fell upon the sorcerer who had devised the fell plan and had brought about the condemnation of the soldier of Christ. I have written of his horrible end in full detail in the account which follows. This poisonous individual of ill-omened memory was detested for his many vices and crimes. Amongst his vile habits was a criminal lust for material possessions and love of slander. These were the things which roused up a great host of the people to kill this vile monster. For one day while he was standing in the presence of his patron, Theuderic, he was dragged to his destruction by a rioting mob of Burgundians. His bloody corpse was ripped apart and left scattered around.[17] In this way the wretch lost both his life and his damnable soul and on the point of his death of his own free will entered the gates of Hell.[18]

9 What shall I say of her who was unjustly called Justa and might justly have been called Injusta? Whom the bloody one had carried off as if she were his own possession? At the same time when he of whom we have just spoken rightly perished, with equal justice a evil spirit entered her and this deadly slave coming again from his hellish dwelling place drove out the entire stock of lies which she had once devised; the confession produced was as follows: 'I know that I have done wrong to a servant of God, I know the cause of this, and I know all the more the penalty that I deserve. Let the Almighty Avenger allot the blame for these things to their deviser, Brunhilda. Let Him bring down this penalty on her in His vengeance, and let His avenging right hand inflict on her the torments of torture; she whose fleeting blandishments dragged me to my doom, whose damnable gifts brought me to death, and whose fatal promises to being beyond hope of salvation.' When she stopped speaking, the author of all sin put an end to her life, bound and

---

[17] Protadius was lynched by Burgundian troops at Quierzys while campaigning with Theuderic II against his brother, Theudebert II, in 605 AD, Psuedo-Fredegar, *Chron.* 4.27.
[18] Presumably Sisebut is implying that as a sorcerer Protadius, when attacked, called on the devil to deliver him.

choked as she was, and carried her off with him to burn for ever among the flames of vengeance.

10 On hearing of their agents' death, both Brunhilda and Theuderic were panic-stricken.[19] They were all the more afraid as they thought that these things had been brought about by divine judgement, and, lest they should pay a similar price, feigning piety, ordered that the man of God who had been taken from his See in vain should be appointed once more to govern the church for which he longed. Desiderius did not heed their pleas and declared firmly that he would stay where he had been exiled. Again and again they begged him not to deny them his presence, to be clement, and to forgive their deceitful scheming. This sincere repentance softened his sincere heart and its abundant benevolence opened the way for the servant of God's return.[20] When the blessed man appeared before them, these wretches flung themselves at his feet, striving to be well thought of by a man whom they had once exiled through a fraudulent judgement and that he might expiate from so great a crime certain others whom a deadly association had involved in their crimes. He in his clemency pardoned what they had done and, as the Lord tells us to, did not remember the trespasses of those who had wronged him, but forgave them.[21]

11 Then when Domnulus and his great host had been expelled from the church in dishonour, Vienne rejoiced and received back her steersman. They rejoiced that the sick had found their doctor, the oppressed their consolation, and that the hungry now had food. The Lord granted a host of blessings to the church at Vienne; for the presence of the holy man, bringing God's mercy on them, put an end to the calamity of natural disasters, the many terrible plagues, and the wild riots which afflicted the whole city: things which had indubitably befallen them because of their shepherd's absence when he had been banished.

---

[19] In fact Brunhilda managed to bring about the demise of two of those who took the lead in killing her favourite, having one, Uncelen, mutilated and stripped of his wealth (Pseudo-Fredegar, *Chron.* 4.28) and another, the Patrician Wulf, executed (Pseudo-Fredegar, *Chron.* 4.29).

[20] Desiderius was recalled from exile in AD 607, Pseudo-Fredegar, *Chron.4.32.*

[21] *Luke* 11.4.

12 I have decided to speak of three of his miracles, though my feeble narration afflicted as it is by a lack of skill will scarce manage to achieve this. Once when a huge crowd came to visit him and he ordered that they should be furnished with food and drink as is the custom, he was told by a servant that the wine most in demand was the shortest in supply. He swiftly ordered that the jar from which this wine had come be shown to him and, when he had made the sign of the cross over it, through the grace of the Saviour it became full of a noble, fragrant wine.[22] In this way the crowd which had gathered were filled by both his blessing and this wondrous drink.[23]

13 Again when he had mortified his body through a long and rigorous fast and punished it by reining in the desires of the flesh for a time, not because of his worldliness, but to discipline himself, a fellow priest came to visit him in a place not far from the city. Amongst the other topics in their friendly conversation was one about divine portents. And when Phoebus passed through the day's span and had crossed the meridian of the hours[24] and the appointed time to eat was nigh, suddenly, cutting through the heavens a she-eagle, the queen of birds, appeared in the shimmering sky, flying swiftly with her whirring wings.[25] She was carrying prey from the sea and set a creature of the waters[26] before them. They took it with great joy and dined upon it, giving thanks to the Lord our Provider.[27]

14 Some time before his glorious martyrdom, it happened that he lit a lamp by the altar, filling it with his own hands, whence it poured forth afar its beams of light. Though no one had refilled it, the oil grew

---

[22] cf the wedding at Cana, *John* 2.6-10.

[23] cf *Passio* 5.

[24] cf Virgil, *Aeneid* 6.535-536. The emphasis may reflect Sisebut's own interest in astronomy.

[25] cf Dracontius, *De Laud. Dei* 1 240-1 (= *PL* 60 711) 'then departed through the heavens the feathered flying tribe in whirring flight, striking the air with their wings.'

[26] cf Ausonius, *ep.* 24.19.

[27] cf the Crow which brought bread to Saints Paul and Antony in the desert, Jerome, *Vit.Paul.*10. The *Passio* makes this link with Antony explicit. See also *I Kings* 17.6 where ravens feed Elijah as he makes his stand against King Ahab. The parallel is particularly apt for Sisebut given the influence of Jezebel over Ahab.

greater and became too much for the vessel.[28] Indeed the lees of the overflowing oil is gathered with great veneration and through God's grace puts to flight the pain of sickness, restoring those suffering from illness and bringing them health once more. Let these outstanding events which my feeble style has been able to outline suffice as an account of his life.[29]

15 Now with the Lord's aid, I will give an account, as it has been reported to me, of his sufferings and how he commended his blessed soul to our almighty Lord. When Theuderic and Brunhilda were seen not to be helping, but harming their realm, ruining rather than ruling it, to be full of vice, and, falling back into the sin of perjury, sacrilegiously abandoning the promises of their oath, treacherously not attempting to live up to it, nor leaving one single crime or evil unattempted, the martyr of God, bishop and examiner of their sins, sounded forth the trumpet blast in the manner of the prophets and whole-heartedly took himself off to drive out all their sins in order that he might make God's people those whom the devil had made strangers to him,[30] mindful of this saying of divine authority: *He which converteth the sinner from the error of his ways shall save a soul from death, and shall hide a multitude of sins.*[31] But the *vessel of wrath,*[32] the fomentor of vice, and fruit of damnation brought them bitterness not sweetness, harshness not gentleness, and balms that brought death instead of salvation. The enemy besieged their hearts all the more fiercely and the cunning serpent held them captive in his power. Nor were they whom the deadly brigand had bound in ever tighter chains able to walk freely to the gate of salvation. Sated with his lethal drafts, they began to bark out rabid rantings against the servant of God, spewing forth their disgusting words in raucous tones. But mortal threats did not break the martyr of God, nor did the wrath of perjurers weaken him, nor the frenzy of the mad

---

[28] cf the miracle performed by St Martin of Tours, Sulpicius Severus, *Dial.*2.3, where the saint makes oil flow from a phial sent to him.

[29] cf *Passio* 3 where the miracle is said to have happened in Desiderius' period of exile.

[30] cf Pseudo-Fredegar's account of St Columban's encounter with Theuderic and Brunhilda. This also involves a capitulation by the secular rulers to the holy men followed by their reneging on their undertakings, Pseudo-Fredegar, *Chron.*4.36.

[31] *James* 5.20.

[32] *Romans* 9.22.

move him. He held himself immobile to suffer in order that justice be carried out until he should receive from the Lord the promised heavenly realm.

16 The enemy of mankind, on seeing his steadfast constancy, occupied completely the hearts of Brunhilda and Theuderic which he never left, treating them as if they were his own home, and in imperious tones drove them all the more to the doom which they deserved, for he promised them the foremost place in the execution of justice if they could extract the soul of Christ's soldier from its mortal chains.[33] Straightaway the king's sacrilegious mouth, full of foul speech and ever ready-armed with impiety in debate, snarled out his sentence: 'It pleases us to see Desiderius, critic of our life[34] and enemy of our deeds, stoned[35] and afflicted with all manner of tortures.'[36] Swiftly his servants and accomplices in crime who were sinfully to carry out the command to do this vile deed gave their word that they would do so without as much as listening to the sentence. Nor did the struggles of his task lie hidden to the martyr of God, who had been marked out, or rather forewarned, to receive as his prize the crown of martyrdom.

---

[33] Sisebut's pun here is that Theuderic and Brunhilda will indeed have the foremost place in imposing their justice on Desiderius, but they will also find themselves to the fore when divine judgement is meted out.

[34] According to Dill [1926] 193, 'Merovingian Kings enjoyed all the freedom and variety of the East in their conjugal relations.' In fact the Merovingians do not seem to have abandoned polygamy until the seventh century, NcNamara and Wemple [1976]. Theuderic, while never marrying, sired four bastards. It is unsurprising, therefore, that Desiderius found much about which to complain. The king was also criticised for living with concubines by St Columban who refused to bless his bastard children and was exiled as a consequence, Jonas, *Vita Columbani* 32-47 (= *PL* 87 1029-1038). Sisebut may have intended his readers to draw a parallel between Theuderic's treatment of Desiderius with that of Herod Antipas towards John the Baptist described at *Matthew* 14.3-12, both being sinners and under the control of a woman.

[35] For stoning as a punishment in Merovingian Gaul, see Gregory of Tours, *HF* 3.36 (the lynching of the tax-collector Parthenius), 4.49 (an official military punishment inflicted by Childebert on some of his own troops), 9.35 (a mob attack on Count Waddo), and 10.10 (a civil punishment inflicted by Childebert on his major-domo, Chundo).

[36] Pseudo-Fredegar, *Chron.* 4.32, makes Brunhilda and Aridius of Lyons the prime movers in Desiderius' condemnation.

17 When he saw his pre-ordained day, he was dragged all of a sudden from the bosom of his church by the hands of infidels[37] and led to execution like an innocent man condemned to die. A huge crowd wept piteously that the care of so great a shepherd had been taken from them, crying out thus: 'Why holy father do you desert your sheep? Why are you leaving your flock to perish? Do not, we beg you, send us into the jaws of wolves, lest we, your sheep, who until now have fed on the sweet nectar of flowers, should, without our bishop to watch over us, be cut and blooded by tearing thorns and sharp briers. For this will surely happen and is in accordance with scripture which says that the absence of the shepherd scatters the sheep for his presence is their greatest boon.[38] In no wise will we let you be torn from us. And if the life we desired is denied us, we can endure with you a glorious death.' To this the blessed martyr replied calmly: 'Your resolve is to be admired, but your devotion to me cannot be praised. For if the Tartarean portals of Hell besiege us, the gates of that deadly inferno try to close upon us, if the terrible crackling flames of the pit attempt to overwhelm us, it will be better to fight the enemy with spiritual weapons. Now since we are summoned to serve in the heavenly host, we all believe truly that we shall return among the gleaming squadrons of angels, the apostles and those who took up their teaching, and the resplendent companies of martyrs. Allow, I beg you, your shepherd to go to the shepherd of all shepherds so that the whole flock, its shepherd going on before them, might more easily come to the place which has been made ready for them.'

18 So he spoke, and suddenly a raging throng of madmen appeared, bringers of death, terrible to look upon, with savage expressions, brutal eyes, of hateful appearance, and terrible in the way they moved. They had twisted minds, depraved morals, lying tongues, spoke in obscenities, and while haughty in appearance they were empty of substance and thus vile both within and without. Paupers in goodness, but wealthy in evil and enslaved to wickedness, they were enemies of God, though eternal friends indeed of the devil, men all too willing to be damned. This

---

[37] The *Passio* says that Desiderius was arrested by three Counts: Effa, Gaisefred, and Beto.

[38] cf *Matthew* 26.31, *Mark* 14.27, *Zechariah* 13.7.

accursed band, vile madness giving them their arms,[39] seized him and their stony heart poured a rain of stones over the martyr of God. The terrible missiles flung by the madmen missed him: the harsh nature of flints turned aside in its flight, and the very sound of the stoning showed itself to be the servant of the servant of God. The stones, though not living, were alive to God's laws and yielded to the Deity. Human hearts, which could have turned and drawn near to pity, alone remained unmoved. As he breathed out his spirit, one of them seized a club and broke the holy man's neck.[40] Thus his soul abandoning its fleshy guise and freeing itself from corporal chains, joined triumphant with its colleagues in the starry heavens.[41]

19 In this unskilled way I have given, to the best of my ability, an account both of the life and of the death of Christ's soldier, which, although it may displease the learned through its excessive crudeness, shall nonetheless, having cast aside verbal pomposity, ennoble the humble and the believer. And now we have told of his life, miracles, and his most glorious end, it remains to describe the perdition and death of the sinners. When Theuderic, abandoning God or rather having been abandoned by God, rejoiced at the news that the servant of God had died, he was seized by a disease of the bowels, ended his vile life and a friend of death came to possess it for eternity.[42]

---

[39] cf *Aeneid* 1.150. The context of this quotation seems particularly appropriate given Sisebut's description of Theuderic's men, but it is unclear whether the King would have known the whole Aeneid or just snippets of it.

[40] cf *Passio* 9. This locates Desiderius' place of martyrdom at Calonera, the modern St-Didier-sur-Chaleronne. The account of the martyrdom is slightly different in form - Desiderius is struck by a single stone and then beheaded with a sharpened rock. The implications are also perhaps different; while in Sisebut's account Desiderius is stoned to death by decree of Theuderic, in the *Passio* it appears that he is lynched by Theuderic's troops because they cannot take him through the massed ranks of the local populace.

[41] 'Joined... heavens' - forms a hexameter.

[42] Theuderic died in AD 613, Pseudo-Fredegar, *Chron.*4.39. Prior to this he had defeated Theudebert II and managed to reunited Burgundy and Austrasia, Pseudo-Fredegar, *Chron.* 4.37-38. His death here sounds similar to the death of Arius as reported by Socrates, *Eccl.Hist.* 1.38 (which in itself carries overtones of the death of Judas as described in *Acts* 1.18), given that the Visigothic Kingdom had only converted from Arianism in AD 579 the allusion would not have been lost on Sisebut's audience.

20 Brunhilda, already lost and doomed to die, lost her source of consolation[43] and in her fear was tortured within by pangs of conscience, knowing that as her guilt placed her amongst the foremost in committing the crime, the vengeance which followed would demand her punishment all the more. While she pondered on these dark matters, she declared war on her closest neighbours.[44] When the time of battle came and the arrayed hosts came together, a terror inspired by God fell on the troops of this most wicked woman whence their cowardly limbs followed the fatal policy of seeking safety in flight.[45] So while they fled in disorder before the face of their foes, the enemy of the Christian faith and the deviser of all these crimes was taken by her enemies.

21 Concerning her end, it will not irk me to relate what I have learnt from common opinion.[46] There is a hunched beast[47] with a huge body and naturally possessed of certain humps (the top of its back is thick and broad, higher than the rest of its frame, and very well fitted for carrying loads) and is more useful for carrying loads than any other animal.[48] She was stripped of her clothes and raised up onto this proud

---

[43] She attempted to impose Sigebert, the eldest of Theuderic's bastard children, though only eleven years old, as king of Theuderic's realm.

[44] Sisebut is a little disingenuous here; Chlothar II of Neustria was invited into Austrasia by a group of disaffected Austrasian aristocrats led by the founders of the Carolingian dynasty, Arnulf of Metz and Peppin. Sigebert and Brunhilda were thus forced to defend themselves against external invasion supported by disaffected elements in their own kingdom.

[45] This battle took place on the River Aisne near Châlons-sur-Marne. According to Pseudo-Fredegar, *Chron.*4.42, Sigebert's army fled on a pre-arranged signal. The king was probably betrayed by Wornacher, who was rewarded by Clothar by being made *Major Domus in perpetuo* in Burgundy. It is intriguing therefore that Sisebut does not dwell on how the unjust Queen was abandoned by her people, but rather implicates them, albeit as cowards, in her crimes.

[46] Sisebut's account of the death of Brunhilda varies slightly from that of Pseudo-Fredegar. While both agree that she was paraded naked on a camel, Pseudo-Fredegar, *Chron.*4.42, adds that prior to this she was tortured for three days and afterwards she was bound to a single unbroken horse by her hair, one arm and one leg. The end result was, of course, the same.

[47] cf Jerome, *Ep.*107.3, 120.1.

[48] For camels in Merovingian Gaul see Gregory of Tours, *HF 7.35.* Sisebut seems confused here as to whether he means a dromedary or Bactrian Camel. Both beasts were known at the time; see Isidore, *Etym.*12.1.35-36.

central place and paraded in humiliation before the gaze of her enemies.[49] For a short while she offered this sorry spectacle to her onlookers, then, bound to some unbroken horses, she was dragged over some pathless rocky terrain. Thus her body, already broken by old age, was plucked apart by these spirited horses and her limbs, bloody and nameless, scattered abroad.[50] And so her soul freed from its mortal flesh was deservedly cast down to eternal punishment and to burn in seething waves of pitch.

22 A more detailed account of these events and a fuller account of their causes have escaped us. But lest I should anger the fastidious by being long-winded, let us add some small things and then put an end and call a halt to our tale, begging everyone as a community not to be unwilling to accept that which our Lord Jesus Christ did not disdain to condone through his martyrdom. Christ gave such a quantity of holiness to his most venerable corpse that whenever anyone troubled by illness or afflicted by a sickness of the flesh called with all his heart on his divine spirit there, shaking off every disease and lesion, he came hale and hearty to the health for which he had longed through the grace of God, the one in three and everlasting. May He grant me, all unworthy, eternal life and you, my audience, an abundance of grace.

---

[49] George of Cappadocia suffered a similar fate in Alexandria, see Socrates, *HE* 3.2. The practice was a standard form of Byzantine humiliation which parodied the consular investiture ceremony and is last recorded as being inflicted on Andronicus Comenus in AD 1185. It was imposed on the Armenian Arsaces in Byzantium by Justinian as the penalty for treason, Procopius, *BG* 7.32.3. Thence it seems to have been adopted in the Latin West. Count Argimund who was caught conspiring against Reccared in AD 590 suffered this fate, though he was paraded through Toledo on an ass rather than a camel, see John of Biclarum, *Chron.* 94, and Duke Paul who led a rebellion against Wamba in Septimania was, like Brunhilda, exhibited on a camel, Julian of Toledo, *Hist. Wamb.* 30 (= *PL* 96 796).

[50] cf *Aeneid* 2.558.

Braulio of Saragossa

THE LIFE OF ST AEMILIAN THE CONFESSOR, CALLED THE HOODED

To the priest Fronimian

1. Braulio, unworthy bishop of Caesaraugusta, to the man of God, my Lord and brother, the priest Fronimian, greetings.[1]

In the time of Bishop John, my lord of pious memory, an elder brother by birth,[2] a man who shared our common holy calling and was a teacher of the faith, I had intended in obedience to his orders and your injunctions, along with my trust in the account which I had obtained from the testimony given by the venerable abbot Citonatius, the priests Sofronius and Gerontius, and Potamia,[3] that devout lady of holy memory, to trace out with my pen, as far as my abilities and weakness of health permitted, a clear-cut life of our exceptional Father and patron, a man singled out by Christ in our times, the Blessed priest Aemilian. But because a whole page containing the list of his powers was lost through the negligence of my administrators when I was beginning to work on what I should say, and I was then occupied by a succession of disasters of all kinds and because of the troubles of the times I lost the wish to write, so that, although you urged me on, I was unable to give my heart to the task. But now, by God's will, as it seems to me, when I wanted to look at a certain book on something that had occurred to me

---

[1] There is no need to take the use of brother here as indicative of anything other than a spiritual bond between Braulio and Fronimian. Braulio was bishop of Saragossa from c.AD 631 to AD 651. In his correspondence with Fronimian he refers to his colleague as a 'priest and abbot'. The absence of the title here suggests *VSA* was written before Fronimian's elevation and that there was no monastic foundation on the site of Aemilian's tomb as sometimes claimed. Eugene II of Toledo (see *DVI* 13) refers to a church of holy Aemilian (*Carm* 11) our earliest evidence for monastic activity dates from the tenth century AD.

[2] See *DVI* 5.

[3] A short life, probably entirely inspired by *VSA*, exists for Potamia, see Férotin [1902] & [1902a]. No material concerning the other three individuals named here has survived.

15

and ordered it found and the pile of books was gone through, that long-lost account, all unsought for, since even the eagerness of those looking for it had come to an end through despair of ever finding it, was suddenly found. However, as the prophet says, '*I was found of those that sought me not*'[4] *my heart is glad and my glory rejoiceth*,[5] not through zeal to light a candle, but with the joy of coming across a silver piece.[6] And so at last, believing this task not to be without divine dispensation, I have steeled my soul that I might pluck the fruit of obedience and comply with your frequent petitions.

2. Therefore I have written to the best of my ability and in a plain and open style such as befits these matters,[7] a short tract on the life of this holy man, in order that it might be read out as swiftly as possible at the Mass held in his honour. I have sent it to you, my Lord, and taken care to put this letter of mine at its head, committing it to your judgement for approval. I have one reservation. If anything in it displeases you, correct it or excise it. But if it pleases you as it is, and your good will allows it, let it be published and give thanks on my behalf to our Creator, to whom all good things belong. I wish, moreover, that as that most Holy man, the priest Citonatius, and Gerontius are still alive, that they should review beforehand all that I have written and thoroughly discuss it. Let them confirm that I have made no errors either of names or events. I have also added at the end of this little book, just as you told me of them, those miracles worked in that same place which I

---

[4] *Romans* 10.20.
[5] *Psalm* 16.9.
[6] cf *Luke* 15.8.
[7] This is a reference to Braulio's use of the *sermo humilis*. The self-conscious use of 'lowly speech' was a deliberate rejection of classical rhetorical standards. Initially a defence of the style of Christian writings, always regarded as of a low standard by pagan opponents, the espousal of the *sermo humilis* evolved into a fully-fledged doctrine where it was argued that only a lowly style would make divine glories accessible to man. Moreover the *sermo humilis*, it was argued, was not devoid of profound thought, but eschewed an 'arrogant' style which would put its teachings beyond the reach of the common man. Thus it allowed anyone who approached it in a spirit of humility to reach its inner doctrines. For a lengthy discussion see Auerbach [1965].

learned about from you last year.[8] In addition, I have sent a hymn written in Senaric iambics for the feast of the Holy man as you asked.[9] I thought it superfluous to compose a sermon for the same day, since I can think of no greater exhortation to the good life than an account of his virtues and it would take a whole hour if a sermon were added and so burden the spirits of those who are listening.

3. Therefore I beg that what I have composed be accepted both by yourself with whose instructions I have complied and by him the love of whose powers has roused the aforementioned men to testify to these noteworthy things and made all of you witnesses everyday to similar acts. You have succeeded in your request that these things ought to be recorded by me and I myself am seized with the desire of receiving my reward, as I have done as you have commanded. In order that Low Mass might be recited on the same solemn occasion, I have given this task to my beloved son, the deacon Eugene,[10] thinking it would not be out of character for me if, for the honour of this most blessed man, the tongue of a man whom I consult in all my plans and counsels should give life to my task, bearing in mind that as I have him as a confidant in all other matters I should enjoy his sharing the reward in this task.[11] May the grace of Christ deem it worthy to keep your blessed self safe and mindful of me.

---

[8] i.e. at San Millán de Suso where Aemilian was buried. There is no reason to think that this was a monastic establishment. Eugene II of Toledo (see n.1 above) mentions a 'basilica of Holy Aemilian' in his eleventh poem.

[9] *PL* 80 713-716. Senaric iambics (a six-footed line where the basic rhythmic unit, the iambus, is a foot composed of a short followed by a long syllable) had been a common metre of the Roman theatre. St Hilary adopted it for some of his hymns, e.g. his *fefellit saevum* (*PLS* 1 275-6), it was however the stricter Iambic Dimeter, used by Ambrose (see *PL* 1171-1222), which became the normal metre of hymns in the West. See *DVI* 11 for the fame of Braulio's hymns.

[10] Later Eugene II of Toledo, see *DVI* 13. Again there is no need to see anything other than affection for a younger colleague in Braulio's use of 'son'.

[11] An office for S Millán can be found in Férotin [1912] 603-8. Lynch [1938] 223-4 argues that this is by Eugene.

Preface

4. The newness of the outstanding miracles of the apostolic and most pure man, the priest Aemilian, which were performed in almost in our own times urges me to write of them, but the immensity of the task of telling the tale is foreboding. For can the pen of a man given over to earthly things be brought to set forth in a worthy fashion the deeds of a heavenly man, who when compared to bygone ages shines forth gleaming like the brightest star, and in comparison to men of the present day is outstanding in his inimitable virtue? Nor do I think if the springs of Tully[12] were to pour out the tale and come gushing forth in copious streams of eloquence and a host of ideas create a lush supply of words, could all those things from the time when he spurned earthly things down to his leaving of his body and our world which Christ *who only doeth wondrous things*[13] has and is working by grace through him be expounded. When I look upon this, fear fills my soul, since I have not an abundance but a lack of learning, a dearth not a plentitude of words, and am much practised in being unpracticed. However the truth of Christ's promise drives out my fear, Who promised us and taught us this, saying: '*Open thy mouth wide and I will fill it;*'[14] and elsewhere: The Lord shall give words to evangelists, words of great worth.[15] He also said this: '*It is not ye that speak but the spirit of your father which speaketh in you.*'[16] These words are most fitting in my case, and so the soul is uplifted and the dart of fear turned aside. And, behold, what the soul once feared it is eager to start upon with firm tread, comforting itself with Your great power, Christ, because You Who allowed a beast of burden to speak with the words of a man,[17] can grant that a man should speak in a manner befitting his task. To which reasons can be added one that seems especially to touch upon the citadel of my soul and the anchor of my hope: that without undertaking this work and receiving the reward for my labour, I believe that I shall not obtain any

---

[12] i.e. Cicero.
[13] *Psalm* 72.18.
[14] *Psalm* 81.10.
[15] cf *Psalm* 67.12.
[16] *Matthew* 10.20.
[17] cf *Numbers* 22.28.

means by which, as if with a sort of soap, I shall be able to cleanse my vile and polluted life.[18] As once one of the old poets most eloquently put it, 'This work, this perhaps will deliver me from the fire.'[19]

5. It finally remains to say that I prefer to hand down an account in these wretched pages than hide these deeds in a smothering silence, lest the long reticence of their ancestors should make posterity doubt the truth of these matters. But in order to reply briefly to those who struggle to display their eloquence, let them know that the abuse of detractors has but little weight, as the law of the Church does not set empty verbosity as something for humble and lowly Christians to pursue nor the superficiality of human complaints, nor yet bombastic ostentation, but the sober, modest, and weighty profundity of the truth. It is indeed better to tell the truth in a less than educated fashion than eloquent fictions, as can easily be learnt from the Gospels of the Saviour which preach to the people in simple language. I do not because of my ineptitude revile the eloquence of wise men, but will not at all condone the fleeting frivolity of bickerers. For I do not think that noble, wise, and mature men could be angry with me because of my appetite for this task: men who are in no way ignorant that in the house of the Lord it behoves each one of us to offer that which his faculties provide, even down to *all work of goats' hair*.[20] If they too wish to say something about this matter, as I have said, not only will they not fall short of material, but in fact they will be unable to expound it all. Wherefore although I have in part cleaved to the study of the things of this world, here I have altogether spurned them, lest I should make my account difficult to understand for the less educated and throw the camp of Israel into confusion with the language of Jericho.[21]

6. Therefore, as I am about to relate the things of which I have decided to speak, I wish to warn my readers and listeners to come and hear not from an eagerness for fine words, but full of faith. If there is someone looking for the former, let him get hence lest he should tarry fruitlessly.

---

[18] cf *Jeremiah* 2.22.
[19] Juvencus (*fl.* AD 330) *Libri Evangeliorum, praef.*,1.22.
[20] *Numbers* 31.20.
[21] cf *Joshua* 6.18.

But if he wishes to know about the things which follow, let him come devoutly to learn of them. First, let him know that there are certain deeds in this account which most certainly ought to followed by us or by anyone, but there are others which were bestowed singularly upon that most worthy man and cannot be imitated by anyone without bringing about their own destruction: acts which however ought through admiration to make us eager to praise God.[22] For the generality of mankind should keep to our general precepts, and only those upon whom almighty God has decreed that special gifts be given ought to take hold of these gifts, as indeed is the view of those learnèd in law concerning benefits obtained through the decree of earthly rulers.

7. I shall not go back far into the past, nor shall I follow the rules of the orators[23] and set forth the praises of his grandfathers and great-grandfathers, since, as these selfsame men would say, if he was sprung from lowly stock, he ought be praised all the more as he adorned the lowliness of his birth with the nobility of his way of life. Let us therefore begin our tale, with Christ's favour and the prayers of the blessed man himself aiding our efforts, from the time of his conversion which occurred in the twentieth year of his life. The venerable priests of the churches of Christ, Citonatius, a man of a holy and most pure life; and Sofronius and Gerontius, presbyters in whom the church has no small faith, gave me a reliable account of what they themselves had seen. To these most worthy witnesses can be added the testimony of the most devout Potamia of blessed memory, who ennobled the nobility of her birth with a yet more noble way of life.[24] I have chosen to take these four as witnesses of the miracles which he performed in the flesh, setting aside the testimonies of towns and provinces on matters of this sort to which almost all of Spain bears witness. For we must pass over those deeds which happened so frequently that they were almost a daily occurrence, since it would be impossible, as I have already said, to include them all. If anyone wants to know about them, he will believe more easily those that he has seen.

---

[22] A similar warning is given in chapter 23 of the *Life*; cf Gregory the Great *Dial* 1.1.6.

[23] Another reference to Braulio's use of the *sermo humilis*; see n.7 above.

[24] Was Potamia one of the 'maidens of Christ' with whom Aemilian spent his declining years?

The Life

I. Of the conversion of the Holy Man

8. Therefore, as I had started to say, my witnesses relate that he was converted and came to the religious life in the following way. The future shepherd of men was a shepherd of sheep which he used to drive into the depths of the mountains and, as is the custom with shepherds, he took a harp with him,[25] lest tiredness should impede his idle mind, left with nothing to do, from guarding his flock.[26] When he arrived at the place ordained by heaven, a divinely-inspired sleep flooded over him. Then that craftsman who makes hearts clean performed his task with his customary dedication and turned the material of the cithara into an instrument of learning and roused up the mind of a shepherd to the contemplation of heavenly things. When he woke, he thought on the heavenly life and leaving the countryside went off to the wilderness.

II. He goes to a monk at Buradón

9. Rumour had told him that a certain hermit called Felix,[27] a most Holy Man, to whom he could not unworthily offer himself as a disciple, was then living in Buradón.[28] He hurried to him, and when he had eagerly entered his service, was taught by him how he could guide his wavering

---

[25] 'Cithara' the same instrument that King David, also a shepherd in his youth, is said to play in the Bible, *1 Samuel* 16.

[26] The thirteenth-century poet Gonzalo de Berceo whose *Vida de San Millán de la Cogolla* is heavily based on Braulio adds, stanza 3, that Aemilian was born in Berceo, a village approximately one mile from San Millán de Suso, the probable site of Aemilian's oratory. This could of course be pleading by a *parti pris* as Gonzalo was a monk at San Millán de Yuso. For commentaries on Berceo's work see Dutton [1967] and [1992] both in Spanish.

[27] St Felix's remains were transferred to the monastery of San Millán de la Cogolla in AD 1090.

[28] 'Castrum Bibilense'. This is the point where the River Ebro enters the plains of La Rioja in the province of Logroño. A further modern name is Las Conchas de Haro.

footsteps towards the heavenly kingdom.[29] By this act he teaches us, I believe, that no one can successfully journey towards the blessed life without the instruction of teachers.[30] This man did not do so, nor was this the command that Christ gave to Paul nor did the Holy Spirit allow Samuel to do this. This man was told to go to the hermit, Paul to Annias,[31] and Samuel to Eli,[32] although they had all been roused up by signs and words.

III. He comes to the place where his oratory is built

10. After he had been well taught the paths of life by this man and been greatly enriched by the wealth of instruction and treasures of salvation, he returned to his own country, full of the grace of religious learning and thus came to a place not far from the village of Berceo[33], where his glorious body now lies.[34] He did not delay there long, for he saw that

---

[29] Berceo, stanza 14, adds that the saint went by Valpiri - the site of the battle which liberated Fernán González, Count of Castile, in AD 945. The Count who was a benefactor of the monastery of San Millán (if the 12th-century copies of the charters referring to him in the monastery cartulary are to be trusted), had adopted Aemilian as his personal saint. Berceo's addition here could simply be an attempt to link the count and his saint. However, if the poet is preserving a genuine link between Aemilian and Valpiri, it would help to explain González's attraction to San Millán.

[30] Such self-inspired hermits or Sarabaites were strongly frowned on by the early church, see Benedict, *Rule* 1 and Isidore, *De Eccl. Off.* 2.16.9 (=*PL* 83 799). For attempts to suppress such hermits see *4 Toledo* 53 (AD 633) & *7 Toledo* 5 (AD 646).

[31] *Acts* 9.10-19.

[32] *1 Kings* 3.

[33] 'Vergegium'. Berceo, *op.cit.* stanzas 27-28 adds a description of the valley of San Millán de Suso. A fifteenth century Spanish translation of Braulio's *Life* (*Real Academia de Historia Ms Emil.59* fol 127v) identifies this place with San Millán de Suso, located above the site of the monastery of San Millán de la Cogolla. This identification appears to be secure. However a rival cult of San Millán arose in Aragon in the fifteenth-century which asserted that his birthplace was Torrelapaja near Berdejo. For this dispute see Gaiffier [1933].

[34] Berceo *op.cit.* stanza 31 adds that Aemilian cleansed the area of snakes which became fused into the rocks. The body of the saint was transferred to the lower church of San Millán de Yuso which formed part of the monastery of San Millán de La Cogolla in AD 1030, see Dutton [1967].

the crowd of men who came flocking to him would be a hinderance to him.

IV. He goes hence to the wilderness and spends forty years there

11. He sought the heights, his eager spirit taking his steps lightly over the difficult terrain, so that marching through the vale of sorrow[35] not only with his heart but also with his body and going from virtue to virtue, he seemed as if he was climbing Jacob's Ladder.[36] When he came to the more remote, secret places of Mount Dircetius,[37] staying as near to the summit as the nature of the weather and the woods would allow, he became a guest of the hills. Set apart from the company of men and busying himself only with the consolations of the angels, he dwelt there for the passage of 40 years.[38] What invisible, what visible battles, what varied and cunning temptations, what mockeries of the Ancient Wretch, he experienced there, they alone best know who say that they themselves have experienced such things. He directed all his desire, all his inclinations, all his aspirations, in sum, his entire life, to his irrevocable first intent to be a devotee of the Holy. O how great a gift! O how singular a man! O how outstanding a spirit! He was so given to divine contemplation that it seems that this age can claim nothing of him for itself. How many times, I imagine, did he, filled with divine ardour, raise up his voice among those thick, lofty forests, the towering summits of the hills, and the crags which reach towards

---

[35] cf *Psalm* 24.3.

[36] cf *Genesis* 28.12-13.

[37] Probably located in the Sierra de la Demanda. *Codex Misc.* in the Archivo Historico Nacional, *ms.*1007B f 69ᵛ-70, dating to AD 932, refers to Mount Dircetius as the site of the head-waters of the River Duero. Berceo, *op.cit.* stanza 47, refers to the saint living in caves here. The region is full of rock-cut hermitages, see Azkarate Garai-Olaun [1988].

[38] A clear parallel with Christ's 40 days in the Wilderness and the Israelites' 40 years of wandering in the desert of Sinai. Berceo, *op.cit.*, stanza 49 refers to altars said to have been built by Aemilian here. This tradition either grew up after Braulio's life was written or was suppressed by him. Similarly stanza 57 refers to a hermitage built by Aemilian which is not found in Braulio's *Life*. A sixteenth-century note appended to manuscript F folio 128v of Berceo's work at this point identifies the hermitage with a chapel of St Laurence built on the summit of Mt. San Lorenzo, the highest point (7475ft) in the Sierra de la Demanda, 2 miles south of San Millán de Suso.

heaven, saying to Christ 'Woe is me that my sojourn is prolonged',[39] How many times sighing and groaning did he cry out, '*I have a desire to depart and be with Christ.*'[40] How many times, moved in his innermost being, did he most vehemently make lament, saying, '*While we are at home in the body, we are absent from the Lord.*'[41] Meanwhile he was shaken by the cold, abandoned in solitude, soaked by the unforgiving rain, and buffeted by blasts of the wind, but through the love of God, the contemplation of Christ, and the grace of the Holy Spirit, he not only tolerated, but willingly and eagerly endured the violence of the cold, the desolation of loneliness, the onslaught of the rain, and the harshness of the winds. However, since *a city that is set on a hill cannot be long hid,*[42] fame of his holiness spread to such a degree that it came to the notice of almost everyone.[43]

V. The Bishop Didymus assigns a church to him

12. When this news was brought to Didymus who then held the office of bishop in Tarazona,[44] he pursued the man, wishing, as he was in his diocese, to put him into Holy orders. At first it seemed a harsh and hard thing to Aemilian to flee back, to return, to be, as it were, dragged from heaven to earth, from the rest which he had now almost obtained to wearying tasks, and to be taken back to the active from the contemplative life.[45] Finally, he was unwillingly compelled to obey,[46]

---

[39] cf *Psalm* 120.5-6.

[40] *Philippians* 1.23. Braulio's selective quotation of Paul here is of interest. Paul is torn between martyrdom and living to help the Philippians and concludes 'I know that I shall abide, yea, and abide with you all, for your progress and joy in the faith'. Braulio completely suppresses the Apostle's conclusion and hence reverses the sense of the passage.

[41] cf *2 Corinthians* 5.6.

[42] cf *Matthew* 5.14.

[43] Berceo, *op.cit.* stanza 67, places the limits of Aemilian's sojourn in the wilderness in the Moncayo hills which form part of the Cordillera Ibérica in the provinces of Soria and Saragossa. The nearby church of San Millán de Verdejo in Aragon was to lay claim to the saint.

[44] The town lies some 50 miles West North West of Saragossa.

[45] The contemplative life was frequently regarded as far superior to that of a priest ministering to a secular flock. See Athanasius, *Letter to Dracontius* (= *PG* 25 523-534) and Gregory the Great *Hom. Ezekiel* 2.4.5-6 for attempts to refute this point of view.

and so performed the office of presbyter in the church of Berceo.[47] Then setting aside those things which men of that order, the men, that is, of our day, are accustomed to dedicate themselves, he imparted his holy care on this life to which he had been dragged back. In this however through continual prayer, week-long fasts, perpetual vigils, true discernment, sure hope, great frugality, kindly righteousness, firm endurance, in short with the greatest austerity he tirelessly kept himself from all evil things.[48] He so plucked flowers of knowledge from the meadows of the ineffable Godhead that he who had scarcely committed the eighth psalm to memory,[49] far surpassed without compare the ancient philosophers of the world in practical knowledge, wisdom, and sharpness of perception;[50] and not undeservedly, as what they had obtained by worldly labour the Godhead gave him through heavenly grace. Indeed, I conjecture, he was altogether like Saint Antony[51] and Saint Martin in his calling, training, and performance of miracles. But, in order to pass over many things, among his acts as a priest, this, I declare, was his greatest labour: to drive Mammon out of the temple of the Lord with vigour and wisdom as quickly as he could.[52] Wherefore

---

[46] cf *VSD* 3 and the fate of Martin of Tours who was made a bishop against his will, Sulpicius Severus, *VSM* 9. For problems between bishops and holy men see Robles [1963].

[47] Berceo, *op.cit.*, stanza 106, states that the church was dedicated to Sta.Eulalia.

[48] cf Sulpicius Severus, *VSM* 10 where St Martin continues his ascetic life while a bishop and Bede, *Life of Cuthbert* 26 (= *PL* 94 766), where the same is said of St Cuthbert. For this theme in general see Rousseau [1971].

[49] Illiteracy in the priesthood was frowned upon, but seems to have been a common problem. *Narbonne* 1 (AD 589) forbade bishops to ordain illiterates as priests and ordered that any presently illiterate priest must learn to read and would suffer a loss of income if his progress was deemed too slow. *2 Toledo* 2 (AD 527) forbids educated priests to move to another church to prevent a neighbouring diocese poaching them without paying for their initial education. *4 Toledo* 26 (AD 633) provides for a book of offices to be given to priests in order that they can perform their duties correctly. This step, however, clearly did not solve the problem as *8 Toledo* 8 (AD 653) paints a dismal pictures of priests who were ignorant of the Psalter, Canticles, hymns, and the service of baptism.

[50] Braulio here emphasises that Aemilian outstripped his secular rivals in both the classical divisions of knowledge, i.e. the theoretical and practical.

[51] Antony was famously dismissive of book-learning, but unlike Aemilian had the entire bible by heart (Augustine, *De Doctrina Christiana* 1 *praef.*4).

[52] cf *Matthew* 21.12, *Mark* 11.15, *John* 2.14.

he shared the substance of Christ with the innermost parts of Christ,[53] making the Church of Christ wealthy again in virtues rather than riches, in religion rather than rent, in Christians rather than chattels. For he knew that he could be accused before Christ not for casting aside temporal things, but for casting aside men.

VI. Clerks accuse the Holy Man before the bishop

13. Because of this, as is the custom among the worst sort of clerk, some of his clerics came before Didymus to attack him on the grounds of harming their communal property.[54] Slandering him, they declared that the losses of the church were clear to behold and that the goods which it had received had on all sides been diminished. Now the aforementioned prelate was inflamed with torches of anger and eaten through with envy because of Aemilian's virtues. Looking at him, he vehemently assailed the man of God. When he had belched forth the intoxication of his anger (as a soul drunk with fury is want to do), the man of God, fortified by his sanctity and protected by his forbearance, stood there unmoved with his accustomed tranquillity.[55] After this he was released from the ministry he had taken up, and passed the rest of his life beyond reproach in the place which is now called his oratory.[56] Thus far his conversion and his life. Although those acts of grace which were concealed are the more beautiful (those which the Lord established

---

[53] Normally interpreted as meaning the poor.

[54] cf Sulpicius Severus, *Dial.* 1.9, where St Jerome is said to have been hated by clerics because he censured their depraved way of life. The alienation of church property was later formally forbidden by *3 Toledo* 3 (AD 589), however the principle would have been in operation prior to this date.

[55] cf *VSD* 15. The imperturbability of martyrs is a common theme in martyr accounts, running back to the first martyr's, St Stephen's, steadfast calm in the face of his Jewish opponents, *Acts* 7.55.

[56] Berceo, *op.cit.*, stanzas 106-107, assumes that this was a return to his early haunts and identifies these with San Millán de Suso. This is also the view of the fifteenth century Spanish translator of the *Life*, *RAH, Ms Emil.59* 128v. The church of San Millán de Suso is described by Gómez Moreno [1919] 288-309 & *lam.* 112-118. Further work on the site was undertaken by Iñíguez Almech [1955]. The present church which probably dates to the late 10th century AD incorporates rock-cut structures which may well have been Aemilian's oratory. It was severely damaged when it was sacked by Almanzor in AD 1002.

in these new struggles and which we have been taught in faith and truth by Paul the teacher and captain[57] of the Gentiles) than those which have brought themselves to light through various gifts of virtue, even these latter are too many to be able to be written down. However I must set down by what signs his glory shone forth, even if I proceed to do so in an unworthy fashion.

VII. He wrestles with the devil

14. It came to pass one day that Enemy of the Human Race met the Wrestler[58] of the Eternal King on the road, and addressed him with these words, 'If you want, let us fight and discover what each of us is able to achieve with his strength.' He had not finished saying this when he advanced upon him and laid hold of him visibly and in the flesh. For a long time he belaboured Aemilian who was scarcely able to fight back. But when he earnestly called upon Jesus in prayer, divine aid strengthened his trembling steps and he immediately vanquished the fugitive,[59] apostate spirit, turning its body into air.[60] If, by chance, it should seem incredible to anyone, that an indisputably invisible spirit can, except in a mystical understanding, take physical form, let it be revealed to him how the pages of Divine Scripture relate that Jacob struggled with an angel, albeit a good one.[61] I, however, would say this: that it took less audacity for Satan to tempt a servant than the Lord, Aemilian than Christ, a man than God, a creature rather than the creator.

---

[57] 'Magister' which would have both these overtones to Braulio's audience.

[58] cf *Ephesians* 6.12 and *Passion of Sts Perpetua and Felicity* 10.

[59] Fugitive, 'refuga' had strong pejorative tones in Visigothic Spain, see *5 Toledo* 12 & *8 Toledo praef.*, 1.

[60] cf *VSF* 11 where the devil vanishes not into the air, but the earth. Berceo, *op.cit.* stanza 207, states that this was a famous encounter which took place by the church of San Pelayo (now destroyed) located just below San Millán de Suso. *Ms Emil* 59 agrees and adds that this church was founded to mark the event. A stone here reads 'Here San Millán vanquished Satan in the flesh.' The church itself must have postdated Aemilian by at least some 300 years as San Pelayo was born in Saragossa in AD 911 and martyred in Cordoba on the 26 June AD 925.

[61] *Genesis* 32.24-32.

VIII. He cures a monk

15. To return to the thread of my account: there was a certain monk, Armentarius by name, afflicted with a painful swelling of the stomach who came devotedly to Aemilian asking that his innermost parts be cured.[62] When he had put his hand on the lump and traced the sign of the cross there, the sickness left him at once and, having recovered his health, he blessed the Lord.[63]

IX. A paralysed woman is healed

16. A certain woman called Barbara who had contracted a paralysing disease and was greatly afflicted by it, was brought to him from the territory of Amaia,[64] and restored to her lost health by a prayer of the holy man.

X. A lame woman walks

17. Another woman from the same place was brought borne on a cart, since she was long since lame having lost the use of her feet and, although it was Lent, asked to be cured by him.[65] He did not wish to see her out of his reverence for the season (for it was his custom during these days to be content to be alone in his cell and see no-one except for a single individual out of his attendants[66] who brought him a minuscule quantity of cheap food that he might continue to live). Since, as I said, he refused to see her, she fervently pressed him that he grant her merely to kiss his staff. When the man of God heard her in his kindness, he immediately saw to it. When she saw this had been done,

---

[62] The disease appears to be dropsy.

[63] *Armentarie* appears as a graffito on the rock-cut church, la Iglesia superior de Nuestra Señora de la Peña. Azkarate Gara-Olaun [1988] 489-490 tentatively suggests that this could have been Aemilian's centre of operations.

[64] A village near Villadiego some 40 miles North West of Burgos and the main centre of Cantabria in this period.

[65] cf *Luke* 5.18ff.

[66] It appears therefore that Aemilian did not live entirely alone as a hermit. The same is true of St Fructuosus who while living as an anchorite had a servant called Baldarius.

she kissed the staff and stood up safely with firm and solid feet and, having given thanks for the divine gift, departed at once rejoicing.[67]

XI. He gives sight to a Senator's maid

18. The maid of the Senator Sicorius,[68] long deprived of the light of day, asked that he restore to her the use of her eyes. Then the man of God by word and touch, and with Christ as his guide, asked for her health and straightaway his request came to pass: her sight returned and she saw the shapes of things in a very clear light.[69]

XII. He cures a possessed deacon

19. A certain man ejected from the office of deacon was violently possessed by a most shameless demon.[70] Bound by his friends he was placed before Aemilian's face to be cleansed. While he was convulsed by his madness as if he was rabid, raving and lashing out, the unclean spirit was ordered by the most blessed man to leave him. There was no delay: the disobedient learnt to obey, the demon was stricken with invisible punishments and made a stranger to the dwelling it had seized. It abandoned the man, who spoke and shouted out his praises to God.

XIII. He heals another slave

20. The slave of a certain Tuentius, Sibila by name, had been seized by impure spirits.[71] He was dragged to the blessed man by his family, who, when he saw him, asked by how many demons he was possessed. They

---

[67] cf *Matthew* 9.20ff., 14.36.

[68] A member of the mysterious senate of Cantabria found in chapter 33?

[69] cf *Mark* 8.23-25.

[70] It is unclear whether the man was expelled from his office because he was possessed or that the demon found such a sinner a particularly easy target.

[71] These two names may cast some light on the status of languages in this period. 'Tuentius' is a semi-Romanised Gothic name, suggesting that this noble thought it worthwhile to present a veneer of Roman culture to the outside world. His slave's name however is firmly Gothic and hence it appears that the veneer was strictly for external purposes only. For nomenclature in Visigothic Spain see Claude [1972].

told him that they were five and each one gave its name.[72] He commanded them through the power of Jesus Christ and straightaway they all departed, screaming in great terror. The slave, cured, returned happily to his own.

XIV. He heals another: the slave of a Count

21. And he restored to health and safety through the incomparable power of divine omnipotence, a slave of the Count Eugene who was possessed and afflicted by a demon which had long held him in slavery by a lengthy occupation of his body.

XV. Likewise he heals a married couple

22. Now what am I to say about the senator Nepotian and his wife Proseria? Save that as they had been joined in marriage, so they were jointly possessed by a demon, with the result that the flesh which had become one with his wife was believed to be dwelt in by one spirit which in its twofold possession seemed to have perverted the law of marriage for its own use.[73] How obvious their condition was can be learnt from the fact that news of it spread everywhere so that it did not slip from peoples' minds for generations.[74] Hence it may seem that I have added this account superfluously because there is no Cantabrian who can have failed to have seen or heard of this incident.[75] When news of this occurrence came to our Aemilian he ordered his unclean foe to leave the bodies of the couple. It was in no way able to resist his command and freed them as it had been ordered. They on their liberation sounded forth their praise to the King of heaven.

---

[72] cf the Legion of demons in *Mark* 5.9 and *Luke* 8.30.

[73] i.e. Christ's law of marriage, *Matthew* 19.5-6.

[74] A somewhat unfortunate statement given Braulio's opening comment that Aemilian's miracles were almost contemporary with his own day.

[75] An important notice as it implies that Aemilian's acts were widely known in Cantabria. As the saint's centre of operations is to be found in the modern province of La Rioja, not Cantabria, this perhaps implies that sixth century Cantabria covered a much larger area than the area later denoted by this term. It is of interest that Berceo omits this detail in his poem and the fifteenth century Spanish translation of Braulio *RAH Ms Emil 59* refers to the Navarrese at this point not the Cantabrians.

XVI. Likewise he cures another woman

23. In the same way a demon had possessed in a horrific fashion the daughter of the curial Maximus called Columba, producing an unforeseen weakness in her limbs. She was placed in great expectation before the servant of God to be cured. When he made the sign of the cross on the threshold of her brow, the demon was soon driven out and ejected and she obtained a remedy for her ill health.

XVII. He casts out a demon from a senator's house

24. The house of the senator Honorius gave shelter to a most wicked and rebellious demon who most monstrously attached itself to his house and everyday perpetrated some disgusting and vile deed so that no one could endure this servant of the devil. Worst of all, often when the master of the house had sat down to feast, the impure spirit would put the bones of dead animals and frequently manure in his dishes. Often too at night when the inhabitants were asleep, it stole the clothes of men and women and hung them from the roofs as if they were veils of some foul deed. Not a little anxious and not knowing what to do, Honorius kept calm amid his anguish, having a sure faith in the virtues of Aemilian and heartened by this hope, he sent for him to be brought to him, despatching carriages to aid him on his way. The messengers arrived and implored him to come and drive out the demon with whatever power was at his disposal. At last worn down by their entreaties he set out to show the power of our God, but did so on foot not in a carriage.[76] When he came to Parpalines (where these things took place),[77] he found everything had happened as he had been told, and he

---

[76] cf *VSF* 12.

[77] An alternative ms reading is Pamplona, this is the version followed by the fifteenth-century Spanish translation of Braulio, *RAH Ms Emil.59* fol.132r. The location of Parpalines is unknown. A note by Toribio Minguella on the *Memorias* of P.Romero (ms de San Millán) places Parpalines in the Ocón Valley near Ausejo, a view followed by Orlandis [1992] ch.10. This identification coincides with that found on a document on folio 50v of one version (the *Becerro Galicano*) of the *Cartulario* of the monastery of San Millán de la Cogolla, dated to *era* 958, i.e. AD 920 (Ubieto [1976] 68, Serrano [1930] 16) in which King García Sánchez I of Navarra grants to the monastery of San Millán de La Cogolla the village which Sicorius gave to the saint to thank him for curing him and

himself endured some lawless acts. He ordered a fast and gathered to him the congregation[78] of priests who lived there. On the third day, having fulfilled the vow of the fast he had ordered, he exorcised some salt and mixed it with water according to the teachings of the Church and began to perform an aspersion of the house.[79] Then the hateful being burst forth from the bowels of the house. Seeing itself ejected and cast out of its dwelling place, it threw stones at Aemilian but he, fortified by his unconquerable shield, remained safe.[80] Finally put to flight, the demon spewing out flames with a most nauseating odour sought the wilderness.[81] And so the inhabitants of the house rejoiced that they had been saved by Aemilian's prayer.

XVIII. Divine Protection Guards Him

25. What more is there to say? There was so great an abundance of sanctity in that man, so great a store of divine power, so much puissance of divine authority that when a multitude of madmen ran to him, not only did he not show the slightest trace of fear, but even locked himself in alone with all of them in the place where he was to cure them through divine grace.[82] Often when he lay down on his bed, they tried to burn him and brought burning straw up to his bed. But when they tried to set the bed alight with it, it lost its heat. They persisted in this all through the night, labouring in vain. Therefore when Aemilian realised this, at his command the madmen bound one another

---

giving sight to his servant girl. This is described as 'The village of Parperinense called Buengua...'. The notice, however, is of awkward phraseology, not found on the other version of the Cartulario (the *Becerro Gótico*), and the name of the senator concerned should be Honorius not Sicorius. It appears therefore that we are dealing with a pious *post eventum* forgery where chapters 18 and 24 of the life have been confused. Serrano [1930] xxiii n.12 notes another document of AD 1074 found on the vellum manuscript of Valvanera n°10 which mentions a village of Parpalines near Ocón. It is however a later addition to the manuscript.

[78] Lat. 'ordo'.

[79] For these rituals see *Liber Sacramentorum* ed. Férotin [1912] 11-22.

[80] cf *Ephesians* 6.16.

[81] cf *Luke* 11.24.

[82] cf Sulpicius Severus, *Dial.* 3.6.

with chains, their hands providing a means of safety, since their hearts were full of madness.[83]

XIX. A beam lengthens at his prayer

26. I ought not to be silent about this matter which I see is already known throughout the world. I am talking about the beam which shaped by the hand of some carpenters was taken to build a granary,[84] but was found to be too short to fit with the other beams being used for the work. When he saw this, he ordered the carpenters to eat with easy minds, while he himself withdrew to plead before the eyes of the creator. When he had finished the *synaxis*[85] at the sixth hour in his own special customary style,[86] it was revealed to him that what he had asked for had been granted and he returned to these hired workers. 'Do not think that you will lose the money for your work.' he said, 'Set the beam in its place.' They lifted it and set it up as he instructed, and found that it was longer than the rest, having grown by more than a palm's breadth.[87] In that place he made a mark which can be clearly seen to this day. So through his prayer, the workmen did not waste their

---

[83] Oddly this, rather than the division of his tunic, is the commonest depiction from the life of the saint. The saint does not seem to have been able to cure the madmen and the miracle must lie in the fact that the lunatics willing bound themselves rather than having to be constrained by others. Their binding was to prevent them harming themselves or others; see Bernardo de Gordonio's early fourteenth century work, *Lilio de la Medicina*, cap.19 *De Mania & Melancolia* which prescribes this treatment if all cures have failed.

[84] Traditional horreos are still a common sight in North West of Spain. Berceo, stanza 225, and the fifteenth-century Spanish translation of the *Life*, *RAH, Ms Emil.59* fol.133r, state that Aemilian commissioned the granary himself to store food for the pilgrims who flocked to visit him. This is an unwarranted internal inference from chapters 28 and 29.

[85] *Synaxis* originally meant 'congregation'; it came however to take on the meaning of 'divine service' including both ones containing the eucharist and, especially in the West, a non-eucharistic service composed of psalms, prayers, and lessons from Scripture.

[86] This is an example of the things which Braulio warns his flock not to imitate in chapter 6 of the *Life*.

[87] This miracle is very different from the normal ones of healing and exorcism. An eleventh-century catalogue of relics from Oviedo also lists a piece of wood which miraculously grew to the right size in the building of a church, see De Bruyne [1927]. This may represent an embroidered version of our story or suggest that such miracle accounts were common in Northern Spain. There is a possibility that the account attempts to supersede or Christianise the pagan cult of trees found in this area.

labour nor were they cheated of the wages for their task. The very wood even now cures the devout who are ill, and is said to have so much power that almost daily it gives health to the sick.[88] For this reason my account would drag out to an enormous length, if I wanted to repeat all the acts of healing which have been recorded there and lie open to inspection. But now I think it worth saying a little of his liberality and chastity.

XX. He gives the sleeves of his tunic to the poor

27. Once a crowd of the poor came to him[89] asking for their normal subvention and though he was lacking in goods or could not find anything which he could give them, he was not found lacking in his innate piety. For he cut the sleeves from his tunic and generously handed them over along with the cloak he was wearing. Then one of them who was more importunate than the rest, as is the way with beggars, went in front of all the rest, took these and put them on. O here was another Martin who in clothing the poor man clothed Christ![90] Not undeservedly have they obtained the same reward, for they had the same spirit of liberality. However lest this striking importunity in front of so great a man should go unavenged, the rest of the beggar's colleagues on seeing his act became envious and indignant at the presumption of one man. Armed with their sticks, they rose up and fell upon him in a horde and drove him all over to wherever anger prompted them individually. And clearly he deserved this trouble which was brought on by his own lack of foresight.[91]

---

[88] It was placed in a reliquary in one of the columns of San Millán de Suso. The fifteenth-century Spanish translation states it was working miracles 'to this day' as does a note to manuscript S of Berceo. There is no indication of when the beam was moved from the granary. Manuscript *RAH XXIV* f 155v, dating from the thirteenth century, lists a 'pitatium' of the wood amongst the monastery's treasures.

[89] Berceo, *op.cit.*, stanza 239, again presents this crowd as one of pilgrims coming to visit the hermit.

[90] cf Sulpicius Severus, *VSM* 3. The division of his cloak was St Martin's most famous act of charity. Here Braulio makes Aemilian trump Martin as he gives away all his cloak and the sleeves of his tunic.

[91] Aemilian's act is tempered by Braulio's sense of social propriety.

28. I shall tell of another incident which I would like the grasping to hear in order that they should not think on the morrow. It happened that a crowd came to the blessed man when he did not have enough wine for them.[92] But because those who ask of the Lord shall not be lacking in any good thing,[93] a huge multitude drank to its fill from scarcely, as it is reported, a *sextarius* of wine.[94] However they say a greater miracle occurred on another occasion.

XXII. He is aided when food comes to him

29. As fame of his sanctity spread, crowds of visitors came to see him daily and he, of his own free will, urged them with all his heart to stay as his guests and refresh themselves from his charity. When his servant learnt this clearly, he told the holy man that there was nothing left for them to eat. Aemilian reproached his servant with a gentle rebuke, criticising his lukewarm faith[95] and prayed to Christ to provide the necessary food. He had not finished his prayer when, lo, suddenly carts generously loaded down with food sent from the senator Honorius came through the gate.[96] The man beloved of God took the gift and gave thanks to the Creator of the World for having heard his prayer. He set a sufficient amount of food before his invited guests and saw that the rest be saved for those who might come later. Thus he trod a middle path between performing the duties of common hospitality and his own practice of abstinence, so that his table would be found set for a feast for guests no matter the time of day, while he, on the other hand, was so sparing with food that he was never seen save sober in mind and mortified in the flesh. He replenished the bodies of his guests with food and their souls with his words. He was so eloquent in his analogies and

---

[92] Berceo, *op.cit.*, stanza 247, casts this incident in a monastery of the kind of his own day.

[93] cf *Matthew* 7.7.

[94] approximately one pint. The incident carries strong overtones of the feeding of the five thousand, *Matthew* 14.13-21, *Luke* 9.10-17, *John* 6.1-13 and the wedding at Cana, *John* 2.1-9.

[95] cf *Matthew* 8.26, 14.31, 16.8; *Luke* 12.28.

[96] This in fact seems a lesser miracle than the one Braulio described in the preceding chapter. Christ's feeding of the masses is parallelled, but the element of the miraculous is at a much lower level.

so subtle in his advocacy of the spiritual life that whoever came to him for whatever reason left him a better and contented man for he never departed from his precepts in either his life or his words. Lest I drag out my account into a long tale, he gained the palm of victory over his vanquished flesh in such a way that his North was never conquered and used to warm a cauldron,[97] nor to provide kindling for the fires of Nebuchadnezzar.[98]

XXIII. He is slandered by a demon because he lives with women.

30. Now those apostate spirits, when they wished in the cunning of their evil to harm him through the slander of madmen, because they could find nothing of which to accuse the servant of Christ, they merely attempted to reproach him by asking why he cohabited with maidens of Christ.[99] So the Enemy plays with his ancient art: a man he is not able to cast down in deed, he presses on to besmirch through rumour; a man whose conscience he cannot overcome, he defames. It is as if he can offer through his beguiling temptations examples of consolation, while men think that there is no good man to be found and despair of finding a man whose good deeds they should imitate. When this is the case, they almost think it a remedy for themselves if no innocent man can be found and are consoled to their own damnation by the thought that the multitude too shall perish. What use, Devisor of Evil, can the ill repute of the servants of Christ be to you, since our Lord and Redeemer has promised his own the heavenly kingdom *by honour and dishonour, by evil report and good report,*[100] But this holy man even in his old age was devoted to abstinence and common decency. He lived with holy maidens from his eightieth year onwards: bound down by his holy work

---

[97] *Jeremiah* 1.13: a prediction of disaster coming to the kingdom of Judah from the north.

[98] cf *Jeremiah* 21.7, 21.14.

[99] The celibacy of the clergy made such accusations both frequent and plausible. The *Cantiga de los Clérigos de Talavera* in Juan Ruiz' *Libro de Buen Amor* and the preface to the *Friar's Tale* in Chaucer's *Canterbury Tales* capture the thoughts behind them. St Cyprian, *Hab.Virg.* 19, remarks on the trouble that virgins cause to the church. Gregory of Tours (*HF* 6.36) records similar accusations made against Aetherius, the bishop of Lisieux, adding that since the bishop was nearly 70 at the time he was astounded that such allegations were made. See also *VSD* ch.4.

[100] *2 Corinthians* 6.8.

and pain, he happily accepted from the maidens of God all the ministrations that a father may accept. But, as I have already said, he was so far from sinful temptations that he never experienced a trace of a disgraceful urge in that part of his life. Now because he had reached so advanced an age, his needs increased proportionately so that when he suffered from the sickness of dropsy, he allowed his body to be washed by these same holy women, but he himself was a stranger to all illicit passions. This truly was a special gift which we find granted to few, and which ought to be tried by no one lest they come into danger of temptation. For every individual is called to his own vocation, let him remain in that vocation before God.[101] For David said, *'neither do I exercise myself in great matters or in things too high for me.'*[102] He indeed walks in things too high for him who tries to do things which the Godhead has not granted to him.

XXIV. A horse stolen by robbers is restored to him

31. But I shall relate how even brigands feared him and how he made thieves wary. A certain Sempronius and Thuribius, driven on and tempted by the devil came to the dwelling of the man of God to rob it. And although it is written concerning the Just Man *'There shall no evil befall thee, neither shall any plague come nigh thy dwelling'*,[103] these two either for their own chastisement or to provide an example were allowed to draw near to Aemilian but forbidden to chastise him, indeed they were caught and themselves felt the chastisement of God. The thieves when they reached dwelling of the holy man, came across outside it the beast upon which he was accustomed to ride to church and stole away with it.[104] They did not enjoy their ill-gotten gain for long. For after a little while, they came, each having lost the use of an eye, begging for pardon and bringing back the animal. The holy man of God took back the horse, rebuked himself for having ever owned it, sold it

---

[101] cf *I Corinthians* 7.20. Braulio is eager here to discourage any thought among his readers that they should become solitary hermits.

[102] *Psalm* 131.1.

[103] *Psalm* 91.10.

[104] Berceo, *op.cit.*, stanza 271, refers to the incident taking place in the 'pasto de la Varga', unfortunately this has not been identified.

straight away, and gave its price to the poor. However he did not restore the thieves' sight, prompted, I believe, by his spirit of discretion reasoning that unless they were deprived of their eyes they would not cease from deeds such as that they had perpetrated on him, and that if they wished to do something similar again, they would swiftly be betrayed from their lairs by the marks on their bodies and their ill-repute. For who would think that a man who both alive and dead often restored sight to the blind could not have obtained this boon from the Lord? But it was better for them to pay the price of their deed in this life rather than after it, as it is said, '*it is better for thee to enter into life with one eye, rather than having two eyes to be cast into hell fire'.*[105]

XXV. He learns of the day of his death

32. When in the hundredth year of his life, about a year before he was to pass on from the body, it was revealed to him that his human labours would be brought to an end and that he would receive the most holy promises of the Almighty, he turned to a stricter way of life. A man who had dried up his limbs through vigils and fasting, now entered this new campaign like a veteran soldier, so that his end might be the more outstanding and of a kind that is always held better and more praiseworthy by Christ, Who says '*he that shall endure unto the end, the same shall be saved.*'[106]

XXVI. He predicts the Doom of Cantabria

33. During Lent in the same year the doom of Cantabria was revealed to him. Therefore he sent a messenger and instructed the senate to meet

---

[105] *Matthew* 18.9, *Mark* 9.46. Aemilian's harsh approach runs contrary to normal hagiographic accounts which tend to emphasise the forgiveness of the saint. This may well be a reflection on Braulio's unease at the notion of forgiving bandits who were rife in his area, see *Ep.*3. Forgiveness is a virtue attributed to St Martin, said never to have judged any one by Sulpicius Severus (*VSM* 26), and to St Augustine whom we are told turned a blind eye to his monks' lapses (Possidius, *V.Aug* 18.8).

[106] *Matthew* 24.13.

him on Easter Day.[107] When they gathered at the appointed time, he told them what he had seen, and reproved them for their crimes: murder, theft, incest, violence and other sins, and told them to make penance for all of these. Although they all listened to him reverently (for they all regarded him as a venerable man and almost as if he was one of the disciples of our Lord Jesus Christ), a certain Abundantius said that he had gone senile in his old age.[108] But Aemilian told him what he in

---

[107] There has been great debate as to whether 'Cantabria' here refers to a city or a district. *RAH Ms Emil.39* fol.245r, dating to the eleventh century, contains the following gloss referring to these events: 'Of Cantabria. In the *Life of Saint Aemilian* it speaks of *The doom of Cantabria which was foretold by him*. King Leovigild invaded and slew the raiders of the province. He occupied Amaya, took their wealth and brought the province back under his sway... Cantabria is sited on Mount Iggeto next to the source of the Ebro. Leovigild, the heretic king, destroyed it'. Berceo, *op.cit.*, stanza 292, also assumes that a town is intended and notes that the city was never rebuilt, but that three towers could still be seen on its site. Berceo is probably referring to a hill which is still known as Cantabria which lies to the North of the Ebro near Logroño between Rioja Alavesa and Navarre. John of Biclarum on the other hand, while recording Leovigild's campaign (*Chron.* 32 (AD 574)), makes no mention of a town called Cantabria. Isidore while saying that the Cantabrians are named from a town and the river Ebro, *Etymologiae* 9.4.113, a statement which might seem to support the notion of a town Cantabria, also states that Cantabria is a region, 'such as is commonly called a *conventus*' of Galicia. The seventeenth century authors Moret [1655] and Oihenart [1638] denied the existence of the town, and apart from the references listed above there are no sources attesting its existence. Madoz [1846] 10.35, however was inclined to believe in the town, as was Dutton [1967] & [1992] who cites Madoz's description of the site with approval. The evidence of Isidore and John, however, appears to be decisive in ruling out this interpretation.

The issue is not without importance as if a district rather than a town is meant 'Cantabria' in this period appears to have been a term with a far wider geographical scope than the Cantabria of the Roman period. This is the conclusion drawn by Barbero and Vigil [1965] & [1974] and Pérez Bustamante [1974] who envisage Visigothic Cantabria embracing the area of Burgos and La Rioja. This view has been challenged by González Echegaray [1976-7], [1986] ch.3, and Besga Marroquín [1983] ch.4. who believe that the change in the meaning of 'Cantabria' did not come about until the 10th century. As Braulio does not make it clear whether the council travelled to Aemilian or Aemilian to the council, it could be argued that a Cantabrian regional council might still have travelled outside its own bounds to the audience with the Holy Man.

Leovigild did not capture all of Cantabria as a small area which gave its allegiance to the Franks was finally conquered by Sisebut in AD 607, see Pseudo-Fredegar, *Chron.* 4.33, Azkarate Garai-Olaun [1993], and Larrañaga Elorza [1993].

[108] The description of the sins of Cantabria and the ridicule poured on Aemilian has echoes of Job and the destruction of Sodom in *Genesis* 19.

person was going to suffer. And events bore him out, for he was cut down by the avenging sword of Leovigild.[109] He attacked the rest too in equal measure for their perjury and treachery, predicting the coming wrath of God since they did not repent of their former works, and was anointed with their blood.

XXVIII. His death and burial

34. Now when the time of his death was approaching, he summoned the most holy priest Asellus who had been his colleague and in whose presence his most fortunate soul was freed from the body and returned to heaven.[110] Then, through the care of that most blessed man, his body was carried with great devotion being paid it by the devout and laid where it remains to this day in his oratory.[111] Farewell, Farewell, Blessed Aemilian, freed from mortal cares, take hold of your good fortune among the company of saints, and mindful of the teller of your life, the worthless Braulio, come forward as his intercessor, so that through you I, who am unable to flee my evil deeds, might find pardon and earn this vicarious reward: that my prayers for indulgence for my sins be heard through the favour of him whose virtues I set down with

---

[109] Leovigild's expedition against Cantabria took place in AD 574, John of Biclarum, *Chronicle* 73. For the 'avenging sword', cf the avenging wrath of God at *Romans* 13.4. If the account is taken literally, Abundantius may have been the leader of the Cantabrians. Berceo, *op.cit.*, stanza 291, makes him the first to die in the battle, though this could easily be a *post eventum* deduction from Braulio's account. The religious affiliation of Cantabria is unclear, but if it was Orthodox Braulio is placed in the awkward position of having to endorse an Arian conquest of an Orthodox area. He sidesteps this problem magnificently by making Leovigild an instrument of God's wrath.

[110] Breviaries place Aemilian's death day on 12 November, AD 574, cf Berceo, *op.cit.*, stanza 363.

[111] Berceo, *op.cit.*, stanza 313, adds that the tomb was carved out by Aemilian himself during his lifetime. The relics of the saint were transferred in AD 1030 to the church of San Millán de Suso built by the saint's oratory. In AD 1053 they were said to have miraculously resisted the attempts of García III of Nájera to take them to the Collegiate church of Sta María la Real in Nájera. The king consequently built the Church of San Millán de Yuso, which is identical to his foundation in Nájera, in the valley below San Millán de Suso and the saint's relics were laid to rest there in AD 1067. This church was entirely rebuilt in the sixteenth century. Apart from relics of Aemilian and Felix, others belonging to Adelphius, Braulio, Conantius, Eugene II, Eulalia, Fructuosus, Ildefonsus, Isidore, Leander, and Montanus were also to be found here.

my pen, and that along with these men over whom I unworthily exercise pastoral care, I might be found justified at the last judgement. I feel that this small work is coming to its close, but after speaking of the miracles he performed while alive, should we be silent about the acts of grace performed by him when dead? I shall bring forward two or three miracles, so that those told to us by the testimony of others and attested to in writing might be made all the more credible.

XXVIII. The blind receive sight at his tomb

35. An account of how many blind men have had their sight restored at his tomb, how many of the possessed have been purged of their troubles, or how many men suffering from all kinds of disease have been cured there which began from the time of this saint's death and ran down to our times would be too long to add this to this little book. But I think that this one example is worthy to be written down: that immediately after his passage to heaven two men deprived of sight were restored to the light.

XXIX. A lamp-wick of God was lit

36. Indeed this last year, close to the feast of St Julian the Martyr, there was no *oil for the light,*[112] and its wick remained unlit. However when they rose for their vigil they found the lamp full of oil and burning. It not only provided light until the morning, but from the great amount that remained this wonder produced further wonders.[113]

XXX. A blind and lame woman is healed

37. A woman, Eufrasia by name, was brought there from Banonicum.[114] She was blind and lame, but upright and clear-sighted in faith as can be deduced from this tale. When she had been anointed on her eyes and feet,[115] straight away the propitious Godhead gave her the ability to see

---

[112] *Exodus* 25.6.
[113] cf *VSD* 14.
[114] Location unknown, the fifteenth century translation reads 'Bannos.'
[115] Presumably with the oil mentioned in the preceding chapter.

and walk. Let men believe these things told through the testimony of witnesses who have seen the deeds done in our times. Indeed the place where she lives, and the woman, once an invalid, but now cured, are known.

XXXI. A girl is raised from the dead

38. Again another girl, about four years old, from Pratum which is not far from his oratory,[116] was taken by sickness and brought by it almost to the end of her life. Her parents moved by piety and fearing that they would be bereaved, decided that she should be taken to the tomb of the blessed man of God. As they carried her she seemed to die on the journey. Nevertheless as they did not lack in faith, they brought the dead girl to the place and placed her by the altar. Then, as the day was drawing to a close, they withdrew thence, leaving no-one there. When three hours had passed, they returned partly from curiosity and partly overcome by grief to see what it had pleased the Creator to do with her. They found alive she whom they had left dead and not only living but playing with the altar cloth. They glorified Christ who establishes all things and who had looked with favour on their devout grief. Behold, here at the present and in our times is another Elisha, whose dead bones bring lifeless limbs to life![117] But while the men of old fled in fear, these folk bore the girl and placed her at the altar full of faith. From this we can see that there is one and the same God in the Old and New Testaments, our Lord Jesus Christ, *who only doeth wondrous things.*[118] He hid the hope of happiness from those fearing him,[119] men panic-stricken under the law of fear, and not yet strengthened by charity which *casteth out fear: because fear hath torment,*[120] but now that Power Which alone gives life to the dead has made those who believe in Him and live trusting in Him whole through the Grace of Faith. The Power that raises the dead is one and the same, but manifests Itself differently at different times, just as the motives of those bringing the

---

[116] Possibly Pradilla located near San Millán de Suso.
[117] cf *2 Kings* 13.21.
[118] *Psalm* 72.18.
[119] cf *Psalm* 31.20.
[120] *1 John* 4.18.

dead were different. For one group brought the corpse that they might bury it, the other to receive it back again living. Hence we are given to understand how great is the rest of blessedness possessed by Holy men at whose tombs the Almighty Lord performs such wondrous deeds.

We have honoured our promise, it remains to bring the course of our tale to an end and give thanks to Christ, the King of heaven, by Whose aid and inspiration we have seen this work begun and ended, Who has granted us, for the consolation of our present sufferings the contemplation of the life[121] of holy men, Who lives with God the Father and the Holy Spirit, one God, world without end. Amen

---

[121] Braulio's use of the singular here is deliberate as all holy men were regarded as living the divine life which was a unity; see Gregory of Tours, *Life of the Fathers*, Preface where Gregory defends his use of the singular and an anonymous monk of Whitby's *The Life of Gregory the Great* 30 (edition by Colgrave [1968]).

[Paul the Deacon]

THE LIVES OF THE FATHERS OF MERIDA

In the Name of the Lord here begins the book of the lives of the Holy Fathers of Merida

PREFACE to this book

1 No Orthodox believer and above all no Catholic ought to disbelieve in the miracles which that most holy and famed bishop, Gregory, Bishop of the city of Rome, fired by the grace of the Comforting Spirit, set down in his books of *Dialogues,* writing them with a pen which told the truth:[1] miracles which in olden times Almighty God thought it fit to work for the glory of His name through humble servants who were indeed pleasing to Him. **2** Let no one's mind be troubled by this doubt: that these things appear to have happened in ancient times, and so perhaps not believe in them completely, thinking that this holy man of divine election, a tabernacle of the Holy Spirit, has obfuscated some points with empty and nebulous language. For through the authoritative words of the evangelists it is made clearer than the light of day to everyone that the Lord had always worked miracles and works them to this day.[2] **3** Wherefore in order that the faith of all those reading or listening may be strengthened with greater and stouter belief, I shall tell of the things that have happened in the city of Merida in our present times: which are not events we have learned about from the tales of strangers or from contrived fables, but which we ourselves have heard with our own ears from those who have left the body in wondrous fashion and who we have no doubt have reached the heavenly realms.

---

[1] Gregory I 'the Great', Pope AD 590 to 604. Gregory's four books of *Dialogues* which deal with miracles performed by mainly Italian saints were written between AD 593 and 594; for a detailed discussion see Petersen [1984].

[2] See especially *Mark* 16.17-18, the words spoken by Christ just prior to His ascension: 'And these signs shall follow them that believe; In my name shall they cast out devils; they shall speak with new tongues; They shall take up serpents; and if they drink any deadly thing, it shall not hurt them; they shall lay hands on the sick, and they shall recover.'

1. Here begins the account of the death of the young boy Agustus

1 There was a young boy, not yet of advanced years, in fact still but a youth, called Agustus.[3] Innocent, artless, unlearned in letters, while he was faithfully performing with his fellow youths the tasks laid upon him by the venerable man in charge of the convent in the House of the glorious virgin Eulalia, he suddenly happened to fall ill.[4] 2 When many came to visit him, as is the custom - I myself often went there - , it happened that one night, when the solemn vigil had been completed, (for in winter it is the practice in this holy church to celebrate, with the Lord's help, the offices of Matins and Lauds separately with a short interval between them[5]), 3 I rose to see him and, entering the cell where he lay on his bed, found all who were there so deep in slumber that none of them were wakened by my entry. Indeed, I found the light which had been lit there had gone out. 4 Straightaway I told all those lying before him to get up and commanded that the light which had gone out be relit. When we had light, I asked this boy Agustus how he was. 5 He replied, 'As regards hope for this present life, I confess that all the limbs of my body are undone and no strength remains to me. However, as regards hope for the life eternal, I rejoice that I have not only hope, but say that I have seen that very author of life eternal, the

---

[3] The dropping of the classical 'u' is common in the Visigothic period.

[4] For the training of young boys destined for the priesthood in an ecclesiastical house see *II Toledo* 1 (AD 527) and *IV Toledo* 24 (AD 633) where the institution is called a 'domus ecclesiae'.

Boys placed in such an institution by their parents would remain there until the age of eighteen when they had the choice to leave or continuing their religious career. A prayer and benediction for new entrants have survived in the Mozarabic *Liber Ordinum*, see Férotin [1904] 38, 39. For a general discussion of education in this period see Riché [1962].

It is unlikely that the inscription cited by Garvin [1946] 275 = *ICERV* 348 (Kindly Martyr Eulalia hold this house under your rule so that the Enemy knowing this might flee in confusion and this house and its inhabitants flourish with your aid. Amen) refers to a specific house of Eulalia. It appears rather to be an apotropaic inscription for an ordinary dwelling place (cf the Mozarabic prayer for entering a house, Férotin [1904] 176). The strength of this belief in Eulalia's powers can be seen throughout *VPE*.

[5] cf *Rule of St Benedict* 8. For a detailed discussion of ecclesiastical offices in the Visigothic Church see Férotin [1912] col.54-71. These are the two offices combined by Cranmer in the *Book of Common Prayer* to produce Morning Prayer.

Lord Jesus Christ, with the hosts of angels and innumerable throngs of all the saints.'[6] 6 When I heard this, I was astounded, trembled greatly, and begged him to tell me all that he had seen as it had happened. To this he replied, 'I call the Lord of Heaven and Earth as my witness that I will not tell you of some fantastical vision, but that you might believe more fully, I tell you that I have not slept this night.' 7 When he had said this, he began his tale as follows, 'I was in a beautiful place where there were many fragrant flowers, the greenest grass, roses, lilies, many crowns of gems and gold, countless silken trappings, and a gentle breeze which cooled everything with its refreshing, airy breath.[7] There I saw innumerable seats to the right and to the left and in the middle a seat set forth much higher than the rest. There were countless serving-boys, all well-dressed and handsome, preparing the tables and a glorious feast. The rich dishes were not of meat, but all of fowl and everything which was being prepared was white like snow[8] and they were awaiting the coming of the Lord, their King.' 9 Then I, though unworthy, thinking that it would be worthwhile for me to hear him speak more fully of this great wonder, said to him, 'Tell me, I beg of you, while this of which you speak was being prepared, what were you doing?' 10 He replied, 'I kissed all their feet, and they said to me, 'Blessed is God Who has done well bringing you here.' 11 While they were saying this and finishing all their tasks, suddenly there arrived a great multitude of men dressed in white, all adorned with gold and precious stones, and wearing gleaming crowns.[9] And one division of this multitude came on from the right and another from the left and thus hastening from both sides they offered their king ineffable homage. 12 In their midst came a most splendid and incredibly beautiful man, well proportioned, glorious to

---

[6] cf *Daniel* 10.8.
[7] There are strong verbal echoes here of Prudentius, *Apotheosis* 841-2. For the *locus amoenus* see Gregory the Great, *Dial.* 4.87 and the vision of Saturus in the *Passio of St Perpetua and Felicity* 11. The entry of the dead into the garden of Eden was also a common feature of Jewish funerary imagery in this period, see Roth [1948].
[8] This insistence on the whiteness of everything Agustus sees may explain the absence of red meat. However, it may also reflect the view that the monastic rule Agustus knew was meant to mirror the heavenly life. We know that red meat (*quadripedum carnes*) was banned, save in exceptional circumstances, by the *Rule of St Benedict*, ch.39.
[9] cf *Revelation* 4.4. The whiteness of the elect is a common topos in early Christian thought.

behold. He was taller than all the others, brighter than the sun and whiter than snow.[10] **13** When they came to the seats which had been prepared for them, this more beautiful man sat in the higher place and the rest fell down and adored him and then sat in their places. Straightaway he blessed them all and they adored him once, twice, three times over. Then the dishes which had been prepared were set before them. **14** When they had begun to eat that distinguished personage who sat in the high place said to those who stood by him, 'Is there not some sojourner here?' and they replied, 'There is, my Lord.' Then he said, 'Let him be brought into my sight.' I, indeed, was standing far off and watching. **15** When I was brought before his gaze, I began to tremble violently.[11] He said to me 'Do not be afraid, my son. Go behind me and stand here.'[12] and added, 'Do not be afraid. Know that I will be your protector.[13] You shall never lack for anything. I will always feed you,[14] I will always clothe you, I will protect you for all time, and never leave you.'[15] **16** And straightaway he ordered that food and drink, the like of which I had never seen, be given me from that self-same feast. Taking it, I received it with all joy. And truly I tell you that I was so refreshed by the grace of that food that thereafter I had no desire for any other kind of food save it alone. **17** So when the feast had come to an end, he said to me, 'Let this multitude depart. You will come with me by another route that I might show you the garden which I have in my keeping. And again when the banquet had ended all fell down and adored him, and the king blessing them gave them permission to leave. **18** As they were going, they dragged some men, I know not whom, before his tribunal who were crying out and wailing. When he heard their cries, he said, 'Drag the wicked servants outside, they are not worthy to see my face.' When he had said this, they were taken away

---

[10] Christ. Tallness is a common attribute of superiority in antiquity - see *Passio of St Perpetua and Felicity* 4. It is also found in pagan contexts, e.g. the depiction of Trajan on Trajan's Column.

[11] cf. *Isaiah* 6.5 and *Hebrews* 10.31: 'It is a fearful thing to fall into the hands of the living God.'

[12] To stand behind a noble was an act expressing both loyalty to and dependence on that person, cf the behaviour of Witteric at 5.10.10.

[13] cf *Genesis* 15.1.

[14] cf *Genesis* 50.21.

[15] cf *Joshua* 1.5.

wondrous swiftly so that I could not see them clearly nor recognise them.'[16] 19 Questioning him again, I said, 'I beg you, my son, to tell me if you recognised anyone among them of those who were known to us in this world and who, summoned from the light of day, have passed on.[17] To which he replied, 'The men whom I saw there, were very different from the men we see here,[18] for they were all of a different form[19] and clothed in a different sort of dress.' 20 Then he added, 'After they dragged those men outside, the Lord who was more handsome than the rest, rose up from his seat and, taking me by the hand, led me to a most beautiful garden,[20] where there was a river with water the colour of glass[21] and along its bank were many flowers and woods scented with incense and smelling of various pleasing fragrances. 21 Thus going along the bank we came to the place which I now see as I lie on my bed.' 22 These are the things that the boy remembered and told me in the presence of many people. Wherefore I, though unworthy and to the fore in all manners of sinning, a Levite[22] of Christ, chose to write it down as he told it, albeit in different words, but nevertheless ones carrying the same meaning. 23 Then I took care to tell everything that I had heard to that most holy man, my Lord the abbot. When he heard these things, being, as ever, full of piety in his innermost soul, he hurried as quickly as possible to that same Agustus and questioned him eagerly about what he had seen, wishing to hear tale he had told from his own lips. And Agustus repeated in the same fashion what he had said, intimating it to his blessed ears. Then he repeated once more to a kindly and most blessed Levite and all the brethren who were questioning him what he had said a little while before. 25 Soon his soul began to burn with a desire to receive penance.[23] As soon as he had

---

[16] cf *Matthew* 25.30. The banquet scene and judgement carry slight overtones of *Daniel* 7.10.

[17] For the notion of death as a summons see *Matthew* 24.26, 25.1, 25.13.

[18] cf Gregory the Great, *Dial.* 1.10.

[19] cf *1 Corinthians* 15.40-55.

[20] Perhaps a reference to the Garden of Eden.

[21] cf the glassy sea in *Revelation* 4.6.

[22] i.e. a deacon. This is the only autobiographical note we have for the hagiographer.

[23] The sacrament of Penance, or the forgiveness of sins committed after baptism could only be granted once (Hermas, *Shepherd*, *Mand.*4.1.8 and Tertullian, *De Paenitentia* 7.9.10) Any lapse thereafter would be mortal and therefore the rite which entailed absolute

received it, I went out and hurried to pray at the Basilica of Holy Mary Ever-Virgin which the common people call to this day the church of Her Who Brings Rest, and which lies five miles from the city of Merida.[24] When, as dusk was drawing on, I returned thence I found him dead. 26 Since it was already evening, he could not buried that day.[25] That night while his little body lay unburied in the cell where he had died, in the stillness of the night that same Agustus standing outside called out in a great voice to another youth of his own age, Quintilias. 27 After his voice had been heard and recognised, an artless and truthful boy called Veranian at once got up, went outside, and was permitted to see Agustus himself standing there clothed in white.[26] Petrified by fear, he did not presume to draw closer to him whose face he testified on

---

and perpetual chastity and renunciation of the world (see Tertullian, *De Paenitentia* passim, Councils of Elvira, c.AD 306, Saragossa, AD 380 and *I Toledo* c.AD 400) was normally only performed close to death. Those who recovered from illness after penance were excluded from further worldly activity as King Wamba found to his distress in AD 680 when he found himself debarred from being king (see *4 Toledo* 17 and *12 Toledo* 2). The rite for penance can be found in the *Liber Ordinum* = Férotin [1904] 87-93. See *ICERV* 42 for a Saturninus who died at Merida after receiving the rite.

For a brief general discussion of penance in the early church see *Di Berardino* [1992] vol.2 sv Penitence. For a more in-depth discussion centred on Visigothic Spain see González [1950] Martínez Díez [1968], and Lozano Sebastián [1974], [1980].

[24] Following the minority reading of manuscript O 'quietissima'. Other manuscripts refer to an otherwise unknown saint, Sta Quintisina. Given the context of the passage, it would have made sense for the hagiographer to go to pray in a church associated with a cult of the dead and one of the prime functions associated with the Marian cult is that of bringing comfort to the dying; see, for example, the last line of the rosary. The location of the church might also suggest that it was connected to an extra-mural cemetery which would explain how the unofficial epithet 'quietissima' might have been attached to the Church. The church itself is probably to be identified with La Ermita de Nuestra Señora de Ureña situated in the Campos de Judíos.

[25] Burial on the same day as death was the normal custom. *VII Toledo* 3 (AD 646) refers to the requirement of *Valencia* (AD 546) that bishops should be buried within a day and a night of their death. This may have been to cut down the opportunity for relic hunting, see Prudentius, *Peristephanon Martyrorum* 6.130-141.

[26] Sulpicius Severus (*Ep* 2.3) had a vision of St Martin who appeared before him dressed in white and with a 'fiery face.' For the 'whiteness' of the elect see Gregory of Tours, *VP* 1 praef.

oath was snowy white.[27] **28** The following day his little body was entrusted to the grave according to custom in the basilica of the most blessed virgin my Lady Eulalia.[28]

2. Here begins the account of the death of a Monk of Cauliana

1 Very many worthy men say that a good many years before our time, a miracle of Our Saviour was graciously worked through His divine clemency in the province of Lusitania. **2** It happened in the monastery of Cauliana which does not lie far from the city of Merida, being some eight miles distant, when that most reverend man of pious memory, the abbot Renovatus, presided over it, having already shown himself a wondrous bishop of the city of Merida.[29] While he, as befitted a far-sighted man of the sharpest intellect who was most zealous in every discipline and in his fear of God, continually called all the monks dwelling there to their heavenly home by his wise care, the goodness of his life, and his example of performing good deeds, and all the flock was following their shepherd, who went before them, along the narrow

---

[27] cf accounts of the transfiguration, esp. *Luke* 9.29 and of Moses' face glowing after he had spoken with God, *Exodus* 34.29. A mysterious man who appeared to and cured a female cripple in a dream at Brioude had a complexion 'brighter than a lilly' (Gregory of Tours, *Virt.Jul.* 9.) Gregory of Tours describes Gregory of Langres' body after his death as having a rosy face and a body as white as a lily 'so that one would have said that he was already prepared for the glory of the future resurrection' (*VP* 7.3).

[28] This church, as we later learn, lay outside the walls of the town. Recent excavations make it clear that it occupied the site of the present-day church of the same name, see Cabellero Zoreda & Mateos Cruz [1992] and [1993]. Prudentius refers to a 'tumulus' of Eulalia, *Peristephanon Martyrorum* 3.191-200, in terms which would apply to a richly decorated church. However the poet must have been exaggerating as the remains from this period are of a small apsed mausoleum surrounded by a necropolis. For a discussion of Prudentius' account of the site see Arce [1982] and [1992]. The mausoleum was replaced by a larger basilica in the fifth century. The church remained in use through the Visigothic period, but fell into disuse during the Arabic occupation of the town. The present church dates from the thirteenth century.

[29] The site of Cauliana is generally accepted as that of Santa María de Cubillana, see Garvin [1946] 313, for a more sceptical attitude see Puertas Tricas [1975]. A local legend records that Roderic, the last king of Visigothic Spain, fled here in the hope of rallying his troops after his defeat by Arab general Tarik Ibn Ziyad at Guadalete, see Menéndez Pidal [1906].

tracks and roads to heaven,[30] a ravenous wolf striving with all its might, tried to rip away one little sheep with its snapping jaws. **4** For while the whole throng of the congregation continued in their praise of God and walked in the path of righteousness through fear of the Lord, a certain monk found fault with their most holy life and gave himself up to gluttony and drunkenness beyond measure, handing himself over to perdition. Thenceforth he persisted ever more in his intent and began to steal whatever he could find. **5** The man of God rebuked him in a kindly fashion on very many occasions, but did not easily prevail upon him. Again and again Renovatus earnestly rebuked him with his words, but when he would not abstain from the seductive pleasure of gluttony[31] or his designs to steal and thieve, the abbot ordered him to be flogged, put on iron rations, and thrust into a punishment cell.[32] **6** But the monk in no way returned to enduring his old devotions, and not only in no way ceased from his sins, but, soiling himself every day, hastened to entrust himself ever more quickly to the Tartarean caves of Hell.[33] **7** When Renovatus saw that he was so determined to press on down this route and that although he had been rebuked and flogged very many times, he had no wish to mend his ways, touched by sorrow in the depths of his heart,[34] he dismissed him to live according to the desires of his heart.[35] **8** He gave this instruction to those in charge of the monastery's stores: that whenever this monk wished to enter, no one was to stop him eating or drinking, to the point of being sick, whatever good and sweet food he found in the cellars. Even if he wanted to steal and hide some of the provisions, as was his custom, he was to have the liberty to do so, in order that they might see more clearly what he would soon do after he had sated his throat and belly. **9** He, indeed, on finding the doors unbolted in obedience to the abbot's instructions, stealthily and with great care entered the cellars of that most wealthy (as

---

[30] cf *Matthew* 7.14.

[31] cf *Philippians* 3.19.

[32] cf Fructuosus' *Rule of Compludo* chapters 15, 16 (English translation in Barlow [1969])

[33] The word for 'hell' used here is the classical 'Avernus'. The passage may be meant to echo the Sibyl's famous address to Aeneas at *Aeneid* 6.125*ff.* which contains the phrase 'It is easy to go down to Hell' (*facilis decensus Averno*) and also makes use of 'Tartarus'.

[34] cf *Genesis* 6.6.

[35] cf *Psalm* 81.12 and the Fructuosian *Common Rule* ch.14.

they say)[36] monastery. However, he was surrounded a little way off by guards on all sides who, cunningly hidden, watched him, all unawares, waiting to see what he would do. He devoured and gulped down everything he found that was sweet or pleasant to eat or drink, until, having lost his wits, he was scarcely able to walk. 10 Then furtively carrying off some food and flasks of wine which are commonly called gills or flagons,[37] he took them to the garden which adjoined the monastery and hid them in a secret place among the thick bushes or clumps of reeds. 11 Then sated from his surfeit of food and stricken from the volume of wine he had drunk, he lay down to sleep setting by himself the things he had stolen. For although it now gave him no pleasure and his overloaded stomach was belching, he still lusted to eat and drink. 12 But when the weight of his stomach made him too ill to eat, straightaway he became drowsy and fell asleep. Dogs then came and ate everything he had carried off, and the guards who had looked on from a distance came and took the vessels he had stolen back to the cellars while he slept. 13 When this had gone on for a long time and everyone thought that he would never be reformed, the Shepherd and Good Saviour delivered him out of the mouth of the lion.[38] 14 For it happened one day that when at first light he came out of the cellar the worse for drink as was usual, some little boys who were studying letters with their teachers in the schoolrooms[39] saw him drunk and at once cried out, 15 'Mend your ways, hard-hearted one, mend your ways at last. Think on the terrible judgement of God. Think on the fearful sentence of His terrible scrutiny. Think on the frightening and horrible severity of that judge's vengeance. Think too on your years and at last change your ways for the better and set your life to rights for at least one day before you die. For if what you do is not permitted to us children, it is all the more forbidden to you who are now full of

---

[36] This qualification is curious. Perhaps the hagiographer means to imply that the true wealth of Cauliana was to be found in the spirituality of its monks rather than its cellars.
[37] Isidore, *Etymologiae* 20.6.2 says that 'flask' is a Greek word. The hagiographer is drawing attention to the size not the name of the vessels.
[38] cf *2 Timothy* 4.17.
[39] This is ecclesiastical schooling of the same form as that found in the House of Eulalia in section 1.

years.[40] **16** When he heard this, he blushed, and filled with great shame was cut to the quick on the spot. Weeping and wailing he lifted his tearful eyes to the heavens and said, *'Lord Jesus Christ, Saviour of souls, who desireth not the death of sinners, but rather that they may turn from their wickedness and live*[41] I pray you correct me and take this shameful dishonour from me or, indeed, if you so wish, take me now from this wretched life, that I might no longer hear reproaches to my face'. **17** Straightaway the Pious Godhead did not disdain to hear him, but at once in that self-same place struck him down with sickness and caused him to burn with a powerful fever. **18** His mighty right hand worked such a change in him, turning him to a better life[42] that, abhorring all delights of the flesh and with his mind afire, he at once sought the remedy of penance: that is he fervently sought the sacrament of the body and blood of his Lord. **19** But while the gentle abbot thought he was asking for this because he was fevered or with profane intent he did not give him full penance, but merely ministered to him the grace of the *viaticum*.[43] But after three days and as many nights of weeping and by a wondrous confession, the monk convinced him of his sincerity. **20** Three days later when he was on the point of journeying from his body, he made his farewells to all the brethren, saying 'Know that all my sins have been forgiven. And, lo, before the gates of heaven the most holy apostles Peter and Paul with the blessed Laurence, archdeacon and martyr[44] with an innumerable host dressed in gleaming white are waiting for me, with whom I must go to the Lord.' And so speaking he passed from the body which was buried according to custom. **21** Fifteen years later *that noteworthy river, the Guadiana,*[45]

---

[40] The phrase 'full of years' presages the monk's imminent demise. It is found in the account of Abraham's (*Genesis* 25.8) and Isaac's (*Genesis* 35.29) deaths.

[41] The prayer of absolution, based on *Ezekiel* 33.11. This is still found as the Prayer of Absolution for Morning and Evening Prayer in the Book of Common Prayer.

[42] cf *Psalm* 77.10-11.

[43] Communion given in the face of death.

[44] A deacon of Spanish origin martyred at Rome in AD 258 and the subject of Prudentius, *Peristephanon Martyrorum* 2. His cult remains popular in Spain to this day. There is a service for his feast day (10th August) in the *Gothic Breviary*, *PL* 86 1178-1183.

[45] Taken directly from Prudentius, *Peristephanon Martyrorum* 3.188: 'memorabilis amnis Ana'.

flooded and having broken its banks, spread its waters far and wide, laying in ruins many buildings in the little villages by its stream and in similarwise overturned the cells of the monastery at Cauliana.[46] **22** When the monks wished to restore them, it came to pass that while they were laying the foundations upon the cell where this monk lay, they came across his tomb. And straightaway a heavenly odour came from it.[47] He himself was found to be whole and uncorrupted as if he had been buried that very hour nor were his vestments or hair found in any part to be corrupted.[48]

3. Here begins the account of the death of abbot Nanctus

1 While we have been trying to relate these recent events, we have passed over the deeds of our ancestors. **2** A great number of men say that many years ago in the time of Leovigild, king of the Visigoths,[49] an abbot called Nanctus came from the lands of Africa to the province of Lusitania.[50] After he had lived here for some time in a most holy fashion, he eagerly came through his devotion to the basilica of the most

---

[46] The last devastating flood was in 1947, see Alvarez Martínez [1983] lam.2.

[47] cf *2 Corinthians* 2.15. The smell was a clear sign of sanctity - see Gregory of Tours' account of the discovery of the grave of St Mallosus at Metz, *GM* 62.

[48] cf *1 Corinthians* 15.52. For a similar sweet-smelling, uncorrupted corpse see Gregory of Tours' account of that of St Valerius of Saint-Lizier, *GC* 83.

[49] Joint ruler with Liuva from AD 568-572, sole ruler from AD 572-586.

[50] We are given no reason for Nanctus' departure from Africa. It may have been provoked by the growing instability of the area, cf Donatus, *DVI* 4. Alternatively he may have left as a consequence of the 3 Chapters controversy. This was provoked by Justinian's clumsy attempt to bring monophysite sects back into the Orthodox fold. To do this the emperor attempted to unify the church around a condemnation of Nestorianism. Therefore in AD 543/4 he issued an edict (now lost) condemning the writings of Theodore of Mopsuestia, Theodoret of Cyrrhus, and the letter of Ibas to Mari (the 'Three Chapters'). All of these works had been cleared of heresy at the Council of Chalcedon in AD 451. The edict was confirmed at the controversial 5th ecumenical council held at Constantinople in AD 553. Despite the reluctant acquiescence of Pope Vigilius, the Western churches reacted with hostility to what was perceived as an attempt to move the church in the direction of monophysitism whose adherents were not in fact mollified by Justinian's actions. The strongest reaction came in Africa, see Markus [1966]. In these circumstances flight to Spain, which, while ruled by an Arian, had an Orthodox church hostile to Justinian and the Three Chapters (see Isidore, *DVI* 18) and was outside the ambit of Imperial persecution, may well have seemed highly attractive.

holy virgin Eulalia where her most holy body lies at rest. **3** It is said that he avoided the sight of women above all things, just as he would a viper's bite,[51] not because he despised the sex, but because he feared that through looking on their beauty he would fall into the sin of temptation.[52] So wherever he went, he arranged that one monk should walk a short distance in front of him and another a little behind so that on no occasion should a woman see him. **4** When, as we have said, he came to the basilica of the holy virgin and martyr Eulalia, he begged with many prayers that most reverend man, the deacon Redemptus[53] who was in charge of the place, to station guards in such a way that no woman might see him from afar when he went at night from his cell to the church to pray. **5** After he had tarried for some days in that holy church, a most noble and holy widow called Eusevia desired with all her might to see him, but he would in no way suffer to be seen by her. **6** When various men had repeatedly asked him that he might deem it fit to see her and he would not at all consent, she formed a plan and asked deacon Redemptus to arrange that the holy man be surrounded by bright candlelight after morning prayer when he was returning from the church to his cell, so that she, standing in a hiding place, might be able to see him, albeit from afar. And so it came to pass. **7** But when the woman's gaze fell upon him, although he was not aware of it, he prostrated himself on the ground with a great groan, as if he had been struck by heavy blow from a great stone. Then he said to the deacon, 'May God forgive you, brother. What have you done?' **8** After this he immediately

---

[51] Perhaps a reference to the serpent of the Garden of Eden.

[52] See Gregory the Great, *Dial.* 3.16 for Martin of Campania who vowed not to look on a woman. Conversely St Martin of Tours found a female hermit who refused to have contact with men, including St Martin himself, Sulpicius Severus, *Dial.*2.4.

The Apophegmata of the desert fathers contain the story of a monk who left a road when he saw a group of nuns coming along it. As he passed, their superior shouted out to him, 'If you were a true monk you would not have noticed that we were women.' (Nau, *Revue de l'Orient Chrétien* 1908, saying 155 or, more accessibly, Ward [1986] saying 22). Perhaps an example of such holiness is recorded by Gregory of Tours (*VP* 1.2, 1.6) in his life of St Romanus. Romanus we are told, although his colleague St Lupicinus vowed never to meet a woman, ministered to men and women alike in his 'simplicity' and asked not to be buried in a monastery where his corpse would have been inaccessible to women in order that both sexes could be healed at his tomb.

[53] Possibly the Redemptus of 5.11.20-21 in charge of the convent of St Eulalia and Masona's bank.

left and with a few brothers set out for the wilderness where on his arrival he built for himself built a lowly dwelling place. When his fame spread because of his many virtues, news of it came to the hearing of Prince Leovigild, 9 who although he was an Arian nevertheless, in order that Nanctus should commend him to God through his prayers, made over to him by written decree a special part of the royal estate from which he along with his brothers could obtain food and clothing.[54] 10 The man of God altogether refused to accept this boon. But when he persisted in his refusal, the messenger sent by the king came to him and said, 'You ought not to despise your son's gift' and through his persuasion Nanctus at last accepted the grant. 11 After some days had passed, the men who lived in that place began to say to one another, 'Let us go and see what this master we have been given is like.'[55] When they went and had seen him in his wretched clothes and with his hair uncut,[56] they despised him and said to one another, 'It would be better for us to die than serve such a master'.[57] 12 Some days later when the holy man of God had set forth to graze his few sheep in a copse, coming across him alone, they broke his neck and killed him. 13 Not long afterwards, they were taken on a charge of murder and brought before king Leovigild in chains. He was told that these were the men who had killed the man of God. 14 He, although he was not of the right faith, rightly sentenced them, saying, 'Free them from their chains and let them go. If they have killed a servant of God, let God avenge the death of His servant without recourse to my vengeance.' 15 When he said this, they were set free and at once seized by demons who afflicted them for many days until they drove their souls from their bodies through a cruel death. Thanks be to God.

---

[54] This neutral depiction of Leovigild contrasts sharply with the hostile light in which he is later portrayed. Leovigild's attitude to the Catholic church seems to have varied, Gregory of Tours, *GC* 12, tells us he restored everything his troops had plundered from a Catholic monastery dedicated to St Martin of Tours in the province of Valencia. However there can be no doubt that later in his reign he persecuted the Catholic church severely, see Gregory of Tours, *HF* 5.38.

[55] This exhortation bears strong verbal parallels to that of the Shepherds in Luke's account of the Nativity, see *Luke* 2.15.

[56] A sign of a slave, see *LV* 9.1.5.

[57] Given the verbal echoes above the hagiographer wishes the reader to recall *John* 1.10-11 here.

4. Here begins the account of the deaths and miracles of the holy bishops of Merida

Preface

1 Leaving aside the bedecked tropes of speech and discarding the long-winded froth of eloquence, we shall relate to simple folk in a simple and truthful fashion things which are altogether true. 2 For if we should wish to wrap up in darkly obscure speech those things which can be learnt more clearly by the light of day, we should weary, not instruct the minds of our audience, since when the uneducated masses do not understand the sense of the words used, listening becomes wearisome for them. 3 Therefore, as we have promised, we shall relate the miracles performed by the holy fathers of old in simple fashion, just as they were handed down to us by the reports of many men.[58]

1

1 It is often told how a holy man called Paul, a Greek by nationality[59] and a doctor by trade, came from the lands of East to the city of Merida. 2 When he had lived there for a long time, gaining a good reputation from his sanctity and many good deeds, and surpassing everyone in his humility and kindness, the Lord granted him the gift of becoming bishop of the town. 3 When, with God's favour, he was ordained bishop, at once God did away with all the storms of strife which had troubled the church in the time of his predecessor and through Paul's prayers granted his church the greatest tranquillity.[60]

---

[58] For a parallel to the tropes used here see *VSA* 2 & 5.

[59] It is unclear whether this is a reference to Paul's race or the fact that he is a Greek-speaker (cf. the Greek Syro-Phoenician woman of *Mark* 7.26) There is no reason to infer a substantial Greek colony was present in Merida from the few inscriptions written in Greek found there, see Arce [1982].

[60] Unfortunately nothing is known of these events. Possibly there is an allusion to the civil war between Agila and Athanagild (AD 551-555) which led to the murder of Agila by his own men in Merida, Isidore, *HG* 45-46. However as we know that Masona was bishop by AD 573, the implied long incumbencies of his two predecessors make this chronology very tight if not impossible, see Garvin [1946] 359. It is more likely that internal ecclesiastical strife is being hinted at by the hagiographer; see *VPE* 4.4.5 below

2

1 While he, with God's favour, was peacefully and benignly presiding over all the citizens and showing the sweet-flowing care of his holy heart in return for the affections of all, it came to pass that the wife of a most noble man, one of the leading citizens of the town who was born of senatorial stock fell ill.[61] She too was of glorious descent and a noble family. 2 She had conceived after her wedding, but the child had died in her belly. Many doctors had tried a variety of treatments on her, but she felt no improvement in her body and was in grave danger, daily drawing closer to death. 3 There was nothing dearer to her illustrious husband than his wife, whom he had recently taken in the sacrament of matrimony, so spurning all doctors, he rushed to the holy man in the hope of restoring her health and cast himself at his feet. He tearfully begged him, that, as he was a servant of God, he should intercede in his prayers for the health of his wife, or surely, as he was a doctor, not think it unworthy for him to give the sick woman the favour of being cured by his own hand. 4 But straightaway the man of the Lord replied to him, saying, 'I am not permitted to do what you ask of me, for, although unworthy, I am a priest of the Lord and offer sacrifice to the Lord with my hands, and so am not able to do what you implore me to do, lest afterwards I should come to the holy altar with polluted hands and incur forthwith the wrath of the divine Godhead.'[62] 5 To which he added, 'We will go in the name of the Lord to visit her and entrust her to the doctors of the church[63] that they might give her medicine and to the best of our knowledge we will show them how they might effect a cure. I, however, cannot treat her with my own hands.' 6 The nobleman knowing that no other doctor could produce a cure and that his wife was already close to death, began to weep greatly and earnestly begged him

---

for further hints that these problems in fact continued during Paul's episcopate and *DVI*, *preface* for an account of similar problems at Toledo.

[61] Presumably this is the senate of the town. Cf the senate of Cantabria, *VSA* 33.

[62] Our earliest indication of the prohibition of the medical profession for priests which remained in force in the Roman Catholic church until 1983.

[63] This reference shows that the doctors of Masona's *xenodocium* were not an innovation for the Meridan Church. *ICERV* 288 records a doctor [Reccar]edus from the town. The inscription probably dates to the sixth century. For a general discussion of the practice of medicine in Merida in the Roman and Visigothic periods see Sanabria Escudero [1964].

not to send anyone to his house, but to come himself and apply his knowledge with his own hands. 7 When he would not agree or in anyway consent to this, all the brethren who were by him also begged him with tears in their eyes to go. He then said, 'I know the great compassion of the Lord and believe that if I go, he shall restore to this sick soul her former health, and straightaway grant me pardon for my presumption. But I have no doubt at all that wicked men will hold up this case against me in the future.'[64] 8 To which all his brethren replied. 'None of us shall say anything on account of this. But go, master, and perform with all haste that which will bring you rewards.' At last, overcome by their prayers, he promised to go, provided that beforehand he might ask permission of the Lord, lest rashly embarking on this task he might easily perform something, for which, if he was condemned by the judgement of God, he would only obtain pardon with difficulty. 9 Therefore he went at once to the basilica of the most holy virgin Eulalia and prostrating himself on the flags[65] lay there for a whole day and persevering in tireless prayer remained there the following night too. 10 Here he was given instructions by a divine oracle and at once rose and went without delay and in haste to the house of the sick woman, where he poured forth his prayer, and in the name of the Lord placed his hands on the sick soul. 11 Placing his hope in God, with wondrous skill he made a most skilful incision by his cunning use of the knife and extracted the already decaying body of the infant limb by limb, piece by piece and, with God's aid, restored forthwith the woman who was on the point of dying and only half alive, safe and sound to her husband. 12 He told her that she should have no further knowledge of her husband, for if at some time in the future she should know his embrace, worse troubles would soon befall her.[66] 13 But nonetheless they fell at his feet, thanked him, and promised that they would obey the man of God in everything that he commanded, begging God to inflict worse suffering on them in the future if they did not keep their promise. 14

---

[64] An insight into the ecclesiastical politics of the day and a hint perhaps that Paul's rule was not as calm as the hagiographer implies.

[65] Though Prudentius (*Peristephanon Martyrorum* 3.198-200) mentions a mosaic floor in Eulalia's shrine this was probably destroyed by the Vandals in AD 429. Mosaics are very rare in the Visigothic period so a simple flagged floor is more likely here.

[66] It appears that the woman's deliverance is regarded almost as an act of Penance.

There was indescribable happiness and unbounded joy in their house; all acclaimed God with their praise, and, praying and exulting, declared that the Lord had truly sent his angel who had pity on her.[67] **15** Then they drew up a document about their affairs to the effect that the holy man should immediately receive half of all they owned and that the other half should come under his control in its entirety and inviolate after their death.[68] They had such possessions that no richer senator than them could be found in the province of Lusitania. **16** Paul rejected their offer outright, refused it, and had no wish to accept, but they beseeched and pressed him so much that finally he was compelled to accept. On receiving this gift, he saw to it that the wealth served the needs of the poor rather than his own personal expenses. **17** The couple who had made this offering continued in chastity and the fear of God and not long afterwards were called by divine summons to the kingdom above.[69] **18** On their death the most holy bishop Paul received their entire patrimony and while he had arrived as a stranger owning nothing, he now became more powerful than all the potentates of the town so that all the belongings of the church were considered as nothing in comparison to his possessions.[70]

3

1 Finally, when he had passed very many happy years with his people, and living in a way pleasing to God had flourished ever full of virtue, **2** it happened that one day some Greek traders from the region from which he himself had come, arrived in their ships from the East and put in on the shore of Spain. When they came to the city of Merida,

---

[67] cf *Acts* 12.11.

[68] Visigothic women retained control of their property after marriage, including property acquired in the period of marriage, *LV* 3.2.6.

[69] An act of divine mercy as it reduced the time in which they could lapse from their vows.

[70] The point of this comparison implies that the Meridan church owned considerable wealth even prior to this bequest.

according to custom they presented themselves on arrival to the bishop.[71] 3 When they had been received by him in a kindly fashion they left his palace[72] and retired to the house where they were staying.[73] On the following day they sent him a small gift to thank him. It was taken by a boy called Fidel, who had come from their country with them as a hired hand to seek his fortune. 4 When he had been presented before Paul and the holy man had joyfully received the gift he had brought as token of thanks, the bishop began to question him point by point as to what he was called and from what province or town he came. 5 When he told him his name and named his home town, the bishop *seeing the young man that he was industrious*[74] questioned him about everything, taking one thing at a time, and asked the names of his parents.[75] By this questioning the boy revealed to Paul in all honesty his homeland, town, village, and the names of his parents. 6 As he was telling him, Paul recognised the name of his sister. At once he leapt from his seat and in the sight of all fell upon him with embraces, for his bowels yearned upon him,[76] and hanging upon his neck kissed him for

---

[71] The Pulo do Lobo rapids down river from Merida near Mertola, where the river falls some 50 feet means that it would have been impossible for the traders to reach the town by river, see Alvarez Martínez [1983] 10-11 & lam.3. It is more likely that they put in at Seville and travelled along the old Roman Road through the Sierra Morena to Merida. A ship dating from the Byzantine period was found in the Plaza Nueva at Seville during abortive attempts to build a metro for the city. For an enthusiastic attitude towards trade see García Moreno [1972], *contra* Arce [1982]. Byzantine influence was however fairly strong in Visigothic Spain, see Schlunk [1945a] and the remarks of Cruz Villalon [1982] 425 'la base primordial del reportorio iconográfico emeritense es bizantina'.

The traders' reception may indicate the predominant position of the Orthodox bishop in the life of the town (coming from the Orthodox East they would be unlikely to acknowledge an Arian bishop however important in local life) as is sometimes claimed however the hagiographer may simply be uninterested in the secular obligations of the traders such as the possible need to present themselves to the Count of the town.

[72] Referred to as the *atrium*. For this usage see Isidore, *Etymologiae* 15.3.4. The palace may have been built on the site of the Palacio del Duque de la Roca which was demolished in AD 1887, see Alvarez Sáenz de Buruaga [1975].

[73] It is unclear whether this house was a commercial enterprise or a predecessor of Masona's *xenodocium*.

[74] *1 Kings* 11.28 - said of Solomon on seeing David.

[75] cf *Genesis* 43.7.

[76] cf *1 Kings* 3.26.

a good while and wept forth the fullness of his joy.[77] **7** Straightaway he ordered the merchants to come before him and said to them, 'Give me this boy and ask whatever you want of me for him.' **8** They replied, 'This we cannot do for he is a freeman. We hired him from his parents to help us and we can in nowise return to them without him, nor will be able to look them in the eye if we leave him in such a far-flung country'.[78] **9** He replied, 'Let it be clear to you that if you do not leave me him, you shall not return to your own country, but accept a goodly sum of money from me and depart in safety, travelling in peace.'[79] **10** On hearing this, they were no longer able to resist such power and said to him, 'Tell us, Lord, why do you see fit to cherish with such love a man who is unknown to you?' **11** He then replied that he was a relative and indeed a very close kinsman. He added, 'Go in the Name of the Lord, and tell my sister without delay that I have kept her son with me as a consolation in my captivity.' He sent various gifts to his sister through them and also rewarded the sailors generously so that enriched by his presents they returned to their country with great joy.[80]

4

1 When they departed, he had this youth tonsured and brought him to serve almighty God. Like another Samuel he rigorously trained him by day and night in the temple of the Lord so that within a few years he knew perfectly all the offices of the church and the entire corpus of divine scripture.[81] Then, taking him through ranks of the church one by one, he ordained him as a deacon. **2** Made a dwelling place of the Holy

---

[77] cf *Genesis* 46.29.

[78] cf *Genesis* 44.23.

[79] A somewhat surprising attitude from a man of God. The implied power which lies behind this successful threat is unclear. As Orthodox believers from a hostile power Paul may merely have been threatening to denounce the merchants to the Gothic authorities of Merida as spies.

[80] Despite the various biblical parallels it is clear that Bishop Paul all but kidnapped Fidel, unless the story disguises a deliberate act of nepotism on his part.

[81] cf *1 Samuel* 2.18 ff. The ignorance of the clergy greatly exercised the Visigothic Church. St Aemilian when made a priest knew only 8 psalms, *VSA* 12. *IV Toledo* 26 (AD 633) provided that priests be given a Book of Offices to ensure they performed their duties correctly.

Spirit, he was so filled with every virtue that he surpassed all the clergy in holiness, charity, patience, and humility. He made himself so dear and so great a friend to both God and men that he was thought one of the angels. **3** Then, when for very many years he had served God without reproach and obeyed in sweet submission his teacher in everything and, never giving him offence, had in his gentleness gladdened his old age, the most blessed Paul, now that his many years had run their course and as he was verging on man's age of decrepitude, chose him to succeed him and, while still alive, ordained him as his successor.[82] He also made him heir of all his possessions, placing in the codicil of his will the condition that if the clergy of Merida were willing to have him as their bishop, on his death Fidel would in turn leave everything to the Meridan church that Renovatus had left to him, otherwise he would have a free choice to dispose and deal with the aforementioned goods as he saw fit.[83] **5** Truly the holy man made this decree through a revelation of the Holy Spirit,[84] knowing through the grace of prophecy that there would be no lack of wicked men to oppose Fidel through their envy: men, who like dogs, inflamed with the fires of envy would later surround him on all sides and wound him with their bites.[85] **6** Meanwhile, when under God's auspices Paul had made Fidel a priest, Fidel wished to stand by him and serve him as he had when he was a deacon and so taking off his chasuble[86] as if he were but a servant, he stood by him and performed his every chore. **7** Paul forbade him to act in this way and finally admonished him to preserve with constancy the authority of his episcopate, commanding him rather to spend his care on the well-being of his brethren. **8** The most holy old man himself soon abandoned his palace and all the privileges of his office and took himself off to a mean cell by the basilica of St Eulalia. One day while he was there, freed from the tempests of this world and

---

[82] A flagrant breech of Canon Law. The practice had been banned by *Antioch* 23 (AD 341) which is referred to in the Acts of *2 Braga* (AD 572), showing that its provisions were well known in the peninsula.

[83] The hagiographer has no reproach for this act of blackmail which verges on simony.

[84] Our author is embarrassed enough to indulge in special pleading here.

[85] cf *Psalm* 22.16

[86] This garment marked him as a priest rather than a deacon.

being greatly at peace, he passed from the body as he lay in sack-cloth and ashes,[87] praying to the Lord for the sins of the whole world.

5

1 After his death, some poisonous men, just as the man of God had predicted, began to murmur with wicked words against the most blessed bishop Fidel in order to drive him from the place where he had been set whenever the opportunity presented itself. 2 When he learned of this and wished to free himself together with his possessions from their onset, as it became known that he would leave them taking all his possessions with him as was his right under church law[88] and that nothing at all would be left for them, they prostrated themselves, though more unwillingly than willingly, before his feet and begged him with many prayers not to leave them. 3 He showed himself in nowise unwilling to perform the burdens of his office and at the end of his life to leave all his patrimony to the church. And this came to pass, so that in those days the church of Merida was so wealthy that no church in the land of Spain was richer. 4 And so, with the Lord's aid, the pure and sincere love of all for him was made so manifest that everyone of one accord, aflame with their great love of charity, burned for him with the boundless fire of holy ardour and forming with him one heart and one pair of lips they remained in perfect harmony nor did they allow dissention to creep in by turning to another love.[89]

6

1 Since we have made mention of so great a priest, it seems especially worthwhile to put on record some small part of those his deeds through which he frequently demonstrated his virtue. 2 Once on the Lord's Day,

---

[87] For the symbolism of this see Isidore, *De Eccl. Off.* 2.17.4-5.

[88] Another sign of embarrassment? Fidel certainly does not seem interested in a life of apostolic poverty.

[89] cf *Acts* 4.32. Fidel is seen as bringing apostolic fervour back to the church in an early example of religious revivalism. However given what we have just been told above, the hagiographer might be thought to protest a little too much in his assertions concerning Fidel's popularity.

when he was sitting in his palace with many sons of the church, the archdeacon with all the clergy clothed in white came in and stood before him as is the custom. **3** He rose and with deacons carrying censers going before him, as was the custom, he went with all who were present to the church that at God's command they might celebrate the solemn offices of the mass. **4** When they had all left the palace and had gone about ten paces from it, suddenly the whole of this huge edifice collapsed from the depths of its foundations, but God ordained that no one was to be crushed under it. **5** From this fact we should believe that this man was of such merit that by his prayers he obtained from God the boon that the Ancient Enemy should not be given the power to cast down so huge a structure in ruins before he, God having pity on him, had saved everyone by leading them outside without a single one of them being lost. Let no one doubt that this was granted above all through the merits of the most holy virgin Eulalia. **6** When after anxiously making inquiries he found that no one had perished, his soul was not at all sad, but rather he gave thanks to the Lord, joyfully performed the sacrifice to God, and spent that day with all his people rejoicing in the Lord. **7** After a short space of time, he restored the fabric of his ruined seat and, with God's help, made it more beautiful than before. He built an edifice which was enormous in both its length and breadth with a lofty roof. He gave the luxurious halls decorated pillars for their supports and clothed the entire floor and walls in gleaming marbles, placing a marvellous ceiling above them. **8** Then he restored and improved the basilica of the most holy virgin Eulalia in a wondrous fashion, building towers with lofty gables on the high roof of that most holy church.[90]

---

[90] cf The *Passio S Mantii* describing how the chapel built over Mantius' body at Miliana near Evora was replaced by a larger building after the conversion of the Sueves. This is the only passage from the Visigothic period which refers to church towers. These are unlikely to have been bell towers as there are no references to church bells prior to the ninth century. Cerillo [1978] suggests they were analogous to the cupolae found on Byzantine churches, an attractive suggestion given the influence of Byzantine architecture

7

1 Even while still in the flesh this blessed man is said to have often been seen standing and singing in the choir of the church with the hosts of the saints.[91] Many other tales are told about him which we shall decline to relate on account of the length of the telling, lest they should become burdensome to our readers.[92] 2 One day he sent a boy from his household to a place called Caspiana, sixteen miles away from Merida and instructed him to return in all haste. 3 He, when he had gone and was unable to return the same day, stayed there. At nightfall when he was already asleep, he dreamt that the cocks had crowed. Waking at once, he mounted his horse and hurried through the middle of the night until he came to the gate of the city which is called the Gate of the Bridge.[93] 4 When he had been there a long time, he realised that he had risen at an untimely hour and that, though he had shouted, no one would open the gate for him when he called, and so he decided to put his horse to grass for a short while until someone should unbar the gate. 5 And, lo, lifting up his eyes in the stillness of the night, he saw far off a fiery globe[94] coming from the church of St Faustus[95] which lies around a mile from the town. Setting out from there, it passed to the basilica of St Lucretia.[96] 6 He watched this in silence wondering what it might

---

[91] For attestations of choirs as part of a Visigothic church see *ICERV* 312 (Bailén) and *ICERV* 352c (Seville).

[92] cf *VSA* 2 & 5.

[93] A reference to the great Roman bridge across the Guadiana. This was restored in the Visigothic period by the Gothic and the Orthodox bishop of the day, Zeno, in AD 483, *ICERV* 363. For a full study of the structure see Alvarez Martínez [1983]. This means that Caspiana would have been found to the West of the city rather than the North as Garvin ([1946] 398) suggests.

[94] cf the column of fire which preceded Israel by night in the desert, *Exodus* 13.21-22 and Prudentius' account of such a column preceding Eulalia on her path to martyrdom, *Peristephanon Martyrorum* 3.49-55.

[95] Martyred in Cordoba with Ianuarius and Martial in c.AD 304. Prudentius refers to him and his fellow martyrs as the 'three crowns' of the town, *Peristephanon Martyrorum* 4.19-20. Faustus' feast day is 19th October and an office in his honour is found in the *Gothic Breviary* on that day = *PL* 86 1225-1226.

[96] This church was identified with the Ermita de Nuestra Señora de Loreto by Moreno de Vargas [1633] 196, 248, 489 who argued that Lucretia's name had mutated to this form. Despite the stigmatisation of this view as 'weird' by Garvin [1946] 402, it has

be, then all at once there came a multitude of saints whom the light preceded, who crossing the bridge, arrived at the gate and amongst their number walked the most holy Fidel. **7** When they reached the gate, the boy, seeing the columns of white-clad saints had multiplied and that the holy Fidel wearing a white cloak was hurrying along in their midst, was astounded. Petrified, he began to tremble and through his fear became as a dead man.[97] **8** The Deity opened the bars of the gates for the host and they entered the city. When they had gone in, the boy rising up wished to go in after them, but was in no way able to do so, for he found the gate secured just as it had been before. **9** When it was opened at dawn, he went to the palace and straightaway the holy man asked him at what hour he had set out from Caspiana. The boy told him the hour at which he had risen and the delay that he had experienced at the gate. **10** When the man of God then asked him if he had not seen something and he confessed that he had, Fidel warned him to make no mention of it, while he, the Holy man, remained in the body, to avoid coming into great peril.

8

1 Similarly a certain devout man once saw him going with a host of saints one night from the church of the holy Eulalia and journeying to the basilicas of the martyrs, but acting foolishly he at once told many people about it. **2** Finally he came to the man of God and told him what he had seen. Fidel asked him, 'Have you spoken of what you saw to anyone or not?' He at once replied, saying in all honesty that he had. **3** Then the bishop said to him, 'May God have mercy on you, brother, for you have not acted rightly. I know that you will not be blamed for this in the judgement which is to come. But now take communion and give us a farewell kiss,[98] for you are about to go on your journey. Arrange

---

received support from García Moreno [1976] 321. Cruz Villalón [1982] 412 however believes the Visigothic remains here are from a later period. The saint herself is almost unknown, though she does feature in Hagenoyen's additions to Usuard's ninth century martyrology = *PL* 124 732. Her feast day is 23rd of November.

[97] cf *Matthew* 28.4 - the resurrected Christ appears in white and makes the guards of his tomb faint in terror.

[98] cf Paul, The kiss of farewell is referred to by the *Common Rule* attributed to St Fructuosus, 2 and Isidore, *Rule* 6.3.

your household affairs[99] in all haste and if you desire the remedy of penance, take it.' **4** He at once took the rite of penance, ordered his house, bade farewell to all, and the following night passed from his body.[100]

9

1 Once a certain devout man, thinking over the office of the church while he lay in bed, was overcome by sleep in the stillness of the night. He dreamt that the sign for Lauds had been given **2** and rising at once, he went with all haste to the church. In order not to miss the time of the sacred office, he sped on his way running and arrived there breathless. **3** When he entered the Church of St Mary which is now called Holy Jerusalem,[101] he heard the voices of men singing with wonderful modulation[102] and looking towards the choir he saw a multitude of saints standing there. **4** Struck with the extremes of terror and trembling, he took himself off silently into a corner of the basilica. Carefully hidden and looking on in silence, he heard the whole office performed by them in its customary order. **5** When they had finished their office shortly before cock-crow, they went singing praises[103] from the church of St Mary to the little basilica of St John where the baptistery is. This is hard fast by the church of St Mary: there is merely a wall between them, and both are covered by the same roof.[104] **6** When they had finished their praises, they began to say to one another, 'Behold the hour has come when they ought to be given the sign. Therefore we must

---

[99] cf *Isaiah* 38.1.

[100] cf *2 Samuel* 17.23.

[101] The cathedral church of Merida. See 5.6.14. Giving the cathedral church the title Holy Jerusalem was a common Spanish practice being found at Seville, Toledo, and Tarragona. The site of the church was probably that of the present church of Sta Maria, see Cruz Villalón [1982] and Mateos Cruz [1992].

[102] For descriptions of Mozarabic chant see Rojo & Prado [1929], Prado [1928], and Anglès [1940]. *4 Toledo* 13 (AD 633) urged the composition of hymns.

[103] Garvin [1946] 412 wishes *cum laudibus* to be read in the technical sense as Lauds. However the hagiographer has already told us that this office had been completed.

[104] A similar arrangement to that at Merida where cathedral, episcopal palace, and baptistry are found in close proximity is found at Idanha-a-Velha in Portugal, see Almeida [1977]. For a more general discussion of ecclesiastical topography see Greenslade [1966].

first see to that for which we were sent'. **7** When they had said this, there appeared in their sight some hideous and terrifying Ethiopians, giants, most vile to behold in their darkness, so that from their restless gaze and jet-black faces he was given to understand as he saw them clearly that they were beyond doubt servants of hell.[105] They carried sharp scythes[106] in their hands. **8** The saints then said to them, 'Go with all speed to the palace, enter the cell where holy Fidel the bishop lies, and deal him a grave wound to his body so that his soul might swiftly leave the chains of the flesh and be able to come with us to our Lord Jesus Christ and the crown which has been prepared for it.[107] **9** They went at once in obedience to their orders, but returned without striking him, saying, 'We cannot enter his cell for he is not sleeping, but lying prostrate on the ground in prayer. Moreover his cell is full of the sweetest smell of incense and the power of so much fragrant incense which he has offered to the Lord is such that it prevents our entering there. **10** They ordered them again, saying, 'Go and strike him, for the command of the Lord must be obeyed'. When they had gone and were unable to enter they returned again saying, 'His prayer altogether prevents us from entering'. **11** To which they replied, 'Prayer gives way when the call comes. Go and fulfil the command of the Lord which once given can never be ignored.' And when they went a third time by the Lord's permission they entered. There they struck him so fierce and cruel a blow that the devout man who was standing in the church clearly heard his voice coming forth, groaning in great pain. **12** When the dawn came, he went to the holy bishop and told him everything that he had seen and heard. He replied, 'I know, my son, I know, it is in nowise hidden from me'.

---

[105] St Perpetua had a vision in which she wrestled an Egyptian who symbolised the devil, *Passio of St Perpetua and St Felicity* 10. For the black colour of the devil see also Gregory the Great, *HEv* 1.12.7 and Rush [1941] 210-211. For the notion of the Devil as God's agent or *exactor* see Gregory the Great, *HEv* 2.39.5 & *Mor* 4.35.69. The theme reoccurs in *VPE* at 5.6.1.

[106] 'Rhomphaea'. This was a curved, scythe-like pole-weapon used originally by the Dacians.

[107] cf *Matthew* 25.34.

10

1 When he said this and straightaway felt his entire body give way, his limbs losing their strength as the disease fell upon them, he ordered that he be taken to the basilica of the most holy virgin Eulalia. **2** There he first wept for his sins, gaining satisfaction in floods of tears. Then he gave large sums of alms to prisoners and the needy. Finally he remitted everyone's debts, returning their pledges to them. **3** When he had returned these to one and all, there remained the notice of a certain widow which had not yet been returned. He waited for the widow to return it to her, but, like the feeble woman she was, she was unable to approach him because he was surrounded by a dense crowd. **4** When she had come for several days and had been unable to find a place, she panicked, her mind making her sorrowful, and, achieving nothing, she returned grief-stricken to her lodgings. Then one night the most holy martyrs Cyprian[108] and Laurence appeared before her in a dream and said, 'Do you know why you cannot get a place?', and she replied, 'I know not.' They then said to her, 'Why do you often hurry to the basilicas of the rest of our brethren and yet spurn to come to us?' **6** She rose at once and hurried to their basilicas and weeping poured out her prayers, begging pardon for the neglect she had showed in the past. She then went to the basilica of saint Eulalia and with wondrous speed found a place and received her notice without any difficulty. She gave great thanks to God, for she had not only found her appointed place as she entered, but also because it had been so devised by the saints of God that when she had entered the holy bishop had been holding her notice in his hand waiting for the individual to whom he should return it. **8** And it came to pass that after he had in his good will returned it and she had joyfully received what she had long longed for, shortly afterwards the holy man, preceded by the hosts of saints and expectant angelic choruses, passed exultantly to the celestial realms, and joining the heavenly hosts with everlasting joy earned the right, at Lord Jesus' command, to be gathered into the heavenly mansions.[109] **9** His body was

---

[108] Bishop of Carthage and martyred in AD 258. See Prudentius, *Peristephanon Martyrorum* 13.
[109] cf *John* 14.2.

placed by that of his most holy predecessor in one and the same tomb and buried with honour in, so to speak, the same bed.[110]

5. The Life and Virtues of the Holy Bishop Masona

1

1 When that gentle man of whom we have spoken passed to his homeland above, the providence of the Divine Godhead chose as his successor an Orthodox man named Masona, who was his equal in all his virtues. And so a blessed man succeeded a blessed man, a holy man a holy man, a pious man a pious man, a good man outstanding for his kindness and every form of grace succeeded in the line of bishops one who had shone forth with his enormous virtue - in short Masona succeeded Fidel.[111] **2** When his predecessor had been enrolled among the starry citizens in the heavens, his manna-like sweetness and outstanding merits assuaged the grief of all the citizens here on earth so that not only did he dispel the grief of all at the death of so great a bishop **3** but, as once happened with the fathers of old, Elijah and Elisha, the two-fold grace[112] of the Comforting Spirit possessed by the holy bishop Fidel seemed to all who looked on to have settled on the Holy bishop Masona. **4** The result was that the people in no way were afflicted by grief when their shepherd was taken from them, but rejoiced with a twofold joy that God in his mercy had sent one man to heaven for their salvation and had most graciously replaced him with a man of outstanding virtue here on earth.

---

[110] For an inscription referring to Fidel see Sáenz de Buruaga [1970]. The crypt where the bishops of Merida were interred is to be found inside the basilica of Sta Eulalia beneath the southern end of the iconostasis, see Caballero Zoreda & Mateos Cruz [1992] and [1993].

[111] Mentioned by John of Biclarum, *Chron.* 30, as bishop in AD 573 when he was 'held in high esteem as an exponent of our doctrine'. There is no indication that this was the first year of his incumbency. Masona is the first of the bishops listed as signing the acts of *3 Toledo* and of those listed at a synod held in Toledo in AD 597 (*PL* 84, 358). A letter of Isidore addressed to Masona (*PL* 83 899-902) is dated to 28th February of the 2nd or 3rd year of Witteric, i.e. AD 605-606; however its authenticity is disputed. A general though basic account of Masona's life is found in Orlandis [1992] ch.2 For the later cult of Masona see de Smedt [1885].

[112] cf *2 Kings* 2.9ff. 'Two-fold' refers to the ancient Hebrew practice of dividing an inheritance by one more than the number of inheritors and awarding two portions to the eldest son.

2

1 The holy bishop Masona was sprung of what counts as noble stock on this earth, but showed himself more noble still through the good deeds of his life.[113] Although he was a Goth,[114] his mind was completely dedicated to God and manfully steeped in the virtues of the Most High. He was adorned by his holy way of life and handsome with *a most noble bearing*.[115] 2 He had been clothed from birth in the gleaming stole of charity[116] and humility, was stoutly girt with the belt of faith, famously protected by prudence and justice, and greatly honoured by the love of both God most high and his neighbour.[117] For beloved of God and men, the wonder and glory of his age, a lover of his brethren, he prayed greatly for his people, and his name, resplendent from the many miracles he performed, became known throughout all the land. 3 In his time through his prayers the Lord kept disease, plague, and famine far from the city of Merida and indeed from all Lusitania, driving them far away because of the merits of the most holy virgin Eulalia.[118] Moreover, he deemed it worthy to impart such health and such a bounty of every delight to all the people 4 that no one, not even a poor man, was seen to be in need or to be wearied by want, but the poor just like the wealthy had an abundance of all good things and all the people on earth were joyful, as if they were rejoicing in heaven, at the virtue of so great a bishop. 5 Joy entered into all, peace came upon everyone, no one was a stranger to happiness, perfect charity flourished in every heart. The peace that brings joy prevailed so strongly on the passions of everyone that the Ancient Enemy was conquered and the Serpent of olden times overthrown.[119] 6 No-one was troubled by grief or afflicted by sorrow,

---

[113] cf Potamia in *VSA* 7.

[114] There is nothing to commend the theory of Teillet, referred to approvingly by Alonso Campos [1986], that 'Goth' here is an indication of religious affiliation, i.e. Arianism, rather than nationality.

[115] cf *II Maccabees* 15.13 of Onias. The remark about Masona's race may reflect the hagiographer's personal dislike of the Goths or alternatively be intended to emphasise that it was unusual at this period for a Goth to be an Orthodox Christian. It suggests that the hagiographer himself was a Hispano-Roman.

[116] For the stole as the clothing of the elect see *Revelation* 7.14, 22.14.

[117] cf *Ephesians* 6.13ff.

[118] cf *VSD* 11 and Fidel and the collapsing episcopal palace at 4.6.1 above.

[119] cf *Revelation* 12.9, Augustine, *Ad Catech.*4.1.

nor was anyone struck by terror or affected by jealousy or envy so that he shook with the virulent pangs of that cunning reptile, but all were filled with perfect charity. Rejoicing with God's aid through the grace of their pious father and unperturbed, they all continued in constancy with their praise of God free from any fear or dread. 7 And this great love of Masona did not only burn in the innermost hearts of all the faithful, but through his wondrous sweet affection he drew minds of all the Jews[120] and pagans[121] to the grace of Christ.

3

1 Our lack of skill cannot recount in every detail how great and glorious he was; but although we may be silent about his greatest deeds, we shall at least tell of the very greatest of these.[122] 2 Even before he was ordained bishop, this man is said to have lived with the greatest devotion in the basilica of the most holy virgin Eulalia and there served God without reproach for many years. 3 After he was taken by the will of God from that place where he had been spoken of by everyone and had been admired by, and been an inspiration to them all, and ordained bishop, at the very beginning of his incumbency he founded and richly endowed many monasteries, built a even larger number of basilicas of wondrous appearance, and consecrated in these places many souls to God. 4 Then he built a *xenodocium*, enriching it with a large patrimony and appointing ministers and doctors to serve travellers and the sick,[123]

---

[120] For the condition of the Jews in Visigothic Spain see Katz [1937], Rabello [1976], and García Moreno [1993]. A Latin tombstone found at Merida and referring to a Rabbi Samuel and a Rabbi Jacob (= *IHE* 289) has been dated to the Visigothic period by Roth [1948], see also Millás Vallicrosa [1945].

[121] This is the only mention of pagans in *VPE*. Paganism certainly survived in this period in the Basque country and from St Martin of Braga's (*fl.*c.AD 520-580) *De Castigatione Rusticorum* appears to have been present in other northern parts of Spain.
The pagans have vanished in section 5.3.5 below, which suggests that their inclusion here is merely rhetorical or that they were excluded from the *xenodocium*.

[122] A common topos, see *VSA* 13.

[123] Isidore, *Etymologiae* 15.3.13 lists the first *xenodocium* as being founded by the Jew Hyrcanus as a lodging house for poor travellers. The notion of hospitality is as old as classical civilisation, 'xenodocus' appears in the *Odyssey* (8.543, 15.55). The custom was easily incorporated into the Christian tradition. Jerome (*Ep.*66.11) praises the senator Pammachius for establishing a *xenodocium* in Rome by the *Portus Romanus* in the late fourth century AD. Similarly Gregory the Great (*Ep.*13.6) approves of Queen Brunhilda's foundation of one in Autun. Masona's *xenodocium* is probably to be identified with a building excavated in the barriada de Sta Catalina, see Mateos Cruz [1992] and Caballero Zoreda and Mateos Cruz [1993]. It takes the form of a small central apsed chamber

giving them this command: 5 that the doctors should go through the entire city without ceasing and whosoever they found that was sick, be they slave or free, Christian or Jew, they were to carry in their arms to the *xenodocium*, and having prepared there a well-made bed set the sick man on it and give him light and pleasant food until, with God's help, they returned their patient to his former health. 6 And although an abundance of delicacies were to be had from the many estates which had been given to the *xenodocium*, this still seemed too little to the holy man. So adding to all these great benefits still greater ones, he ordered the doctors to ensure with the uttermost care that they should receive half of all the revenues brought into the palace by all the actuaries from the entire patrimony of the church in order that they could give this to the sick.[124] 7 Whenever one of the townsmen or a countryman from the rural districts came out of need to the palace to ask the dispensers for a measure of wine or oil or honey and held out a small vessel into which it could be poured, if the holy man saw him, with a kindly face and a happy smile, he always ordered the vessel to be broken and a larger one be brought out. 8 How generous he was in giving alms to the poor has been left for God alone to know. However let us speak a little of this too. 9 So great was his concern for the tribulations of all the poor that he gave two thousand *solidi*[125] to that venerable man, the deacon Redemptus who was in charge of the basilica of St Eulalia, so

---

flanked at right angles by two much larger aisled rooms. It would have lain outside the walls of the city, the normal location for such buildings, Hubert [1959]. Many of the travellers are likely to have been pilgrims to Eulalia's shrine.

[124] cf 3 *Toledo* 3 (AD 589) which forbids the alienation of church property. An exception is made for provision for strangers, travellers, clerics, and the needy, but only as long as the church suffered no capital loss.

[125] The *solidus* was the standard gold coin of the Byzantine empire. *Solidi* were not struck by the Visigoths so the reference here is to a notional sum of money. The standard Visigothic coin was the *tremiss*, a gold coin worth one third of a *solidus*. The standard work on Visigothic coinage is Miles [1952], see also in Spanish M-J & R Chaves [1984]. Leovigild was the first king to break with the single currency of the Byzantines; prior to this Visigothic kings had only issued imitation Byzantine pieces.

Leovigild's act of national self-assertion is rightly described as 'an epoch in the history of the coinage of Western Europe' by Miles [1952] *ix*. Over 80 Visigothic mints are known, though four, Merida, Toledo, Seville, and Cordoba, account for 60% of the coins found. The nature of the coins is highly controversial. For two articles arguing that they both circulated widely and were commonly used for financial transactions see Metcalf [1986] and [1988]. Until recently only gold Visigothic coinage had been found, but there is now evidence for the striking of copper coin, Crusafont I Sabater [1988]. An idea of the value of the *solidus* can be gained from the Visigothic Lawcode which assumes that a child's maintenance costs one *solidus* a year (*LV* 4.4.3).

that if anyone came oppressed by want, after drafting a notice, he might draw as much as he wanted from this sum without any delay or difficulty in order to deal with his troubles.[126] **10** Nor do I think I should be silent about how generous he was in giving gifts. For he was as generous with his own possessions as he was careful of those of others and excelled in the magnanimous virtue of giving rather than in receiving. **11** For he was more eager to give away his wealth than to seek more, and had learnt that it is a greater good fortune to give than to receive.[127] He gave away much and took nothing away himself, but willingly granted everyone's request. He gave many gifts, more endowments, enriched all through the munificence of his gifts and by that munificence was held to be a great man.[128] All had their possessions increased by his gifts and were enriched by his generosity. He gave gifts which were too large to be believed not only to his brethren and friends, but even to the church slaves.[129] **12** Indeed, in his day they were so wealthy that on the most holy day of Easter he set out for the church surrounded by many boys wearing silk cloaks as if they were in attendance on a king, and wearing this apparel, something that in those days no one had been able or presumed to do, they went before him and paid him due homage.[130] **13** The Almighty Lord showered many great gifts on this deserving man whose heart never became swollen or puffed in the midst of such great opulence and grandeur of his transitory

---

[126] Masona's fund appears to be a continuation of the policy of his predecessor, see *VPE* 4.10.2. As usury was forbidden, we should assume that these loans were interest free. The fund would have posed a strong threat to local secular nobles to whom the poor would have been forced to turn for loans with interest prior to its creation. No doubt its primary purpose was that of relief; however it would also have had the effect of establishing the church as a rival to secular patronage.

[127] cf *Acts* 20.35.

[128] Again, this would have made Masona a rival to secular patrons.

[129] Ownership of slaves by the Visigothic Church was widespread. *Merida* 18 (AD 666) requires parish priests to make suitable slaves curates and the *tomus* of *16 Toledo* (AD 693) describes any church with only 10 slaves as 'very poor'. For a clerical justification of slavery see Isidore, *Sententiae* 3.47.1-3. See Claude [1980] for a modern commentary on ecclesiastical slaves and freedmen.

[130] The hagiographer seems here to assert that the church has almost taken the place of the King in terms of splendour. It is significant in this respect that we are told by Isidore that the king of the day, Leovigild, had also increased the splendour of his appearance being the first Visigothic monarch to employ royal robes and a throne (*HG* 51). The new silk vestments suggest continuing trade with the Greek East; see Isidore, *Etymologiae* 19.22.14.

wealth. **14** His most humble soul was built upon the solidest of rocks,[131] was of unstained conscience, of honest thought which knows nothing of trickery, and while meek in times of prosperity, showed itself of great strength in adversity. Nor did it become arrogant in prosperity, but neither loss nor increase changed his constancy. **15** For he was steadfast in all things and well prepared for any circumstance. A man of endurance and great physical strength, he persevered: constant in every adversity and unperturbed in times of trouble. He never changed his countenance through joy or sorrow, but his ever cheerful face did not change whatever his circumstances. **16** Nor did pride which is the enemy of every virtue carry him off,[132] but he preserved a sincere humility in everything through the sincere and holy nature of his heart.

4

1 When through divine favour he grew strong in these virtues,[133] his fame, as reports grew, spread news of his goodness abroad and brought to light throughout the regions those works of light which had been given to him by the true light.[134] **2** Whence it came to pass that through his reputation his deeds came to the notice of Leovigild, the savage, cruel king of the Visigoths. Then vile serpent of his envy, always envious of good works,[135] pricked him with its sharp goads, struck at the heart of the prince with its viper's venom and poured its poisoned chalice into his innermost soul.[136] **3** At once having drunk of this deadly cup, armed with a diabolical scheme and driven on by his envy, he sent messengers back and forth time and again to the holy man Masona and commanded him to abandon the Catholic faith and turn to the Arian heresy along with all the people in his charge.[137] **4** But he, dedicated to

---

[131] cf *Matthew* 7.25.

[132] cf *VSD* 2.

[133] cf *VSD* 2.

[134] cf *VSD* 2.

[135] A conflation of Christian vice with the hallmarks of a typical classical tyrant.

[136] This hostility of the hagiographer here contrasts sharply with the neutral account of Leovigild in section 3. The account is taken from *VSD* 4.

[137] Leovigild was determined to establish a single religious confession as the state religion of a unified and unitary kingdom. Hence his concern here is not just with the Goth Masona as an 'apostate' from Gothic Arianism, as has sometimes been asserted (e.g. Görres [1873]), but with the conversion of the entire Catholic population of Merida. In

God as he was, made a steadfast response, sending back to the king his messengers twice, nay, three times telling him that he would never abandon the true faith which he had needed to learn but once. Moreover he rebuked the Arian king as was his duty and repudiated his heresy with telling proofs. 5 When the messengers returned to him, Leovigild began to work on his soul with various temptations, in the hope that perhaps in somewise he might bend him to the pleasures of his superstition. 6 Masona, however, spurned these many cunning temptations, cast out his gifts and prizes as if they were so much filth,[138] and manfully defended the Catholic faith. Nor did he choose to keep silent about the heresy lest he should seem to give assent by his silence, but striving against the king's madness with all his might, he sounded out the trumpet blast of truth.[139] 7 When the King saw himself failing and his labour brought to nought, seized by fury, he began to use terror against him, thinking that he would be able to strike down with his threats a man whom he had been unable to overcome with his blandishments. 8 But the holy man was neither broken by his threats nor persuaded by his blandishments, but striving in fierce fight against the vile tyrant persisted unvanquished in his defence of truth.[140]

5

1 When that most cruel tyrant learnt that he could not either by threats or gifts make the soul of the man of God apostatise from the true faith to his heresy, as he was wholly a vessel of wrath, a fomenter of vice, and the fruit of damnation, the Enemy possessed his breast the more fiercely and the cunning Serpent held him captive in his sway so that he brought to his people bitterness not joy, brutality instead of gentleness

---

fact the form of Christianity preferred by Leovigild was a form of Macedonianism rather than Arianism proper, for a discussion of the king's religious policy see the introduction to this volume.

[138] cf *1 Corinthians* 4.13.

[139] cf *VSD* 15. Biblical parallels can be found at *Isaiah* 18.3, 58.1 and with the seven angels of *Revelation* 8.

[140] Leovigild's treatment of Masona falls into a traditional pattern of martyr acts: inveiglement is followed by violence - see the analysis by Maya [1994].

and in place of health salves that brought death.[141] **2** In order to stir up sedition and cause trouble for the holy man and all his people, he appointed a bishop of the Arian faction called Sunna in the city of Merida, a bringer of death who supported the Arian heresy in all its parts.[142] **3** A thorough supporter of this perverse doctrine he was an ill-omened man, vile to look upon with a troubled brow, brutal eyes, hateful in appearance, and horrible in his movements.[143] He possessed an evil mind, was depraved in his habits, had a lying tongue, was foul-mouthed, swollen without yet empty within, outwardly grandiose yet inwardly spiritless,[144] seen from the outside he was puffed up yet inside he had been purged of every virtue, deformed both without and within, he was wanting in goodness but rich in vice, guilty of crime and doomed of his own free will to eternal death.[145] **4** When this deviser of perfidy came to the city of Merida, he took for himself on the order of the king certain basilicas with all their privileges, rashly snatching them from their rightful bishop.[146] **5** Bound all the tighter in the death-bringing Bandit's chains and stricken with his fatal poison, he began to bark out rabid sermons against the servant of God and spew forth filthy language mingling it with raucous threats.[147] **6** But this hangman's threats did not break the loyal servant of God nor did the turbulent wrath of this noxious man weaken him, nor the rage of this raving

---

[141] This passage is almost entirely taken from *VSD* 15. The hagiographer is attempting to show that Leovigild was not a true king according to the standards of his day: see the words of Leovigild's son and successor, Reccared, that 'Almighty God has granted us to reach the height of kingship for the well-being of our peoples', *3 Toledo tomus*. Similar sentiments were expressed by Isidore, *Sententiae* 3.49.3 For a general discussion of Visigothic ideology on kingship see King [1972] ch.2.

[142] It seems inconceivable that an Arian See did not already exist in Merida prior to this appointment. If, as is likely, this passage refers to the aftermath of Hermenegild's rebellion, Leovigild was probably re-establishing an Arian ecclesiastical structure in the town after its destruction by Hermenegild and his followers. If Merida was a centre of Orthodox sentiment - see the introduction to this volume - and had been a centre of support for Hermenegild, winning it over would have been crucial to Leovigild's plan to create a unitary religion in his kingdom. Sunna's convictions were as strong as those of Masona's as can be seen from his refusal to convert to Trinitarianism when Reccared came to the throne.

[143] Hence like Masona, his exterior appearance mirrors his internal worth.

[144] cf *Matthew* 23.27-28 on the Scribes and Pharisees.

[145] This description of Sunna is taken *mutatis mutandis* from that of Theuderic and Brunhilda's men at *VSD* 18.

[146] Alternatively this passage may reflect in Orthodox terms the repossession of Arian churches handed over to the Orthodox by Hermenegild in his rebellion.

[147] taken from *VSD* 15.

damned soul turn him from his purpose, but like a stout wall he remained steadfast in his defence of the holy faith against all storms.[148] 7 When this infidel had tried with all his might to trouble the servant of God and all the faithful by his cunning devices and had failed, relying on royal favour he continually tried to seize the basilica of the most holy Eulalia, so that having snatched it from its rightful bishop he might dedicate it to the Arian heresy.[149] 8 The holy bishop Masona and all the people with him resisted and fought vigorously against him, so the false bishop[150] Sunna wrote a long indictment against the holy man to Leovigild and suggested to him that the holy basilica which he longed to enter be taken from the possession of the Catholics and put under his own control by royal decree. 9 In response to this the following judgement was made: judges were to sit in the episcopal palace and both bishops be summoned and appear before them. Then they were to engage in debate in judges' presence, each setting forth in turn a defence of their position.[151] And so debating one after the other, they were to construct or adduce support for their case from the books of Holy Scripture, wherever there these things might be written and whichever side won the prize of victory, they too would win for themselves the church of St Eulalia. 10 When this decree, as the rumour grew, came to the hearing of the gentle Masona, straightaway he hurried to the basilica of the holy virgin Eulalia, and for three days and as many

---

[148] taken from *VSD* 15.

[149] See above. The strength of the Cult of Eulalia was such that control of her shrine would have been a key factor in winning the dispute between Orthodox and Arian.

[150] 'Pseudoepiscopus.' This was a longstanding term of ecclesiastical abuse, Psuedo-Priscillian (*Tract* 2 p.41 = *PLS* 2 1439) commented 'There is no one who does not feel hatred when he hears about psuedobishops and Manichees'. Similarly at 5.6.29 the Orthodox collaborator with Leovigild, Nepopis, is called a false priest, 'psuedosacerdos'.

[151] Gregory of Tours records two rather bad tempered debates he had with Agila, an Arian clergyman from Spain, *HF* 5.43, 6.40. Clearly the Arians thought they could argue their case successfully. The tradition of such contests has its roots in scripture, see for example, Elijah's showdown with the priests of Ba'al on Mt Carmel, *1 Kings* 18.16-45, and St Stephen and St Paul's expounding the faith to hostile audiences (*Acts* 7, 17, and 22). In the more recent past St Augustine had engaged in public debate in the Baths of Sosius in Hippo with the Manichee Fortunatus (in AD 392) and then in AD 404 in his own church against another Manichee, Felix (Augustine, *Retractationes* 2.7-8 = *PL* 32 632-634) emerging victorious on both occasions. Bishop Fulgentius of Ruspe held an inconclusive debate with the Vandal King and Arian, Thrasimund, at Carthage in the early sixth century. Some of Fulgentius' anti-Arian writings have survived, notably his *Reply to the Arians* and *Against Thrasimund, King of the Vandals*; *PL* 65 205-304.

nights[152] fasted and wept before the altar beneath which the venerable body of the martyr lay, prostrating himself on the flags. **11** Finally on the third day he returned to his palace which was built inside the city walls, coming back with such mental sharpness and constancy that none of the faithful doubted that He Who said: *'Take no thought beforehand what ye shall speak: but whatsoever shall be given to you in that hour, that speak ye, for it is not ye that speak but the Holy Ghost'*[153] was coming to help him. **12** When he came to the city, had entered the palace and sat down, his expression took away the sorrow of all the faithful by its cheerfulness and he told them to have no doubts about his victory. **13** Then waiting for the cursed Arian bishop and the judges, he tarried there a long time. Finally the Arian bishop together with the judges and surrounded by a host of men made his entry swollen with arrogant pride.[154] Then the bishops sat down, as did the judges who in the main were supporters of the Arian sect and of the impious king. **14** When they were seated, the holy bishop Masona as he possessed the utmost gravity and wisdom for a long time kept silent, looking intently towards heaven. As he was silent, Sunna, the bishop of the heretics, rose up to speak first and began to shriek disgraceful things, bawling out jarring words, which were both scabrous and obscene. **15** When the man of God patiently, calmly, and persuasively made his reply and set forth the whole truth in outstanding fashion, Sunna, as if he had a serpent's mouth, hissed out even more disgraceful words and a great debate began between them. **16** But in no wise could the forces of the flesh prevail against the wisdom of God or the Holy Spirit who spoke through His servant Masona. **17** What more is there to say? Defeated in every argument, the vanquished heretic fell silent and blushed in his great shame and the wicked judges who had supported him all in vain were no more able to sustain their case than he: **18** not only did they blush in their confusion, but on hearing the homily on the most glorious faith which came from his mouth in honeyed words, they were astounded and entirely at a loss and praised with great admiration the man whom shortly before they had wanted to defeat. **19** For the Lord had deemed it worthy to grant so much grace to his lips that day that no one had

---

[152] cf *Tobit* 3.10-15.
[153] *Mark* 13.11.
[154] cf Gregory the Great, *Dial.* 3.1.

ever heard him speak so clearly and eloquently before, and although he always spoke well, that day he showed himself more eloquent than in all days gone by. **20** Then the righteous saw what had happened and rejoiced and all evil held its tongue for God had closed the mouths of those preaching iniquity.[155] And all the faithful were greatly astonished because although they had known beforehand that Masona was a most eloquent man they could not remember when he had ever preached such a learned discourse so elegantly and illuminatingly. **21** Then, their foes laid low in defeat, all the Orthodox and Catholic people cried out in praise, *'Among the Gods there is none like unto thee, O Lord; neither are there any works like unto your works'*[156] **22** All of one accord they went to the basilica of the glorious virgin Eulalia together with their triumphant bishop Masona. Loudly exulting in their praise of God they came and rejoicing with much shouting they entered his most holy church and gave countless thanks to the almighty Lord who had exulted His servants on high for the sake of the church of His holy virgin and reduced His enemies to nothing.

6

1 However this heretic bishop Sunna, although he had been defeated in all his arguments concerning the truth, obstinately persisted in his old beliefs and was unable to hasten with willing steps to the gateway of salvation.[157] For with God's permission the Old Enemy had hardened his heart to stone, as he had done to Pharoah's.[158] **2** After the confrontation, on seeing himself utterly defeated he began in his madness to fabricate ever more accusations against the servant of God, adding to them cunningly devised falsehoods. And armed with every kind of weapon he set out to fight the stronger against the soldier of Christ,[159] secretly accusing that most blessed man, bishop Masona, of many crimes to the

---

[155] cf *Psalm* 107.42.

[156] *Psalm* 86.8, cf *Psalm* 71.19.

[157] taken from *VSD* 15.

[158] cf *Exodus* 4.21. However here it is God, not the devil who hardens Pharoah's heart. God's use of the devil is reminiscent of the book of Job. The notion of the devil as God's *exactor* was current when *VPE* was written, see Gregory the Great, *HEv* 2.39.5, *Mor* 4.35.69. See also *Revelation* 22.11 where evil-doers are to persist in evil-doing.

[159] cf *VSD* 4.

Arian king, Leovigild. **3** But the cunning of the Enemy availed for nothing, his dreadful wickedness did no harm to the man of God whom the grace of the Redeemer armed with weapons of the spirit.[160] **4** Finally the evil spirit compelled the oft-mentioned King of the Arians to remove the holy man from his see and bring him into his presence. His ministers sharing in his crime swiftly obeyed his command[161] and coming to Merida forced the blessed man to travel in all haste to the city of Toledo where the king held court.[162] **5** When the most holy bishop Masona was suddenly snatched away and carried off from the bosom of his holy church, and, though innocent, taken into exile like a condemned man, the voice of all the citizens of Merida cried out moaning in unbearable grief, lamenting with great groaning and wailing that the aid of so goodly a shepherd was being taken from them and shouting out at the top of their voices, **6** 'Why are you abandoning your sheep, good shepherd? Why are you leaving your flock to perish? Do not, we beg of you, entrust us to the jaws of wolves, lest your sheep fed until now on flowers and nectar, without their bishop to take care of them should be ripped apart by ravening wolves.'[163] **7** Moved by so much grief and ever full in his innermost soul of piety in the Lord, he is said to have broken out weeping.[164] Then addressing them at great length, he took time to console them with his profound arguments.[165] **8** After this, bidding them all farewell, he set off with God to guide him in his customary manner: with a calm mind, a constant soul, and a cheerful face. **9** When he came to the city of Toledo and stood in the presence of the vile tyrant, the king provoking him with all manner of insults and pressing him with many threats, strove with all the force of his depraved plan to drag him into the Arian heresy. **10** But when the man of God had willing put up with all the insults directed at him and bore everything with equanimity, he began to answer without delay but

---

[160] cf Sword of the Spirit, *2 Corinthians* 10.4 and *Ephesians* 6.13ff.

[161] taken from *VSD* 15.

[162] Relatively unimportant in Roman times, the town was established by Leovigild as the permanent capital of his kingdom.

[163] Taken from *VSD* 17.

[164] cf Sulpicius Severus *Ep*.3.11. The strength of Masona's emotion is underlined by the fact that we have been previously told that he always kept a cheerful appearance in adversity, 5.3.15.

[165] In *VSD* 17 Desiderius does indeed argue with his flock, here the arguments and the threat of violence by the crowd towards the bishop's captors are omitted.

with all gentleness, the things that the rabid dog snarled at him, and, while paying no heed to the insults directed at himself, aggrieved at the injury done to the Catholic faith, boldly resisted the tyrant. 11 The mad king was tormented more and more by his constancy and so redoubled the rabid yelpings of his foaming mouth against the servant of God. 12 He began to threaten him in terrible ways to hand over the tunic of the most holy virgin Eulalia in order that he might hang it in the basilica dedicated to Arian depravity there in Toledo.[166] 13 To this the man of God replied, 'Know that I shall never soil my heart with the filth of Arian superstition, that I shall never befuddle my wits with its perverted dogma, and that I shall never hand over the tunic of my lady Eulalia to be polluted by the hands or even the finger tips of heretics. You shall never have it however long you try.' 14 On hearing this, the profane tyrant flew into a rage of madness and in all haste swiftly sent to the city of Merida, instructing his men to look diligently everywhere for the holy tunic, and search with care both the treasury of the church of Eulalia and that of the senior church which is called Holy Jerusalem until they should find it and bring it to him. 15 When they arrived there, they searched with diligence everywhere, but did not find it and so returned empty-handed to their king. When they told him of their failure, the devil gnashing his teeth raged all the more fiercely against the man of God. 16 When Masona was brought into his presence, Leovigild said to him, 'Tell me where the thing which I seeks lies, and know that if you do not speak, you shall be severely tortured and then exiled to a far-away place, where afflicted with many tribulations and suffering a lack of every necessity you shall die a cruel death.' 17 To this the man of the Lord is said to have replied as follows: 'Do you threaten me with exile?' Know that I do not fear your threats and am in no way troubled by the prospect of exile and so I beg you that if you

---

[166] Possibly the Church of Sta María. This is recorded as being rededicated to Catholicism in AD 587 under Reccared, *ICERV* 302. The cult of relics was extremely powerful in this period. Gregory of Tours ascribed the conversion of the Sueves to Catholicism to the arrival of relics of St Martin of Tours in their territory (*De Virtutibus Sancti Martini* 1.11) and notes that a Frankish army lifted the siege of Saragossa when its defenders paraded the tunic of St Vincent from the battlements (*HF* 3.29).

Braulio of Saragossa received a letter from the priest Iactatus specifically asking him to supply him with martyrs' relics (*Ep.* 9) for his church. Braulio declined the request.

know any land where God is not present, command that I be exiled there.' The king replied, 'And where is God not present, living corpse?'[167] To which the man of God responded, 'If you already see that God is everywhere, why do you threaten me with exile? For wherever you send me, I know that the piety of the Lord will not abandon me. This too I know full well, that the more you cruelly rave against me, the more will His mercy follow me and His clemency bring me comfort.[168] 19 Because of Masona's constancy the mad tyrant was inwardly stricken with a great seizure of his wicked mind and moved by gall and great bitterness said to him, 'Either give me the tunic which you have deceitfully stolen or, if you do not, I shall have your limbs torn apart by diverse tortures.' 20 The soldier of God fearlessly replied, 'I have already told you time and again that I do not fear your threats. Let your twisted mind devise yet more threats against me to the limits of its ability. I shall not fear you nor overcome by fright give you what you seek. Know this, that I have burnt the tunic, ground it to ashes, and mixing its ashes with water have drunk them down.' 21 And rubbing his stomach with his hands he said, 'Let it be known to all that I reduced it to ashes and drank it and, lo, here it is within my belly, I shall never give it to you.' He spoke thus because unknown to all he had folded it up and was wearing it round his stomach beneath his clothes wrapped in linen clothes and so he wore it, as God alone knew. But God so blinded the eyes of the king and all his court that no one discovered the man of God's ploy. 22 While these and similar exchanges were going on, the heavens were completely clear, then suddenly the Divine Majesty thundered on high, letting forth a great crash so that king Leovigild leapt trembling from his throne to the ground in terror.[169] Then the man of God stoutly said with great exultation 'If we are to fear a king, behold the king we ought to fear who is not as you are.' 23 Then the Evil Spirit opened the sacrilegious mouth of the tyrant ever armed as it was with abuse, with these vile words and at once he barked out the infamous sentence devised by his impiety. 'Masona, ever

---

[167] Isidore, *Etymologiae* 10.31, in an astounding misreading of Greek, glosses this word (biothanatos) as 'twice dead', 'bis mortuus'.

[168] cf *Psalm* 23.6.

[169] cf *I Samuel* 7.10 (where the Philistines are terrified by thunder as Samuel sacrifices to God).

opposed to our way of life, enemy of our faith, and opponent of religion, we order you to be taken swiftly from our sight and sent into exile'.[170] 24 When the evil, impious king had pronounced this wicked sentence on an innocent man,[171] his ministers who shared in his crime instantly took him from his sight and on the king's instructions got ready to mount him on an unbroken horse, in order that it might throw him and so falling and breaking his neck he should suffer a cruel death. Indeed this horse was so wild that no rider dared to mount it for it had already flung many men headlong. 25 As it was prepared for the man of God to mount it, the cruel King looked out from the palace window above, hoping that the man of God would fall from the horse and provide him with a great spectacle.[172] 26 But the holy priest making the sign of the cross in the Lord's name, mounted the wild horse which God made as tame as the gentlest lamb for him. Then the creature which but shortly before with great snorting, whinnying, and continually bucking with all its body had refused to carry another as if it despised its would-be riders, set off to take him on his way with the utmost gentleness and care.[173] 27 All who saw this miracle were astounded and greatly amazed, even the king was moved to great admiration. But what help could the glorious radiance of the sun be to a blind man whose heart the savage Enemy had completely darkened?[174] 28 Therefore Masona, the holy bishop of God, accompanied merely by three of his serving boys, came to the place assigned to him along with the men who were to punish him and had been sent by the king to place him in exile in a monastery. His exile took him to sublime heights, the insult dealt him produced outstanding sanctity, his journey great happiness.[175] 29 After this a false priest called Nepopis was set up in his place and

---

[170] Taken from VSD 16.

[171] taken from VSD 4.

[172] There is a slight parallel with Gregory the Great, Dial. 3.11 where Totila baits a bishop with a bear to no avail.

[173] There is a strong resemblance to Alexander's first encounter with Bucephalus here. The story would have been known to the hagiographer's audience from Solinus Collectanea Rerum Memorabilium 45 and Aulus Gellius, NA 5.2. The comparison links to Christian stories of holy men taming wild beasts, leading back as far as the Old Testament account of Daniel in the Lion's Den (Daniel 6.12-22) and also carries overtones of Masona as a soldier for Christ through its allusion to Alexander.

[174] cf Pharoah's reaction to the plagues in Egypt and Revelation 22.11. This attitude may have been a later Visigothic topos about Leovigild, cf Isidore, HG 49.

[175] Taken from VSD 4.

made the man of God's replacement in the city of Merida. He was a profane man, a true servant of the Devil, an angel of Satan, a harbinger of the Antichrist, and a bishop of another town.[176] And just as the man of God flourished with his many virtues, so this man in contrast besmirched himself with his vile deeds.[177]

7

1 In these three years or more of exile the blessed Masona led his blessed life and showed himself an outstanding man there through his many virtues. Every necessity which he succeeded in obtaining for his and his servants' use he gave to the poor. 2 When there was almost nothing left for him to give, a certain poor widow afflicted by many troubles came to him asking for alms. 3 The man of God, who had given away everything in works of this sort, searched diligently for something to give her and when he found nothing asked the servants who were with him if any of them had something that they could in good faith give to him to present to the woman. 4 One of them called Sagatus, who was in charge of the others, said, 'I have a single *solidus*, but if I give you this we will have nothing at all with which to buy food for ourselves and our mule.' 5 The man of God told him to hand all of it over without hesitation and keep nothing back for himself and to have no doubt that the Lord would be with him and see to his every need. 6 But, though chastened by his command he had given the *solidus* to the woman, a little later this Sagatus ran after the woman and begged her as he had nothing with which to buy food for himself to give back at least a *tremiss* of the sum which she had received that he might see to his own needs. She gave him one *tremiss* without any sadness and took

---

[176] Nepopis must have been an Orthodox believer. The phrase appears to be an ascending tricolon emphasising the insult dealt to Merida. The comment that Nepopis was a bishop of another town suggests that Merida lost its status as an episcopal see at this time (see, however, *4 Toledo* 34 (AD 633) which allows a bishop to keep possession of another diocese if he has held it for over 30 years and it is in the same province). Nepopis' rank, possible seniority, and collaboration with Leovigild indicates that the king's religious policy was not completely opposed by the Orthodox in Spain. His name is Egyptian in origin and it is possible that he was a refugee from the Byzantine Empire, his flight perhaps being provoked by the controversy over the Three Chapters, see n.50 above.
[177] taken from *VSD* 4.

the other two off with her, glad at heart. 7 Then, lo, all of a sudden, two hundred loaded asses carrying a variety of foods which some men of the Catholic faith had sent to Masona were found standing by the monastery gates. When this was announced to the man of God and those who had come had made their gift, giving great thanks to the almighty Lord straightaway he ordered that Sagatus be summoned. When he came, the man of the Lord said to him, 'How much did you give to woman who asked for alms?' and he replied, 'I gave her the whole *solidus* that I had as you commanded, but as necessity pressed on us, afterwards I took a single *tremiss* back from her'. Then the man of God said, 'May the Lord forgive you brother, for you have shown yourself weak in faith and despaired of the mercy of the Lord and worse you have sinned against the many poor folk. You gave two *tremisses* and, behold, you have obtained two thousand *solidi* and two hundred asses loaded with many foodstuffs. I have no doubt that had you not taken that third *tremiss* you would have received three hundred loaded asses.' 10 Thanking them and giving his blessing in return for the blessing that they had brought him, he strengthened all who asked him with blessed homilies and epistles. Then straightaway he gave almost all that he had been given to the poor.

8

1 Some days later when he had gone into the church of the monastery to pray, the most holy virgin Eulalia suddenly appeared above the altar of that holy basilica in the form of a snow white dove[178] and addressing him gently like a caring mistress, saw fit to console her faithful servant. Then she said to him, 'Behold it is time for you to return to your city and resume your former service to me.' And when she had said this she swiftly flew from his sight. 2 The man of God exulted that he had been granted so great a vision and consolation yet began to weep deeply because he was to lose the tranquillity of his poverty and exile and be returned to the storms and tempests of the world.[179] For he had no doubt that what he had heard would swiftly come to pass. 3 Then, without any

---

[178] This is the form in which Eulalia's soul ascended to heaven in Prudentius, *Peristephanon Martyrorum* 3.161-165.

[179] For this topos see *VSA* 12.

delay, this glorious virgin wrought retribution with stern vengeance for the wrongs done to her servant. One night she stood by the impious tyrant Leovigild as he lay on his bed and scourging him at length on both flanks said, 'Restore my servant to me. And know that if you delay, I shall put you to death in ways worse than this.' 4 The wretch was so fiercely flogged that he woke and with much weeping showed his weals to all his attendants, crying out that he had been scourged because he had done harm to the holy bishop. For he revealed who had whipped him, her name, her dress, and her beautiful countenance, making everything clear and all the while letting forth great wails of grief. 5 Then, fearing lest he suffer more from the judgement of God, as he was ever a schemer in all his affairs and a deviser of falsehoods, feigning piety he ordered that the man of God who had been taken from his town in vain, should return to rule over his church once again.[180] 6 When the most holy Masona in no way assented to the mad king's request and said that he would remain where he had been exiled, he besought him time and again to deign to return to his city. Finally the piety of God most high softened his sincere heart and through its abundant benevolence opened the way for his servant. 7 When he with God's help returned, the cruel king tried by his entreaties and gifts to win the favour of a man he had just before condemned by false judgement to exile. He spurned his favours, rejected his gifts, but with a forgiving spirit pardoned the crime he had perpetrated and in accordance with the will of God was not mindful of the trespasses of those who had trespassed against him but forgave them.[181] 8 Then accompanied by an enormous retinue he returned from his place of exile to the city of Merida.[182] When his replacement Nepopis heard of his return, petrified by divinely-inspired terror he prepared in haste to flee to the city where he had previously been bishop. 9 But before he left, he criminally despatched to his own city by night and in secret in an enormous number of wagons using men of the Meridan church a great amount of silver, ornaments, and anything else he saw of beauty in the churches in Merida. 10 Then Nepopis driven in disgrace from Merida

---

[180] Taken from *VSD* 10.
[181] cf *Matthew* 6.12. Virtually all of sections 5-7 are taken from *VSD* 10.
[182] A parallel with the *adventus* processions of triumphant kings is probably intended here.

by all its clergy and people,[183] hurried towards his own city and made haste to leave lest the man of God, Masona, should find him in his church and drive him out in the greatest ignominy. 11 And so he fled, leaving the city in disgrace with a few helpers who all belonged to his household and followed behind him.[184] Then scattered, at a loss, and wandering all over the countryside, they made for their own city. 12 While this was happening, it came about through the will of God and the merits of St Eulalia that on this day holy Masona was returning to the city of Merida with a great host on the self-same road along which the wagons loaded with his goods were hastening away. 13 When he met them on the way not far from the city, the holy man asked to be told to whom all these wagons belonged. And they recognising their true Lord were filled with great joy and replied, 'We are your servants, Lord.' Then he asked them once more what they were carrying in their wagons and they replied, 'Holy things which belong to St Eulalia and yourself and which our enemy, the bandit Nepopis, has stolen. We wretches are going into captivity separated from our goods, our sons, and our wives, driven out from the country in which we were born'. 15 When the man of God heard this, he was filled with great joy and said, 'I thank you, good Lord Jesus, because the plenitude of your kindness is so great[185] that you deem it worthy to take such great care of your servants in all things, unworthy though they are, so that now you have restored us, freeing us from all evil and do not hand over your goods into the power of your enemy.' 16 And on saying this, he ordered that they all be taken back to their own city and so he came to the city with all rejoicing in great joy. 17 Just as a thirsty man in the heat of a fire longs for springs of water,[186] so he because of his ardent soul and burning spirit earned the right to come with God's aid to the basilica of St Eulalia. There when he had with his whole heart sated his desire, he entered the city exulting in the Lord and with all his people rejoicing. 18 And so the church of Merida exulted and received back its helmsman with utmost joy. For they rejoiced that the sick had found a cure, the

---

[183] cf VSD 11.

[184] The hagiographer is anxious to assert that Nepopis enjoyed no support among the citizens of Merida, hence his labouring the point that those who went willingly with Nepopis were members of his household. It is possible that he protests too much.

[185] cf Psalm 31.19.

[186] cf Psalm 42.1, a text used in the baptism service at this period, see Puech [1949].

oppressed a consolation, and that the needy would not lack food 19 What more is there to say? Many blessings were restored by the Lord to the church at Merida and the presence of the holy man bringing God's mercy put an end to the disastrous famines, the frequent plagues, and the cruel storms which had swept the whole city and had indubitably been caused by the absence of their exiled pastor.[187]

9

1 Now Leovigild, who hindered rather than helped the land of Spain and was its destroyer rather than its ruler, for whom there was no crime or evil deed that he could not justly claim his own,[188] abandoning God altogether, nay being abandoned by God, wretch that he was, he lost at one and the same time both his kingdom and his life.[189] 2 Through the judgement of God he was seized by a fatal disease, lost his vile life and obtained eternal death for himself. His soul cruelly wrenched from his body, subject to perpetual torments and eternally enslaved in the depths of hell, is rightly bound down there to burn for ever amongst the ever-rolling waves of pitch.[190] 3 After his most horrible death, that venerable man prince Reccared, his son, came, as is the law, to administer the kingdom and by his merits was deservedly elevated to the heights of sovereignty.[191] Through his great virtues he reached the monarch's post with God's aid by the solemn due process of law.[192] 4 Above all he was

---

[187] Sections 18-19 are taken from *VSD* 11.

[188] Taken from *VSD* 15.

[189] Leovigild died in AD 586. The attack on him once again concentrates on showing he was a bad king by the standards of the day. This savage account of the king contrasts sharply with that of Gregory the Great, which would have been known to the author. According to Gregory, Leovigild in the end saw the truth of the Catholic faith and was converted (*Dial.*3.31). This version was also known to Gregory of Tours, who is inclined however to doubt its veracity (*HF* 8.46). The hostility shown by the hagiographer runs contrary with to the general quiet pride taken in Leovigild's achievements by Orthodox Spaniards, see, for example, John of Biclarum's account of his reign.

[190] cf *VSD* 21 where this is the fate of Brunhilda.

[191] Cf the account of Reccared given by Gregory the Great (*Dial.* 3.31). The parallelism with *VSD* would also be apparent to *VPE*'s readers here as the rule of Theuderic and Brunhilda was replaced by that of the highly-regarded Chlotar II.

[192] Garvin [1946] 485 is inclined to think that this insistence on legality indicates that Reccared was elected king. Be this as it may, the purpose here is to emphasise the illegality of the rebellion described in following sections. Again the reader might wonder whether our author protests too much.

an Orthodox believer, a Catholic in all things unlike his treacherous father, and, following Christ the Lord,[193] turned from the depravity of the Arian heresy and through his wondrous guidance brought the entire nation of the Visigoths to the true faith.[194] 5 For he was champion of our divine religion, a herald of true glory, in all things a defender of the Catholic faith, preaching the coeternal Holy Trinity of one virtue and substance, distinguishing its proper persons, affirming that its nature was that of one God, declaring that there was the unbegotten Father, adding to him the Son begotten of the Father and believing that the Holy Spirit proceeded from both alike.[195] 6 Adorned with these virtues, he came to love all who loved God and utterly loathe and curse all whom he knew were hateful to God and so condemned the errors of the heretics' gross impiety. 7 While this policy was carried out with a will and through

---

[193] Here the hagiographer, while closely following Gregory the Great's account of these events (Dial.3.31), has substituted 'Christ the Lord' for Gregory's 'Martyred Brother'. This is a reference to Hermenegild, Reccared's half-brother and leader of an unsuccessful rebellion (AD 579-584) against Leovigild which took on, if it did not have from the beginning, religious overtones. Horror of rebellion against lawful authority was common in Visigothic writers and here while our hagiographer is happy to attack Leovigild as a bad king, he is not prepared to exalt a rebel against regal authority. Significantly Gregory of Tours, despite his intense dislike of the Goths, is equally hostile to regarding Hermenegild as a martyr for the true faith, and simply sees him as a rebel against duly constituted authority (HF 6.43). Some unconvincing attempts were made in the early twentieth century to deny that he was technically in rebellion against his father, see Guillermo Antolín [1901] and Rochel [1903]. Reccared's view of the matter is unclear. However we are told that Sisebert, the assassin of Hermenegild, who was killed while in exile at Tarragona in AD 585 (John of Biclarum, Chron. 74; (see Rochel [1902] for a weak argument that Hermenegild was in fact murdered in Seville), died a 'most shameful death' two years after carrying out his act (John of Biclarum, Chron.84, AD 587) which may suggest that Reccared made some attempt to rehabilitate his half-brother's reputation. Valerius of El Bierzo, De vana saeculi sapientia 6 (= PL 87 426D) lists Hermenegild as a royal saint. Nevertheless it was only in AD 1586 that Pope Sixtus V gave formal backing to a cult of Hermenegild, his feast day being established as 13th April. Hermenegild enjoyed great veneration from Philip II of Spain; see Manuel de Estal [1961]; and the counter reformation painter Juan de las Roelas painted a heroised version of his death which hangs in the Cardinal's Hospital in Seville. For a modern discussion of the rebellion and its problems see Hillgarth [1985].

[194] Reccared I ruled from AD 586-601. According to John of Biclarum he became a personal convert to Catholicism within a year of assuming the throne. In AD 589 he called 3 Toledo at which Arianism was formally renounced and Catholicism adopted as the religion of the Goths and hence all the population of the kingdom. Fredegar Chron. 4.8 tells us that Arian liturgical works were gathered together and burnt after the conversion.

[195] This insistence on the dual procession of the Spirit which was to cause so much trouble for Christendom may have been an innovation of the Visigothic Church. The doctrine is found in the preamble of 3 Toledo of AD 589 (PL 84 343) and those who refuse to accept it are duly anathematised (3rd anathema, PL 84 346). Isidore, HG 53 also mentions the doctrine being adopted at this council. It is included in the description of the true faith at 4 Toledo 1 (AD 633) = PL 84 365.

God's favour great peace was restored to the Catholic church and the calamitous error of Arianism was driven from almost everybody's mind and after all its troubles had been ended, the city of Merida along with its bishop, holy Masona, rejoiced in the grace of such great peace, giving thanks to the Lord without ceasing, once again the Old Enemy roused up anew as his accustomed envy broke forth afresh, brought strife to the servants of God through his ministers.

10

1 Sunna, the Gothic bishop of whom we have made mention above, goaded by the devil won over by a devilish plan certain noble Goths who were most distinguished by birth and wealth, and not a few of whom had been appointed Counts in various cities by the king. **2** He separated these with a countless host of the common people from the ranks of Catholics and the bosom of the Catholic church, devising deceitful plans against the servant of God, bishop Masona - plans designed to kill him.[196] **3** Then he sent some serving boys to him and feigning affection asked him to come to his house with them, with the intention of doing to death there the man of God in the cruellest of ways. When they came and made this suggestion, the blessed man, filled with the Holy Spirit, divined their treachery and said without delay, 'I am in no wise able to go thither, for there is a matter concerning the interests of the Catholic Church which I must see to. But if he wishes to see me, let him come here to the bishop's palace and see me on whatever matter concerns him.' **4** Then the envoys sent by Sunna returned and announced what they had heard. When he heard this, he straightaway summoned to his house the counts I have mentioned with whom he intended to kill the holy man and told them to go together with him to Masona's house. **5** First, he arranged with them that when they entered the palace, one of them named Witteric, who afterwards was King of the Goths, should draw his sword and strike down the

---

[196] John of Biclarum, *Chron.* 88, dates this conspiracy to AD 588. John's account names a secular ring-leader, Segga, as well as Sunna and the conspiracy is said to have been directed against the King Reccared himself rather than just Masona as our hagiographer implies.

blessed man with a blow so violent that a second would not be required.[197] 6 When he had told Witteric of this plan, with one accord and intent they all went to the holy bishop's palace. When they arrived, they wished to enter at once, but were stopped from doing so and told to wait outside for a short time until the holy Masona sent for the nobleman Claudius, the Duke of the city of Merida, so that they might see each other face to face in his presence. 7 Claudius was of noble birth and Roman stock, a strict Catholic, firmly bound to the tenants of the faith, bold in battle, most devout in his fear of the Lord, learned in the theories of warfare and in no way inexperienced in its practice.[198] 8 When the news was brought to him, as his house was adjacent to the palace, he soon hurried there with a great multitude of men.[199] 9 When the noble Claudius entered the palace, those I have mentioned above also went in with great crowds of people and, after greeting the holy man in the customary fashion, took their seats. 10 When they had been seated for a long time debating with one another, Witteric, a strong youth, stood behind the noble Duke Claudius's shoulder, as if as a young man he was paying an older man or his patron his due, 11 and tried with all his might to draw his sword from its scabbard to hack down both holy Masona and Claudius in accordance with what had been planned. But through God's will the sword stuck so fast in the scabbard that he thought it had been fixed to it with nails of iron. 12 While he tried at length to draw his sword, but was completely unable to do so, the authors of this vile plot silently began to wonder why Witteric was not carrying out what he had promised to do. Giving him sideways glances they urged him on more and more to perpetrate this utterly unholy, ghastly, impious deed at once and not to fear to slay these two men with his sword. 13 In response to their wicked encouragements, he

---

[197] King Witteric AD 603-610. Witteric became king after the assassination of Reccared's son Liuva II. A hostile summary of his reign is given by Isidore, *HG* 58.

[198] For a general account of Claudius' life see Orlandis [1992] ch.5. Despite his rank of Duke, Claudius was not a Goth but a Hispano-Roman. He led the Visigoths to a notable victory over the Franks in AD 589 near Carcassonne; see note 220 below. He remained an important force in the Kingdom, Gregory the Great (*Ep.* 9.230) asking him to chaperon one of his envoys to Spain, the abbot Cyriacus.

[199] Various suggestions have been made for Claudius' house. The two most commonly suggested are on the site of the Convent of San Francisco (the present day Parador) and on that of the later Arabic fortress, the Alcazaba. However no firm evidence for an identification exists at either site.

tried again and again with all his might to draw his sword from its scabbard, but to no avail.[200] When this happened to Witteric he realised that his sword was stayed by the power of God so that he was no way able draw the blade which had ever lain ready for his use, thereupon he was terrified and grew pale. 14 But the authors of this great crime when they saw that the machinations of their vile plan had been frustrated by the judgement of God, immediately got up and making their farewells returned bitterly to their homes.

11

1 When they left Witteric did not go with them, but, trembling, flung himself at the feet of the most holy bishop Masona, revealed their entire plan, and told with all sincerity how though he had wished to strike him he had been unable to draw his sword. 2 Then weeping he said, 'I confess my sin, I wished to carry out this evil deed, knowing full well what I was doing, but God did not allow me to do it.' adding, 'They have devised another plot against you so that if the plot failed in the palace today they might succeed in their aims on Easter Day. This is their scheme. When at Easter you have celebrated mass as usual in the Senior Church and after the mass, as is the custom, go in procession singing psalms with all the Catholic people to the basilica of Saint Eulalia, 3 their men will be standing at the gates of the city cunningly disguised as corn merchants with many wagons loaded with *swords and staves*.[201] Suddenly the whole mass of them will fall on you with drawn swords and staves and cruelly slay everyone, men and women, old and young alike. 4 I, a wretch that has implicated myself in this deed, seek pardon from you, my most pious Lord, and beg that through your prayers the Lord grant me mercy. All that I know I have carefully told

---

[200] The word used here is *spata*. Fernandis in Menéndez Pidal [1940] argues that this term shows the sword is a mark of rank. Although the existence of bodyguards named *Spatarii* gives superficial plausibility to this argument, it falls on two counts. First, *spata* is not used consistently in this context, Witteric's sword is also referred to as a *gladius* and an *ensis*; hence the hagiographer is merely employing literary *variatio* here. Second, *LV* 9.2.9 which deals with the number of slaves which nobles had to contribute to the army, states that the majority of these slaves had to be armed with *spatae*, showing that no rank can be intended by the use of the word.

[201] *Matthew* 26.47, *Luke* 22.52 - these weapons are the ones carried by those who arrest Christ in the garden of Gethsemane.

and laid open to you. **5** *Behold I am in your hand: do with me as seemth good and meet unto you.*[202] Lest by chance your holiness thinks me a liar or deceiver, keep me in the palace and hold me under guard as you see fit, until you have closely inquired into all I have said and see it to be true. If you find things otherwise and that I am a liar, I shall have no wish to live.'[203] **6** On hearing this, bishop Masona, a man of the Lord who had always been marked by the virtue of piety, told him in a kindly fashion not at all to be afraid, gave thanks to the Lord who had freed his servants from such great perils, and then summoned Duke Claudius and told him everything. **7** When he heard how things stood, he advised that they should remain silent about the matter for a while in order that the conspirators should not accidentally discover that their plan was betrayed and flee. But then when he investigated the affair closely, he found that what he had been told was clearly true. **8** When these Arian counts tried to bring to fruition what they had previously planned and came to meet the bishop in the customary fashion, a great crowd was set around them in ambush and suddenly Duke Claudius fell upon them. Some of them were taken prisoner, others who wished to indulge in sword-play were killed on the spot.[204] **9** Then Duke Claudius went to the house of the Arian bishop, Sunna, with a great multitude of men and took in the same way that heretical bishop, who knew nothing of what had happened, and sent him to the holy bishop Masona to be placed under close guard. **10** At the same time he gave over all Sunna's colleagues into Masona's custody, but gave instructions that Witteric who had brought to light the plans of these wicked men be set free. **11** Duke Claudius informed the Orthodox King Reccared of all these events and advised him to decree sentence at once and tell him what he was to do with these enemies of the Lord Jesus Christ. **12** The King took his advice and gave the following sentence: that they should all be deprived of all their patrimony and honours, loaded with iron chains, and exiled; that the false bishop Sunna be exhorted to convert to the Catholic faith, and if he should convert, be told to do penance and weep for his sins with a befitting number of tears so that when he had performed his

---

[202] *Jeremiah* 26.14 - Words of Jeremiah to the princes and people of Judah.

[203] Perhaps an official sanitisation of Witteric's participation in the conspiracy.

[204] cf *Matthew* 26.52, *Revelation* 13.10. See also Isidore's remarks on Witteric's demise, *HG* 58.

penance and they knew him to be a good Catholic, they might ordain him bishop in some other town.[205] **13** But although they often told him to do penance for his great sins and appease the fury of the Lord which he had roused up by his evil deeds, he declined to do so and persisting in his old tyrannical fashion replied,[206] 'I have no knowledge of what penance is, so know that I not understand what your penance is and that I shall never be a Catholic, but shall either live by the rite which I have lived by or most willingly die for that religion of which I am a member and have been since my earliest days'. **14** When they saw the obstinacy of his mind and that he persisted in his evil ways, they banished him forthwith in ignominy and the greatest shame from the land of Spain lest he should infect others with his pestilential disease. They set him ignominiously in a small boat and threatened him that though he was free to go to whatever place, people, or land he saw fit, if he was ever found again in the land of Spain he would find himself given a heavier sentence. **15** Then sailing to Mauretania he put in to shore and staying there sometime he soiled many through the deceit of his wicked beliefs.[207] Finally condemned by divine judgement he ended his life by a horrible death. **16** Holy Masona, by decree of that most clement prince Reccared, rightly recovered with all their privileges those basilicas which he had unjustly lost and the entire patrimony of this heretic.[208] **17** The rest of those wicked men we mentioned above were exiled in accordance with the king's decree.[209] One of them called Vagrila escaped from their hands and fled to the basilica of St Eulalia to obtain sanctuary. When that Claudius whom we have often mentioned already

---

[205] A precedent for the problem of converted Arian clergy could be found in *I Orleans* 10 (AD 511) where bishops are allowed to appoint converted clergy of 'good repute' to any function they wish. *2 Saragossa* 1 (AD 592) = *PL* 84 317 states that Arians unless they are 'holy' should be deposed; however the rest could be restored to the priesthood. A similar procedure appears to be provided for in this passage.

[206] i.e. Sunna refused to lay down his bishopric.

[207] Collins [1989] 21 speaks of Sunna's exile as 'Arian missionary activity' in Mauretania. However the text implies that Sunna's mission was in no way a voluntary act. Deportation to Mauretania, at this time held by the Byzantines, may have been an attempt to stir up trouble there in the wake of the Three Chapters controversy.

[208] *III Toledo* 9 decreed that all Arian churches and their contents be handed over to the Catholic church, see also Isidore *HG* 55. John of Biclarum, *Chron.* 87, states that Reccared returned confiscated land to those persecuted by Leovigild.

[209] According to John of Biclarum, *Chron.* 88, Segga had his hands cut off and was exiled to Galicia.

reported this to Prince Reccared he is said to have remarked, **18** 'I am amazed at the effrontery with which an enemy of God most High has presumed to enter His sacred halls and now flees in hope of finding safety to Him Whom just now he in his madness attacked in vain. But as we know God to have great mercy[210] and have no doubt that He despises no one who turns to Him, not even a sinner, we decree as follows: **19** that Vagrila along with his wife, children, and all his patrimony should serve the most holy virgin Eulalia for ever.[211] And we add this sanction to our decree, just as the lowliest serving boys are accustomed to walk before the horse of their Lords riding on no beast whatsoever,[212] so he shall walk before the horse of his master, the priest in charge of the cells of St Eulalia, and putting aside his honour and pride, carry out in all humility every servile task which the lowest slave is wont to perform.'[213] **20** Therefore the holy Masona on receiving this command at once summoned Vagrila to come from the basilica into his presence and, as his innermost soul was always full of piety, told him to be afraid no longer. But obeying the king's orders, he ordered him to comply with his command and come from the basilica of St Eulalia to the palace which lies within the walls of the city walking before the horse of deacon Redemptus. **21** When he had taken hold of the deacon's staff and holding it in his hands arrived at the palace, the holy man at once absolved him from his punishment along with his wife, sons, and all his goods and let him go free.[214] He laid this one condition on him: that in all his doings he was to keep to the whole and complete Catholic faith for the rest of his days.

---

[210] cf *Numbers* 14.18.

[211] i.e. that they become slaves owned by the church.

[212] Or possibly 'in no form of carriage'. The Latin *vehiculum* has both meanings in Visigothic texts. However here 'beast' seems the more likely implying that Vagrila was not even allowed to ride on a donkey.

[213] cf *VI Toledo* 12 (AD 638) where it is decreed that traitors who flee to churches should receive mercy tempered with justice. Vagrila's fate, though grim, was much better than Segga's.

[214] i.e. they became freedmen of the Church. As the church could not die they had no way of escaping from this condition as had a freedman with a secular patron, see *4 Toledo* 70 (AD 633). For a modern account of freedmen in the Visigothic Kingdom see Claude [1980].

12

1 At this time the devil roused up a rebellion against the Catholic faith in the famous city of Narbonne in the Gallic provinces.[215] It would take too long to relate its causes here. If we wished to narrate these events in order, it would seem that we were composing a tragedy rather than a history, but let us briefly give a summary of a small part of what happened. 2 Two counts, famed for their wealth and noble birth but with profane minds and ignoble habits, namely Granista and Vildigern, together with an Arian bishop called Athaloc[216] and many others who shared their errors caused a serious disturbance in that district. 3 Rising up against the Catholic faith they brought a huge host of Franks into the Gallic provinces to restore to power the depraved Arian faction, and, if possible, wrest the kingdom from the Catholic Reccared.[217] 4 In their attempt they slaughtered an innumerable host of clerics, monks, and Catholics of every kind. Their souls, purer than refined gold[218] and more precious than any precious stone,[219] were received as a burnt offering by our Saviour, the Lord Jesus and set among the companies of martyrs in the treasury of heaven. 5 After this, sublime Almighty God did not delay to fight back against his enemies with his celestial power, avenging through the prayers of the most excellent prince Reccared the blood of the innocents, and exacting a wondrous immediate retribution on his enemies with his avenging scythe.[220] 6 When all the enemies of

---

[215] i.e. Septimania.

[216] Athaloc had attempted to stop the conversion of the Goths at 3 *Toledo* and died of a broken heart when he failed (Gregory of Tours, *HF* 9.15).

[217] For contemporary readers the horror of rebellion would be compounded by the alliance formed with the Goths' traditional enemies, the Franks. We learn from John of Biclarum, *Chron.* 91 (AD 589), that these invaders were despatched by King Guntrum of Burgundy under the command of Count Boso. The Franks clearly wished to take advantage of the turmoil caused by the conflict of religious belief in the Visigothic Kingdom: John mentions another invasion led by Duke Desiderius which had been defeated in AD 587 (*Chron.*86); this is placed at the very end of Leovigild's reign by Gregory of Tours, *HF* 8.45.

[218] cf *Psalm* 19.10.

[219] An impassioned reference to *Revelation* 21.11?

[220] A reference to the victory of Duke Claudius over the Franks in AD 589. According to John of Biclarum (*Chronicle* 91) who likens the victory to that of Gideon over the Midianites (*Judges* 7) almost 60,000 Franks were put to flight and the greater part of these subsequently killed. Isidore (*HG* 54) remarks of it, 'No victory of the Goths in Spain was greater or even comparable'. The effect of the victory can be seen from the fact that the Franks never again invaded the Kingdom. However Claudius' victory may have been won

the Catholic faith had been cast down or had been put to flight, the Holy bishop Masona and all his flock reciting the psalms sang mystic praises to the Lord. He then went to the hall of the gentle virgin Eulalia with all the people clapping their hands and singing hymns.²²¹ **7** Afterwards at the solemn feast of Easter all the citizens celebrated Mass with him in great joy, rejoicing after the fashion of the ancients,²²² celebrating with loud cries in the streets, praising the Lord, and saying, 'We shall sing unto to the Lord, for he has been honoured gloriously',²²³ and again, '*Thy right hand, O Lord, is become glorious in power; thy right hand, O Lord, hath dashed in pieces the enemy. And in the greatness of thy excellency thou hast overthrown those that rose up against thee.*'²²⁴ **8** After this the storms cleared from all the land, the Lord thinking it right to lavish a lasting peace on his Catholic people.²²⁵

13

1 The holy Masona when he had ruled the church at Merida with divine aid for many years, tired by his great old age was possessed by a violent fever and suddenly began to lose his strength in all his body. **2** Then calling his archdeacon whose name was Eleutherius he said to him, 'Know, my son, that *the time of my departure is at hand,*²²⁶ and so I beg and ask you to care diligently for the holy church and all her holy congregation, so that you leave me feeling secure in all matters and make it possible for me to weep for my sins in a secret place where sorrow can be consoled before I die.' **3** When he heard this, his archdeacon did not have pity on his sickness and old age nor did he grieve that he would be left without the comfort of so great a father, but rather rejoiced with great joy that his bishop was to about die. His heart

---

with Austrasian assistance and the concession of at least two towns in Septimania to Theuderic and Brunhilda, see Bulgar, *Ep.* 3 = *PL* 80 112.

²²¹ cf *Psalm* 47.1.

²²² A reference to the Israelites.

²²³ cf *Exodus* 15.1: Moses' song after the Red Sea has closed on Pharaoh's troops.

²²⁴ *Exodus* 15.6-7.

²²⁵ Reccared in fact suffered another conspiracy against his life in AD 590 led by Duke Argimund (John of Biclarum, *Chron.* 94). On his capture the Duke was scalped, had his right hand amputated, and was led through the streets of Toledo on an ass, cf Brunhilda's fate, *VSD* 21.

²²⁶ *2 Timothy* 4.6.

was so puffed up in his joy of possessing this fleeting power that he proudly bustled hither and thither on horseback accompanied by a great entourage of servant boys. **4** After a few days had passed, holy Masona wrote a writ of freedom for those slaves who had served him faithfully,[227] gave them a small sum of money to establish them in their freedom and gave them a few small possessions.[228] **5** When Eleutherius was told of this, he at once went to the bishop's palace and asked after the health of the holy bishop. When he was told that the sickness was getting worse and that even now he was close to death he immediately summoned these slaves, and asked them what the holy bishop had in fact given them. **6** When they told him the truth, he was roused to fury and menaced them in his rage, threatening them and saying, 'Behold, guard well what you have been given, for if you do not give me back all of it untouched when I ask for it, know that you will be subjected to the worst kinds of torture.' After saying this he returned to his home in fury. **7** Then the slaves entered the small cell where the holy bishop Masona lay sick on his bed and began to weep bitterly before him, saying, 'In your piety you have had pity on us, unworthy though we are, but it would have been better for us had you not done so. Behold, even while you yet live they hold out great threats against us, when you are dead which of us will be able to free himself from their clutches? They told him this and many similar things as they wept. **8** The bishop on hearing this found it hard to believe, and first of all as befitted his serious nature he made a careful inquiry as to whether what he had heard was true. When he found that it was indeed true, he wept and

---

[227] This writ was to be presented to each new bishop within a year of his consecration or it would become void, *6 Toledo* 9 (AD 638). Ecclesiastical freedmen could not escape the *patrocinium* of their previous master as the church was not a mortal individual like secular masters and thus could not be said to die, *4 Toledo* 70 (AD 633).

[228] Technically speaking Masona's actions were probably illegal. While freeing slaves was regarded as a worthy act, *Formulae Wisigothicae*, ed. Gil [1974], 2 'This deed rouses us that we may be worthy to find some grace before God', the freeing of church slaves was regarded as an excess of zeal. Canon law provided that to free ecclesiastical slaves a bishop had to recompense the church by paying their value to it. Our first evidence for this principle is the local council *1 Seville* 1-2 (AD 590). The principle was established as valid for all of Spain by *4 Toledo* 67-70 (AD 633). Masona's actions would have fallen between these two decrees and so if not illegal would have been contrary to established good practice. Later legislation became even harsher, *Merida* 20 (AD 666) requires each new bishop to conduct an enquiry into the circumstances of all the ecclesiastical freedmen under his charge. If any are found to have been freed irregularly they along with their families and possessions, even those acquired after the manumission, are to become the property of the church.

straight away ordered that he be placed in a litter and taken to the basilica of the most holy virgin Eulalia whom he had ever served with devotion. **9** When the holy old man arrived there, raising his hands before the sacred altar and lifting his venerable eyes which were full of tears to heaven, with a great groan he prostrated himself on the ground and for a long time poured forth his prayers in the sight of God. **10** When he finished his prayer, speaking in a loud voice which all heard he said: 'I thank you, Lord, that you have heard me. May You be blessed through all ages for You have not ignored my prayer nor taken Your mercy from me'.[229] When he had said this, he returned to the episcopal palace restored to his previous health to such a degree that you would not have thought him sick or elderly, but to have gained a renewed vigour and sturdy youthfulness. **11** When he wished to go to Vespers in the normal fashion, all rejoiced greatly. However, the archdeacon on hearing of this was astounded and overcome by guilt when he heard that the man he thought was going to die that very day was going to Vespers. Confused and shamefaced, knowing not what to do, he stood before the bishop along with all the clergy as is the normal practice and offered him the customary incense. **12** The man of God said to him, 'As my soul lives, you shall go before me.' He heard, but did not understand plainly and asked the other deacons what the holy bishop had meant when he said 'You are going before me'. They being ignorant of the reason replied, 'What he said to you must mean that you go before him to the church.' **13** When they were coming to the end of the office of Vespers, the archdeacon was struck down by a most violent pain in the choir of singers and went home gravely ill. **14** When his mother, a most holy woman, saw him, she rushed straightaway to the venerable Masona as quickly as she could and, weeping and wailing, began to beg him to pray to the Lord for her son. To which he merely replied, 'What I have prayed for, I have prayed for.'[230] Three days later the archdeacon died.[231] **15** Then the holy bishop Masona in the many

---

[229] cf *John* 11.41, *Psalm* 66.19-20.

[230] cf Pilate's words to the Jews asking for the inscription on Christ's cross to be changed, *John* 19.22.

[231] Excavations in the church of Sta Eulalia have revealed the tomb of an Archdeacon Eleutherius who died on the 28th December AD 604. This must be the same Eleutherius and shows that the archdeacon clearly commanded enough support to be buried in the church, see Caballero Zoreda and Mateos Cruz [1992].

days which remained to him gave a great amount of alms to the needy and giving larger tokens of his gratitude to his faithful servants saw fit to give them greater gifts than before. Then an old man and in the decrepitude of old age he breathed out the last breath of his long life at peace while at prayer.[232]

14

1 After him a holy man of the utmost sanctity and honesty was elected bishop. He was called Innocent and his worth was shown by his name. Innocent and honest, he judged no-one, harmed no-one, he showed himself an inoffensive and pious man all the days of his life. It is said that at the same time as he was ordained he was considered the lowliest of the deacons.[233] 2 He is said to have possessed so much sanctity and to have been so conscientious that when the rain failed and a long drought had burnt up the land, the citizens of the town gathered as one body and went with him round the basilicas of the martyrs calling on the Lord in prayer. And whenever they went before him straightaway rain sufficient to water the land well would fall in abundance from the heavens.[234] 3 Whence there was no doubt that they had been able to obtain this and greater benefits from almighty God through his tears springing as they did from a man of humble and honest mind. 4 On his death, the holy Renovatus, adorned with all virtues, not undeservedly reached the heights of the bishopric. He was a Goth of noble stock, famed for his glorious descent. Tall of stature, handsome to behold, of noble presence, pleasing to look upon, having an attractive expression on his handsome face: he was altogether admirable in appearance. 5 But although his external presence was a glory for him, enlightened by the Holy Spirit[235] he showed himself more handsome within. He was learned in many disciplines and adorned with all the many virtues. 6 Indeed he gained fame in all his works for he was most equitable and just, possessed a sharp mind, and was deeply steeped in all the

---

[232] The exact time date of Masona's death is unknown, but, given the date of Eleutherius' death, it is most likely to have occurred in AD 605.

[233] cf *Mark* 10.31 'But many that are first shall be last; and the last first', and similar texts at *Matthew* 19.30 & *Luke* 13.30.

[234] cf Gregory the Great, *Dial.* 3.15 and *VSF* 5.

[235] cf *John* 14.26.

disciplines of the church and well read in holy writings. **7** While he showed forth his glory with these many virtues, he taught many disciples our sacred faith giving them a most hallowed example in his own life and through his prudence, sanctity, patience, gentleness, and compassion he fashioned a host of men the same as himself using as his tools the file of justice and his preaching of the holy faith. The church still gleams and shines like the sun and moon from his teaching. **8** Then when he had ruled his church beyond reproach for many years, he was added to the throngs of Angels and made part of the heavenly legions above.[236] Leaving his body in wondrous wise when his limbs lost their strength, he won the right to enter the halls of the heavenly kingdom and to stay and rule there forever with Christ.

15

1 The bodies of all these saints I have mentioned lie at rest buried with honour in one and the same cell close to the altar of the most holy virgin Eulalia.[237] **2** By their venerable tombs Christ daily grants the grace of holiness in abundance so that whosoever was brought here suffering from any disease, even though he had been long afflicted by his illness, as soon as he had called upon the name of God with all his heart there, he would find and discover that all the disease had been driven from him and every illness thrust aside, and so hale and hearty he came by his desired health through the grace of God.[238]

Epilogue

1 My rude story has told to the best of its ability of the number of miracles performed by the soldiers of Christ and of their deaths. Though in its lack of learning it may in its wretchedness displease the greatly learned, eschewing pompous wording it ennobles the humble believer and gathers together something of profit for those who read or listen to

---

[236] cf *Matthew* 26.53.
[237] See note 109 above. Burial within a church was forbidden by *I Braga* 18 AD 561, but this canon was frequently ignored; see *DVI* 13 for a further example.
[238] cf *VSD* 22.

it.[239] **2** I, the lowliest of all men, beg my fastidious readers to read this little work first and then to belittle it. Let them not be seen to be moved by hatred rather than good judgement and damn something of which they have no knowledge. Above all, let them know that driven to write through the love of Christ and devotion to the most holy Eulalia, I have expounded well-known events and set down in truthfulness truths which cannot be doubted. Glory, honour, power, thanks, strength, might, praise and blessing be to the Three in One, Ever-Lord who rules without end, now and for evermore. Amen

---

[239] cf *VSD* 19.

St Ildefonsus of Toledo

ON THE LIVES OF FAMOUS MEN

Preface

It can be said without fear of contradiction that the blessed and learned presbyter Jerome made a list, starting from the apostles soon after Christ's ascension, of those famous men by whose decrees and teachings the Holy Church, spread throughout all the world, gained prestige among good men and was defended from her enemies. Writing in a simple style in order to preserve their praiseworthy and essential memory, he listed the names of each of them individually, the course of their lives, and their books and diverse tracts, concluding with his own life; revealing them by his record and commending them to posterity through his retelling of their stories.[1] He was followed by Gennadius who continued these narrations in a similar style.[2] Finally that wisest of men, Isidore, bishop of the See of Seville, following the same path, added to the list the best men he knew.[3] But he departed this life without having looked into this matter fully. After him negligence has so overtaken everyone in our lands that some deeds have been obscured by their great antiquity and neglect has also buried in oblivion very many recent ones. Therefore I, who am certainly no equal to those whose names the record has preserved nor to those to whom its recounting has given pleasure, certainly unworthy of the task and lacking in the substance of any good work, the successor of Eugene II

---

[1] Jerome's *De Viris Illustribus* (= *PL* 23 607-720) was written in AD 392-393 at the request of Nummius Aemilianus Dexter, son of the bishop of Barcelona. Heavily dependent on Eusebius, it is 135 paragraphs long and begins with the life of St Peter, ending with that of Jerome himself. The best edition is that by EC Richardson [1896].

[2] A presbyter of Marseilles and author of several heresiological works, now lost, and a treatise on Church dogmatics (= *PL* 58 979-1000). Gennadius' *De Viris Illustribus* (=*PL* 58 1059-1120) was a continuation of that of Jerome and circulated along with it; see Isidore, *Etymologiae* 6.6. It contains 101 paragraphs ending again with an account of the author. Gennadius is known to have been alive in the reign of Pope Gelasius (AD 492-496).

[3] Isidore's *De Viris Illustribus* (= *PL* 83 1031-1106) was written c.AD 610 and deals with 46 individuals.

of blessed memory in the glorious See of the city of Toledo, (which I call glorious not so much from its immense throng of people since it is the presence of our glorious princes that gives it glory, but for this reason: that among those who fear God it is considered both a terrible place for the unjust and a place worthy of all veneration for the just[4]) have tried if not in an elegant work, at least by an act of good intent, to add to their glorious memory lest I should be condemned for my silence and for covering the gleaming light of the memory of so glorious a See and such glorious men in murky darkness of silence.

Tales of distant antiquity have been handed down to us which can be seen to have happened from analogy with our present times. For Montanus, the most blessed incumbent of this see, in order to disprove slanders that he was living with a woman, is said to have held glowing coals in his vestments for all the time that he was consecrating the sacrifice to the Lord and while he completed the entire celebration of the mass. After the service was finished, the fire from the living coals had so become one with the adornment of his vestments that the vestments did not extinguish the flames nor did their force harm the vestments.[5]

Again when Justus the deacon had insulted Helladius, the bishop of this See, with his haughty arrogance and after the death of his bishop lived on as the bishop himself,[6] he became ill and mad with the result that he died - he was strangled in his sleep by those who helped him at his own altar because of the intemperance of his ways.

In the same way the presbyter Gerontius, a favourite of the king who treated his successor, Justus, in a contemptuous and hostile fashion, all of a sudden lost his wits with the result that all the attentions of the doctors brought about something in his bones which merely served to make the disease worse. His madness reached such a pitch that until his dying day it was a horrific thing to see or to speak to him.

---

[4] Ildefonsus here is attempting to assert the religious supremacy of Toledo. His technique is to state that the importance of the town lies more in its religious leadership than the fact that it is the secular capital of the kingdom.

[5] For a similar use of fire to prove chastity see Gregory of Tours, *GC* 75 and *HF* 2.1. *2 Saragossa* 2 (AD 592) orders the testing by fire of relics held in formerly Arian churches.

[6] There is much controversy as to whether Ildefonsus is referring to Helladius' successor, i.e. Bishop Justus of chapter 3, or an entirely separate individual. The overall context of Ildefonsus' passage makes the former the more likely option.

Then when the deacon Lucidius had extorted by violence and the intrigues of worldly friendships the honour of the priesthood and various goods from the next bishop of Toledo, Eugene I,[7] his wits were so befuddled and he fell into such a degree of paralysis that when he wished to live no longer his death was no different to the life he had possessed, just as his life had been a wish to die.

I, spurred on by the works of these good men, have set down in the best literary fashion of which I am capable those things that I have found related of the men of old and those which I have discovered by seeing them myself in our present day and age in order that I may become part of the kindly recollection of those with whom through my sinful life I have no affinity. I, who do not bring along with them a wealth of learning into the Temple of God, shall commend to posterity the memory of those who did so in this faithful act of homage, begging all of them to intercede for me before the pious Godhead. For this reason I have made every effort to keep them present in mens' minds from which they could have slipped into oblivion.

[Indeed Isidore had written on the most blessed Gregory of blessed memory, but as he did not say as much as we have learned about his works, we shall remove his account and add what we have learnt about him in a more complete account][8]

1 Asturius was the successor of Audentius in the metropolitan See of the city of Toledo in the province of Carthaginiensis. An outstanding man, he displayed his virtues more through the example of his life than by the works he wrote. Blessed in his ministry and deemed worthy of

---

[7] Lucidius is probably the individual discussed by Braulio and Eugene II after the latter became bishop of Toledo. Eugene's problems arose from his predecessor, Eugene I, confessing that after he had been forced to make the man a priest, he had not laid hands upon him at his ordination and, as the clergy were chanting loudly, had pronounced a malediction rather than a benediction over him. The status of Lucidius was therefore questionable. Braulio's reply was that as Eugene I had acted deceitfully and had not repudiated the priest's status in public Lucidius' orders ought to be regarded as valid; see Braulio, *Ep.* 35-6.

[8] This is a late interpolation into the manuscript as is the account of Gregory at the end of *DVI*. They have been left in here for the sake of completeness. See the discussion in Codoñer Merino [1972].

performing a miracle, he earned the right to have an earthly burial by those with whom he would be united in heaven. For while bishop of his See, it is said that he was told by divine revelation to seek out the tombs of the martyrs of God in the town of Alcala de Henares,[9] which lies some sixty miles from Toledo. Swiftly hastening there, he encountered the remains of men whom the weight of earth and the passage of time had consigned to oblivion and who ought to be brought to the light and the glory of being remembered by men. On discovering them, he declined to return to his See and, binding himself to the continual service of these saints, there ended his days. No-one while he lived, acceded to his seat. For this reason, as the ancients tell us, he is known as the ninth bishop of Toledo and the first bishop of Alcala de Henares.[10]

2 After Celsus, Montanus took charge of the cathedral of the city of Toledo, the foremost see of the province of Carthaginiensis. He was a man outstanding in the virtue of his soul and adorned with the gift of being able to speak as the occasion demanded. He held and laid it down his office in a manner worthy of it and the law of heaven. He wrote two helpful epistles dealing with ecclesiastical discipline. One he sent to the inhabitants of Palencia in which it is said that using his great authority, he forbade presbyters to consecrate chrism[11] or bishops to consecrate churches in dioceses other than their own, asserting with proofs from the Scriptures that it was in no way permitted to do these things.[12] He

---

[9]The ancient Complutum. The martyrs are the boy martyrs Sts Justus and Pastor who were executed under Diocletian in c.AD 302; their feast day is 6th August. Relics of the two saints are preserved in the Collegiate church of the town.

[10] Asturius' bishopric should date to the second half of the fourth century AD. The cult of Justus and Pastor was certainly known by AD 392, when Paulinus of Nola buried his son Celsus beside the martyrs' tomb, *Carm.* 31 610-610. The two martyrs are also mentioned by Prudentius a few years later, *Peristephanon Martyrorum* 4.41-44. Asturius has been assigned authorship of the hymn, 'O Dei perenne verbum' = *PL* 86 1176 in honour of Sts Justus and Pastor. However this attribution is normally rejected, see *PLS* 4 1878.

[11] A mixture of olive oil and balsam used for anointing.

[12] The text of Montanus' letters is printed in *PL* 65 54-60.

condemned and rebuked sympathisers of the Priscillian sect[13] because although they did not practice their beliefs, they cherished Priscillian's memory; recalling that in the works of the most blessed bishop Turibius[14] which he had sent to Pope Leo[15] this self-same heresy of the Priscillians had been exposed and refuted and ought rightly to remain condemned. He wrote another epistle to the devout Turibius in which he praised him for having put an end to the worship of idols and granted him the authority of a bishop through which he might with all vigour put an end to priests consecrating chrism and to bishops consecrating churches in dioceses other than their own.[16] A very old and reliable tale relates that Montanus carried glowing hot coals in his vestments before the altar in his own cathedral until he had completed the entire celebration of the mass in order to absolve himself from slander. When the solemn rites had been completed, it was found that the coals had not lost their fire nor his vestments their beauty. In this way, having given thanks to God, the detestable falsehood of his accuser and the innocence of the blessed priest were brought to light through the pure nature of fire. He led his glorious life in the reign of king Amalaric[17] and held the honour of the bishopric for nine years.

3 Donatus, a monk both in his profession and his deeds, is said to have been a disciple of a hermit in Africa. On seeing the threat of violence from barbarian peoples and fearing that his sheep would be scattered

---

[13] Priscillian, a extreme ascetic, was the first Christian to be executed by a Christian emperor. Put to death by in AD 395 by Magnus Maximus despite intercessions on his behalf from St Martin of Tours, he remains a controversial figure, see Chadwick [1976]. Braulio when writing to Fructuosus (*Ep*.44) warns him of the dangers of Priscillianism, but by this time the word may simply have been a general pejorative term; see Cronin [1985].

[14] Bishop of Astorga in the mid fifth century AD, dying c.AD 460. By the thirteenth century a myth of Turibius travelling to the Holy Land and returning to Spain with a mysterious trunk of relics had come into being; see Walsh [1992]. There appear to have been three separate saints of this name in Spain whose lives were often conflated; see Gaiffier [1941].

[15] Pope Leo the Great, pope from c.AD 440 until his death in AD 461.

[16] = *PL* 65 54-60, repeated *PL* 84 340-342.

[17] Amalaric ruled from AD 511-531. Gregory of Tours (*HF* 3.10) approved of him, but Isidore (*HG* 40) says he died 'hated and despised by all' after his defeat by the Frankish King Childebert at Narbonne.

and the dangers to his flock of monks, he crossed the sea to Spain with around seventy monks and a great collection of books.[18] He was given food and aid by a noble and devout woman, Minicea, and appears to have built the monastery at Servitanum.[19] He is said to have been the first man to have brought a rule for monastic observance to Spain.[20] He was as distinguished in life by his virtuous example as he was exulted in death through the glory of his memory. Both while living in this world and now at rest in the grave, his glory is said to have shone forth through certain miraculous acts of healing and because of this the inhabitants of the region are said to give honour to his tomb.[21]

---

[18] The 'barbarian peoples' are the Berbers. The mid-sixth century saw much warfare between the Berbers and the Byzantines in Africa. It was presumably this that provoked Donatus' flight from his homeland.

[19] No trace of this monastery survives. Donatus's successor, Eutropius, wrote a defence of his monastery's regime to Bishop Peter of Ercavica (= PL 80 15-20) which implies that the monastery was located in Peter's diocese. Some would identify it with the site at Cabeza del Griego (Cuenca). For a description of this site see Fontaine [1978] 391-2 and Schlunk [1945]. Eutropius went on to become bishop of Valencia (Isidore, DVI 32) and along with Leander of Seville played a leading role at III Toledo in 589 AD (John of Biclarum, Chron. 92).

[20] This statement as it stands is simply false. I Saragossa 6 (AD 380) refers to monks in the peninsula, as does a letter from Pope Siricius to Eumerius, the bishop of Tarragona, written soon afterwards (PL 84 632-633). In AD 398, Augustine wrote to abbot Eudoxius who presided over a monastery on Capraria, one of the Balearic islands (PL 33 187-189). Baquarius of Braga writing to a deacon consumed with lust in AD 410, advises him to take himself off to a monastery as a cure (PL 20 1054).

It is possible that Ildefonsus was simply ignorant of the early history of monasticism in the peninsula. Two alternatives present themselves. One, proposed by Fernández Alonso [1955] 458, is that these early references to monks and monasticism refer to hermits rather than organised monastic communities. It is the case that Isidore (De Officiis Ecclesiasticis 2.16.11) remarks that a monasterium can exist for one monk only, in other words mean what we would understand by 'hermitage' and 'hermit'. But as Linage Conde [1973] 219 points out it is unreasonable to assume that all early references to monks are of this kind. The other alternative is that Ildefonsus means that Donatus introduced a rule which had not been used in Spain until his arrival. The Augustinian rule from Africa would seem the best candidate, see Díaz y Díaz [1958] 9-19. However given the early contact between Augustine and Spanish monks this too seems unlikely.

[21] See Jo.Biclar., Chron. 18 - 'Donatus the abbot of the monastery of Servitanum, was held in high esteem as a worker of miracles'.

4 Aurasius, bishop of the church of Toledo, a metropolitan city, was elected to his ministry after Adelphius.[22] A good man, famous for the authority of his guidance, well suited to set the affairs of the church in order and its stout defender against stubborn adversities, the more he showed himself in a kindly light towards the meek, the more courageous he was found to be against the church's enemies. In him was to be found more eagerness to defend the truth than to write books, whence he is considered to be the equal of the holiest saints because the seed that was sown by their words was guarded by his protective custody. He lived as bishop in the times of Witteric, Gundemar, and the beginning of Sisebut's reign, holding office for almost twelve years.[23]

5 John[24] acceded to the seat of the church of Saragossa following the bishopric of Maximus.[25] At first he was a father of monks, he was then made a bishop to guide the common people. A man learned in Scripture, he was eager to teach more by words than through written works and was as generous and jovial in giving as he was jovial in appearance. He so esteemed the blessing of the Spirit of God which nourished him within through the generosity of his gifts as through his cheerful disposition that its Grace made dear what he gave and excused what he had not given. He composed some hymns for church offices which are elegant in both their music and their words. Amongst his works he devised a method of discovering the date of the solemn feast of Easter which was so subtle and useful that both its great brevity and its

---

[22] died c. AD 603.

[23] Aurasius was elected bishop c.AD 603 and died c.AD 615. Three of his letters survive: an *Epistula Apologetica*, *PLS* 4 1593-5, a letter to Bishop Agapius, *PLS* 4 1595-6 and a letter rebuking Count Froga of Toledo for his Judaising tendencies, *PLS* 4 1596.

[24] John was probably the son of Bishop Gregory of Osma, a signatory of *II Carthage* in AD 610. Eugene II wrote a metrical epitaph for him, *Carm.* 21, and mentions him in two other poems (*Carm.* 8, 70).

[25] See Isidore, *DVI* 33. Maximus was present at *2 Barcelona* in AD 599 and *Egara* in AD 614. His letter to Bishop Argebatus, *PL* 80 617-620, is a sixteenth-century forgery, see *PLS* 4 1662. Blume [1897] attributed to him the hymn, 'Nardus Columbae Floruit' (= *PL* 86 1310) in honour of St Columba of Meaux.

obvious correctness give pleasure to the reader.[26] He held his seat of office for twelve years, leading his life in joy and breathing it out in ardent prayer. He was bishop in the reigns of Sisebut and Suinthila.

6 After the death of Aurasius, Helladius occupied his seat. This man while he showed himself a most distinguished member of the royal court and overseer of state affairs, equally fulfilled the profession and life of a monk in a secular habit.[27] For when he came, as he often did, brought by the course of his varied duties, to my monastery (I mean the monastery of Agali into whose safekeeping I was received as a monk and which through God's gifts and the glory of its perennial and clear holiness has renown manifest to one and all),[28] setting aside his entourage and the pomp of worldly glory, he would devote himself to the duties of a monk to the extent that he joined their ranks and carried bundles of straw to the bakery. When amidst the glamour and arrogance of this world he began to love and seek out the secrets of solitude, with a rapid flight and leaving behind everything which he had known, he came to that holy monastery which he had often visited because of his vocation in order to remain there and lead the life for which he longed.[29] There he was made abbot and by his merits and holy

---

[26] The time of Easter was a problem which plagued the church. Roger of Wendover, writing in the thirteenth century, records in his *Flores Historiarum* a typical dispute for AD 573 when the Spanish and Gallican churches celebrated Easter at completely different times. Roger is clear that the Gallican celebration, not the Arian Spanish feast, was the one held at the correct date, and cites as proof the fact that spring water was forthcoming for baptism on the Gallican date but not the Spanish one.

[27] Helladius' secular career was probably under Reccared. His title is obscure: he was possibly a Duke of a province.

[28] The location of this monastery is unknown save that it lay near to Toledo (it is normally identified with the church of St Cosmas and St Damian mentioned as lying 'in suburbio Toletano' in the *Beati Ildefonsi Gesta* written by Pseudo-Cixila in the tenth century AD). One suggested location from linguistic grounds is the Palacio de Galiana; for others see Codoñer Merino [1972] 49 n.110. An unsubstantiated tradition states that it was founded in the reign of the Arian Athanagild. Though it may have been dedicated to Cosmas and Damian who were Eastern saints, Codoñer Merino [1972] 49 n.112 is correct to point out that Braegelmann [1942] is wrong in assuming that it was probably an Eastern foundation.

[29] Codoñer Merino [1972] 53 sees Helladius' retreat to the monastery as resulting from a change of regal policy under Witteric.

endeavours ruled over the monks as was proper: increasing the status of the monastery and the wealth of the entire community. Then, when his limbs were tiring as old age drew on, he was called to the heights of a bishopric and as he had been summoned both by force and without any say in the matter, he showed in this office greater proofs of his virtue than when he had been a monk. For through his virtue he is said to have ruled with great wisdom over the worldly matters which he despised and to have given such comfort and lavish amounts of alms to the needy that you would have thought that both the body and soul of the poor were dependent on his good will. He declined to write as he demonstrated things that ought to be written through the pages of his daily life. Returning to the monastery I have mentioned at the end of his life, he made me a deacon. He died an old man, having held office for eighteen years. The blessed man was a bishop during the reigns of Sisebut and Suinthila and in the first years of Sisenand's reign and after a long old age of goodness earned the more blessed glory of the celestial kingdom.[30]

7 After Helladius, Justus, his disciple, was made his successor: a man who from his physical appearance and sharpness of his mind was both handsome and clever. A monk from his infancy, he had been well educated and instructed by Helladius in the virtues of the monastic life, and was made the third abbot after him.[31] Soon too he was made his successor as bishop. A man of sharp wits and no mean speaker, he would have lived in hope of great things had not his final day cut his life short.[32] He wrote a letter in a fitting and appropriate style to Rechila, the abbot of the monastery of Agali, in which he forcefully urged him that it would not at all be right to abandon the flock of which he had taken charge.[33] He was a bishop for three years and died in the reign of King Sisenand, who died and departed this life nineteen days after him.

---

[30] Helladius was probably bishop c.AD 615-633.
[31] Is this the Justus of the preface who insulted Helladius?
[32] This is quite possibly a euphemism for the violent death recorded in the preface.
[33] This letter is lost. The short tract 'On the Enigmas of Solomon' was assigned to Justus by Heine [1848], but this has been strongly challenged by Díaz y Díaz [1957] and the tract is now normally assigned to Taio of Saragossa, see Vega [1957].

8 Isidore took charge of the Cathedral of the See of Seville in province of Baetica after his brother Leander.[34] A man distinguished both by his looks and intellect.[35] His ability in speaking reached such a pitch of fluency and delight that his wondrous richness of expression left his audience enraptured to such a degree that a man who had heard him would not remember what he had said unless it was repeated many times. He wrote famous works and no small number of them, namely:[36] a book on the nature of church offices,[37] a book of prooemia,[38] a book on the rise and fall of the prophets,[39] a book of lamentations which he himself called the Synonima,[40] two short works for his sister on the iniquities of the Jews,[41] a work of natural history dedicated to king Sisebut,[42] a book of *Differentiae*,[43] and a book of *Sententiae*.[44] Moreover he collected together from various authors a work which he called the *Explanations of the secrets of the sacraments*,[45] which gathered into one book is called the *Book of Questions*. Finally he wrote at the request of

---

[34] See Isidore, *DVI* 41. The elder brother of Isidore, Leander was born c.AD 545 in Cartagena. His family fled from Cartagena at the time of the Byzantine Invasion during Athanagild's rebellion against Agila. His later support for the Catholic rebel Hermenegild led to his exile to Constantinople by Leovigild where he met the future Pope Gregory the Great. Recalled by Leovigild, he became bishop of Seville and presided over *3 Toledo* (AD 589) where Leovigild's son, Reccared, announced his and the kingdom's conversion to Catholicism. Most of his extensive works are lost and only his address to *3 Toledo* and a monastic rule for nuns survive. It is possible, however, that he is the author of the *Liber Orationum Psalmographus*, ed. Pinell [1972].

[35] *8 Toledo* (AD 653) refers to Isidore as the *doctor* of the church, a title officially conferred on him by the Roman Catholic church in AD 1722.

[36] Braulio provides a much better summary of Isidore's works in his preface to them: *PL* 82 65.

[37] = *PL* 83 757-826.

[38] = *PL* 83 155-180. This outlines the contents of the individual books of the Bible.

[39] = *PL* 83 129-156.

[40] A two part work where Reason appears and comforts the Soul giving it the hope of obtaining forgiveness. = *PL* 83 825-868.

[41] = *PL* 83 449-538.

[42] = *PL* 83 963-1018, Fontaine [1960].

[43] This work, in fact written in 2 books, explained the differences between near homonyms such as 'anima' and 'animus' = *PL* 83 9-98

[44] In fact a work of theology in 3 books. The first book deals with dogmatics, the remaining two with personal and social ethics. The work draws heavily on St Augustine and the *Moralia* of Gregory the Great. = *PL* 83 537-738.

[45] = *PL* 83 207-444. The work's alternative title is 'Questions on the Old Testament'.

Braulio, the bishop of Saragossa, a book of *Etymologies* which he tried to finish for many years and appears to have spent his last day working on it.[46] He lived in the times of kings Reccared, Liuva, Witteric, Gundemar, Sisebut, Suinthila, and Sisenand, holding the office of bishop for almost forty years, an outstanding glory and ornament of the Holy Faith.[47]

9 After John,[48] Nonnitus acceded as bishop to the See of Gerona. A monk by profession, outstanding in his honesty, holy in his deeds, he was elected to his bishopric not through the long deliberation of men, but by a swift decree of God enacted through men. He dedicated himself at once to the cult of tomb of the holy martyr Felix.[49] He ruled the church of God by the example of his meritorious life rather than through written edicts. Both while in his mortal body and at rest in the tomb he is said to have worked miracles of healing.[50] He was bishop in the times of kings Suinthila and Sisenand.

---

[46] = *PL* 82 73-1054. For a partial English translation with somewhat unsympathetic commentary, see Brauhert [1912]. A full Spanish bi-lingual edition edited by Oroz Reta & Marcos Casquero [1982] is available.

[47] Isidore was born c.AD 560, became bishop of Seville c.600 AD and died most probably in AD 636.

[48] i.e. the Chronicler John of Biclarum, so called after the monastery he founded (see Isidore, *DVI* 44), who was exiled to Barcelona by Leovigild and became bishop of Gerona between AD 589-592 on the death of Bishop Alicius, a post which he held to his death. This must have occurred after *Egara* in AD 614 to which he was a signatory. For John see Wolf [1990].

[49] This is where Reccared dedicated the votive crown which Count Paul later used to crown himself with in his rebellion against Wamba, Julian of Toledo, *Hist Wamba* 26 (= *PL* 96 791-792). The cult of the martyr Felix (feast day 1st August) was centred on Gerona, see Prudentius, *Peristephanon Martyrorum* 4.29-30, and Gregory of Tours, *GC* 91. Fábrega [1953] attributes the hymn dedicated to Felix, 'Fons Deus vitae perennis' (= *PL* 86 1171-1173) to Nonnitus. The two masses for the saint's feast day (Férotin [1904] 380ff and 583ff) have also been attributed to him by some commentators.

[50] Nonnitus' death is mentioned by Braulio in his letter to the abbess Pomponia, *Ep.* 18. He was present at *4 Toledo* (AD 633) but must have died before AD 636.

10 After Murilas, Conantius acceded to the seat of Palencia.[51] A serious man in the gravity of his thought as much as in appearance, he was eloquent and popular for his simple way of speaking. An enthusiast for and attentive to the rituals of church services, he composed many noble melodies. He also wrote a good short work on the correct use of all the Psalms. He lived as bishop for more than 30 years, holding the office in the last years of Witteric, and in the times of Kings Gundemar, Sisebut, Suinthila, Sisenand and Chintila.[52]

11 Braulio, the brother of John, acceded to his place in Saragossa after his death. As he was bound to him in kinship, so he was no less close to him in his great intellectual ability. He is known for his hymns and some minor works.[53] He wrote a life of a certain monk, Aemilian, which both preserves his memory and praises this holy man in its own style. He held his bishopric for almost twenty years, which when complete closed the span of his mortal life. He was bishop in the time of kings Sisenand, Chintila, Tulga, and Chindasvinth.

12 Eugene, the pupil of Helladius, and a fellow-reader and colleague of Justus became bishop after Justus.[54] He had been educated by Helladius along with Justus from infancy in holy monastic disciplines, and when Helladius was summoned to his bishopric he took Eugene from the monastery with him. Taught by him once again in ecclesiastical orders, he became the third rector of his seat after him. This was the great merit

---

[51] The mentor of Fructuous see *VSF* 2. Murilas was an Arian bishop who abjured his faith at *3 Toledo*.

[52] c.AD 609–c.AD 639.

[53] All that survives today are *VSM*, a poem (whose authorship is disputed, see Barlow [1969]) in honour of Aemilian incorporated into Mozarabic liturgy, and a collection of 44 Letters.

[54] Eugene the first is occasionally known as Eugene II. This is due to the rise of a later cult of a mythical first-century bishop Eugene of Toledo which took root at Deuil near Paris in the twelfth century. Gaiffier [1935, 1965, 1966] believes that the cult was engendered by a confusion of hagiographic traditions; *contra* Rivera Recio [1963 & 1964] who believes, less plausibly, that the confusion arose from the translation of Eugene II's (i.e. Eugene III with the inclusion of the mythical Eugene) remains to France for safety in the eighth century (see review by Gaiffier [1966a]). The confusion persisted for centuries. Philip II escorted the remains of 'Eugene I' back to Toledo from Paris in the sixteenth century.

of the old man - that he managed to leave as his legacy to the church of God two disciples and saintly sons by whom she could be governed. Eugene was stern in the manner of his life and gait, and sharp in mind. He knew with such wisdom the phases, stations, waxings and wanings, cycles and epicycles of the moon that the exposition of his arguments would astound the hearer and lead him to correct belief. He was bishop for almost eleven years during the reigns of kings Chintila, Tulga, and Chindasvinth.

13 After Eugene, Eugene II was elected bishop. He, although he had been a famous cleric at the royal church, took pleasure in the life of a monk. Seeking the city of Saragossa by a wise flight, he dedicated himself there to the tombs of the martyrs and cultivated, as was proper, the study of wisdom and the life of a monk. Through the violence of the king he was brought back from Saragossa and made bishop.[55] He spent his life more by displaying his merits than by being active. For he had a slight body and little physical strength, but his spirit was on fire with virtue and pursued the strength which is to be had from goodly studies.[56] Through his knowledge of music he corrected songs which had been corrupted by continual use, and took care to restore the lost orders of church offices. He wrote a small work on the Holy Trinity which shines with eloquence and is profound in its exposition of truth. This would have been despatched to Africa and the East, had not the straits resounding with storms made the journey perilous for the panic-stricken travellers.[57] He wrote two other short works, one in verse composed of a variety of different sorts of poetry, the other in prose on a number of distinct topics, which have served to ensure a firm memory of this holy

---

[55] AD 646, see Braulio, *Ep.*31-33. The King involved is Chindasvinth.

[56] Eugene alludes to his precarious health in several of his poems, Vollmer [1905] nºs 13,14 and in a letter to Braulio (Braulio *Ep.* 35). He also appears to have disliked hot weather, Vollmer [1905] nº101.

[57] Now lost. Nájera fragment 18 in the library of Santo Domingo de Silos is possibly a fragment of this work which Collins [1989] believes was a Spanish contribution to the Monothelite controversy.

man and been a spur for the work of many others.[58] He took the works of Dracontius concerning the creation of the world, which antiquity had handed down to us in a corrupt fashion and finding the errors in them by removing these or correcting them or adding improvements, brought them into an acceptable form, so that their beauties seem to be due more to the skill of their correction than the hand of the original author.[59] Since Dracontius appears to have left the work half-finished as he is altogether silent about the seventh day, Eugene added a summary of the six days in six individual lines of verse and then added an elegant discussion of what seemed appropriate to him concerning the seventh day.[60] He held the honour and glory of his priestly office for some twelve years in the reigns of Kings Chindasvinth and Reccesvinth. After

---

[58] The extant works of Eugene are edited by Vollmer [1905] and can also be found at *PL* 87 359-368 & 389-400. Messina [1983] believes that the corpus of over 100 poems includes a collection of 40 composed not by Eugene, but an unknown secular poet. The main influence on Eugene's work is Virgil, though echoes of Lucilius, Ovid, Catullus, Juvenal, Perseus, Petronius, and Valerius Soranus can also be found along with those of Christian poets from Prudentius and Juvencus to Venantius Fortunatus. Eugene may have known many of these poets from excerpts in florilegia rather than being conversant with their entire works. The judgement of posterity on Eugene's poetry has generally been negative. Raby [1927] 'His verses with their metrical faults, their barbarism of phrase, their poverty of contents, their characteristics of acrostic, telestich, and epanalepsis illustrate the declining culture of the seventh century' is a typical example. However Codoñer [1981] presents a spirited case for the defence.

In addition, a variety of hymns have been assigned to Eugene such as *PL* 86 913 'Ecce Christe tibi cara' for the consecration of churches; *PL* 86 1123 'Hierusalem gloriosa' for the feast of St Hadrian and St Natalia (17th June); and *PL* 1183 'Adsunt, o populi festa celebria' for the feast of St Hippolytus (13th Augustus, see Gaiffier [1949]). Pérez de Urbel [1926] believes that the three *hymni pro varia clade* = *PL* 86 919-921 are also by Eugene; however, see *contra PLS* 4 1876 which argues for a fifth century date and an Italian author. For a group of prayers attributed to Eugene see *PLS* 4 2012-2016 and Vives [1946] 372.

[59] Blossius Aemilius Dracontius was born c.AD 450 to Senatorial parents in Campania. Transplanted to Africa, he pursued a legal career while writing poetry. Excessive praise of an unknown individual led to him being arrested by the Vandal king Guthamund, though he was freed in c.AD 496 by Guthamund's successor Thrasamund. His poetry edited by Vollmer [1905] (for a poorer edition see *PL* 60 679-932) is wide ranging in style. Eugene's *Metrical Preface to the Works of Dracontius* can be found at *PL* 87 369-372.

[60] *Monosticha recapitulationis septem Dierum* = *PL* 87 388.

passing from this mortal light, he lies in his tomb in the Basilica of Sta Leocadia.

[Pope Gregory, head of the apostolic see of Rome, full of the fear of God and outstanding in his humility, was so endowed through the grace of Holy Spirit with the light of knowledge that not only is no-one of these present times, but neither was anyone of times gone by his equal. For sublime and shining forth in the perfection of every kind of good deed, setting aside all comparisons with famous men, antiquity can show us nothing similar to him.

For he was Antony's superior in holiness, Cyprian's in eloquence, and Augustine's in wisdom. When he took up his bishopric, he wrote a book of pastoral guidance to send to John, bishop of the see of Constantinople, in which he taught which and what kind of man should come to office, and how, when he held office, he ought to strive to live and teach his flock.[61] This most excellent teacher wrote moreover, apart from the small works which Isidore of blessed memory has made mentioned, other books on Morals: namely twenty two homilies on the prophet Ezekiel bound into two books in which he discusses many things concerning the divine scriptures in a brilliant fashion. These works are mystic and moral, but at the same time readable.[62]

On the book of Solomon, whose name is the Song of Songs, how wondrously he writes, going through the whole work and expounding its moral import.[63] He wrote four books preserving the memory of the church fathers of Italy, which he gathered into one volume, which he preferred to be called the *Dialogues*. In these books the conscious reader is easily able to learn for himself how great a quantity of divine mysteries lie hidden there and what wonderful testaments they are to his love of his divine homeland.[64]

There are also extant a great number of his letters to various correspondents, which are edited and written in a clear style, which, if a man reads them, he will clearly see that in Gregory was a goodly longing after God and that he was studious in his care and vigilance for

---

[61] = *PL* 77 13-128.
[62] = *PL* 76 785-1312. In fact the two books contain 52 homilies.
[63] = *PL* 79 471-548.
[64] = *PL* 77 149-430.

the well-being of the souls of others. Gathering these together into one volume, he divided them into twelve books and gave them the name of the *Register*.[65] It is said that he wrote other famous works, but they have not yet come into our possession. Most fortunate is he, exceeding fortunate to whom God has granted the opportunity to study his works in their entirety. This glorious man and most blessed teacher and bishop lived in the reign of the Emperor Maurice.[66]]

---

[65] = *PL* 77 441-1328.
[66] AD 582-602.

[Valerius of El Bierzo]

THE LIFE OF ST FRUCTUOSUS OF BRAGA

1 After the new brightness of heavenly truth flooded in upon the ancient darkness of the world, the grandeur of the teachings of the Catholic faith shone forth from the seat of Rome, the foremost seat of the Holy Church, and most excellent examples of sacred religion blazed out from Egypt, the province of the East, and the edge of this slender Western shore began to shed forth light, divine piety lit two glorious lamps of outstanding brightness,[1] namely Isidore, a most reverend man, bishop of Seville[2] and the most blessed Fructuosus, a man who from his birth was just and beyond reproach. The former was famous for his oratory,[3] outstanding in his labours, and, steeped in the arts of learning, was foremost in renewing the tenets of the Roman church.[4] The latter, set alight by the flame of the Holy Spirit in his most sacred vocation of a religious life, excelled so perfectly in every spiritual discipline and all his holy works that he easily made himself equal in merit to the Theban Fathers.[5] Isidore through the industry of an active life educated all Spain in worldly affairs,[6] Fructuosus aflame with shimmering brightness from his living of the contemplative life, illuminated the innermost secrets of the heart. Isidore, shining out through his outstanding eloquence, obtained fame through his learned books, while Fructuosus, gleaming at the peak of virtue, left us an example of religious living and followed with innocent step the footprints of his master who had gone before him: our Lord and Saviour.[7] So wondrous are the signs of his virtues that our ineptitude is unable to bear witness to them. But from as much

---

[1] cf *Genesis* 1.12 - the creation of the sun and moon, cf *VPE* 5.14.7.
[2] See *DVI* 9.
[3] cf *DVI* 8.
[4] Literally 'the Church of the Romans', possibly drawing a contrast with the Church of the Goths, i.e. the Arian Church. 'Renewal' probably refers to the fact that Isidore's activity took place soon after the conversion of the Goths to Orthodoxy under Reccared in AD 590.
[5] i.e. the Desert Fathers of Egypt.
[6] Perhaps a reference to Isidore's *Etymologiae*.
[7] cf *1 Peter* 2.21.

as I have learnt from trustworthy reports, I shall write of and inquire into a few matters from the beginning and end of his life.

2 This blessed man was sprung from most glorious royal stock, the son of a man of highest rank, a Duke of the Spanish Army.[8] While he was still a little boy living with his parents, it happened one day that his father took him along with him among the mountain valleys of El Bierzo to receive the accounts of his flocks.[9] While his father recorded the flocks and discussed the accounts of the shepherds, the young boy, inspired by the Lord, was thinking that this was a suitable place to found a monastery. He kept this thought to himself and revealed it to no one. After the death of his parents, casting aside the trappings of this world and shaving his head since he had undertaken a religious life, he gave himself up to that most holy man the bishop Conantius[10]to be taught in the disciplines of the spirit. After he had lived under his regime for some time, it happened one day that his fellow monks went on before him and on arriving at a possession of the church had prepared a room for him to stay in. One of the stewards of the place then came up and asked them, 'Who is going to occupy this room', and they replied 'Fructuosus'. Immediately, overcome with mad temerity, he ordered Fructuosus' small pack to be thrown out and the room to be prepared for himself. Fructuosus bore this with patient silence. When all lay at rest in the still silence of the night, suddenly a flame from the anger of the fury of the Lord set light to the dormitory. Since this room did not possess the customary fireplace,[11] it is clear that it was through

---

[8] While Dukes could be of either Hispano-Roman or Gothic descent, the reference to royal stock means that Fructuosus must have been at least half and probably fully a Goth as royalty was reserved to those of Gothic race (*5 Toledo* 3 and *6 Toledo* 17). A poem reputed to have been written by Fructuosus (Díaz y Díaz [1974] 123 = *PL* 87 1129) links his family to that of King Sisenand (AD 631-636), Sclua, metropolitan bishop of Narbonne, and bishop Peter of Béziers, see Díaz y Díaz [1967]. We have no way of determining his date of birth, but given our one fixed reference point, *10 Toledo* (AD 656), the early years of the seventh century seems the most plausible time. The title of 'Duke of the Spanish Army' is not found elsewhere. It may refer to a provincial army or possibly the entire army of the Kingdom which would have made Fructuosus' father second only to the king himself in the military chain of command.

[9] For an extant account of this sort see Velázquez Soriano [1989] nº.97.

[10] Probably to be identified with Conantius of Palencia (AD 610-640), see *DVI* 11.

[11] Díaz y Díaz [1974] 83 believes that this is a reference to a hypocaust.

the righteous anger of the Lord brought on through the prayers of the holy youth that this wretch bloated with arrogance was forced, in fear of great danger and terrified that he might come to harm and lose his possessions, to abandon the room which he had usurped.[12]

3 After this, returning to the place of solitude I previously mentioned, now a grown man he brought to completion the vow he had made as a small child. For he built the monastery of Compludo according to divine precepts, and keeping nothing for himself, but spending all his wealth on it, he richly endowed it and filled it to overflowing with an army of monks who came both from his own household and from the converts who eagerly hurried here from all over Spain.[13] As it is written that 'the envy of the Enemy always pursues sanctity and evil fights against good',[14] straightaway a wicked man, his sister's husband,[15] was roused up by the goads of the Old Enemy, prostrated himself before the king,[16] and on rising took away his wits so that he decreed that half of the inheritance should be taken from the holy monastery and given to him on the pretext of leading a campaign.[17] When this became known to the most blessed man, he at once took down the trappings of the church,

---

[12] cf Sulpicius Severus, *Ep*.1 10-14. For another incident of localised fire bringing divine punishment see Gregory of Tours, *GC* 80.

[13] Díaz y Díaz [1967] places the date of the foundation of Compludo at AD c.640. The site is probably that of an hermitage near the village of Compludo, see Pérez de Urbel [1944] & Flórez Manjarín [1967]. The monastery appears to have been dedicated to Justus and Pastor, the martyrs of Alcalá de Henares (ancient Complutum, see Prudentius *Peristephanon Martyrorum* 4.41-43) hence its name. The *Rule of Compludo*, ch.18, requires the monks to fast during the 40 days leading up to the martyrs' feast day, 6th August.

[14] This phrase is taken from the *Passion of St Eugenia*, ch.28.

[15] According a poem attributed to Fructuosus his name was Visinand. See Díaz y Díaz [1974] 123.

[16] Probably King Chindasvinth AD 642-653. A foundation document for Compludo dated 18th November AD 646 and bearing the names of Chindasvinth and his wife, Reciberga, exists which lists the patron saints of the abbey as Justus, Pastor, Mary, and Martin. Its authenticity was accepted by Pérez de Urbel [1944] 388, but it is normally regarded as a forgery.

[17] The grant of land would have been made *in stipendio*, i.e. in return for service (see *13 Toledo* 1). This has been seen by some commentators as the embryonic beginnings of feudalism, however see *contra* Linehan [1992]. Such grants could be revoked on the accession of a new ruler but in practice this rarely occurred, see King [1972] 62.

laid bare the holy altars and clothed them in hair-cloth,[18] and wrote to his brother-in-law to confound him, rebuke him, and threaten him in the Lord's name. He himself turned to fasting, grief, tears, and fulsome prayer. And so it came to pass that this envier of holy men and enemy of good deeds was at once struck down by divine vengeance and swiftly ended his life. Thus it came about that a man who had wished to take away the offerings of holy men, himself cruelly passed from this world, leaving no children and handing his wealth on to strangers, taking only his perdition with him.

4 The most holy man established a complete rule and chose an abbot known for his great firmness of discipline for the monastery.[19] Then, because he was suffering frequent disturbances from the host of people who came to him from all parts since reports of his wondrous sanctity had spread to all regions, fleeing mortal praise and favour, he set out from his congregation and with unshod feet buried himself in the forests, places full of briars, rough, harsh country[20] and spent his time in caves and among the rocks in threefold fasts, ever more vigils, and prayer.[21]

---

[18] *Cilicium*, so named from its country of origin Cilicia, but by this period simply indicating hair-cloth.

[19] The harsh rule devised for the monastery by Fructuosus has survived (*PL* 87 1099-1110). The influence of the rules of St Benedict, Isidore (see Campos [1971] 130-132), and Augustine are clear, but its largest debt is to Cassian (see de Vogüé [1985]). Fructuosus' interest in Cassian can be seen from the fact that he asked Braulio for parts of his work (Braulio, *Ep.* 43) and that his first disciple was named Cassian, see chapter 19 below. For an English translation of the rule, see Barlow [1969] 154ff.

Two other monastic documents have been associated with Fructuosus: the so-called *Common Rule* (= *PL* 87 1109-1127) which was attributed to the saint by Benedict of Aniane (d.AD 821) and the *Monastic Pact* (= *PL* 87 1127-1130). The former is in fact not a rule at all, but a collection of decisions on various monastic problems apparently taken by a conclave of abbots. The abbots involved were probably those from monasteries founded by Fructuosus. The *Pact* is an agreement between the monks of a monastic foundation and the abbot which limits the abbot's powers. It is normally assumed to reflect Germanic ideals of authority. For 'Pactual' monasticism see Bishko [1951].

[20] 'argis' a near hapax, see Díaz y Díaz [1948].

[21] Fructuosus does however appear to have had a servant, Baldarius with him; see Valerius of El Bierzo, *De Coelestu Revelatione* = *PL* 87 435-6.

5 Once, while clothed in a cloak made of goat skins, he was struggling in prayer on the crags of a certain rock,[22] an archer came and lay in wait for his prey. When he saw him on the crag prostrate in prayer, thinking that he was his rock-dwelling quarry, he bent his bow.[23] When he was about to release the string to send forth the arrow, Fructuosus, inspired by divine providence, raised his hands in prayer to the sky. The archer perceiving that his target was a man, held his fire. Afterwards when he came to Fructuosus and told him all about the incident, the blessed man asked him not to reveal it to anyone.[24]

[As he traversed back and forth across this wilderness without ceasing, the harsh terrain tore the soles of the holy man's feet so that the feet of this innocent man were covered in blisters. Because of this he was for some time unable to rise from where he lay. During these days a harsh drought afflicted the land with the threatening wrath of divine anger. At the most blessed man's command, all the congregations of monks sallied forth with their holy relics to supplicate the Lord at the holy places. After some days they returned to him, worn out by their ordeal, but having obtained no answer to their prayer. He, weeping and groaning, said to them, 'Lift up my hand and support the weakness of my limbs. Great is the mercy of the Lord, perhaps in his own good time he will grant that it shall rain.' Then he set forth with the monks going with him and holding up his right hand. They had gone but a small distance when rain fell in such abundance that they were scarce able to return home. Then all of one accord they glorified the Lord for his mercy, wondering at the merits of his most faithful and holy servant.][25]

---

[22] The standard dress for monks in the rule of Pachomius which would have been known in Jerome's translation to Fructuosus and his biographer.

[23] i.e. an Ibex, still hunted in Spain today. The ibex is mentioned by Isidore, *Etymologiae* 12.1.16 who derives its name from 'avis' or 'bird' because of its habit of living in high inaccessible places; cf Gregory the Great, *Dial.*2.1 where Benedict is thought to be a wild beast because of his dishevelled state; similarly Cassian remarks that the abbot Paphnutius resembled a wild cow, *PL* 49 559ab.

[24] Possibly in imitation of Christ not wishing his miracles to be known but more likely because he did not want his hermitage to be revealed for fear of the consequences - see chapter 9.

[25] This interpolation is found in Manuscript O of the life = *Biblioteca Universitaria de Salamanca, ms.*2537. The manuscript dates from the late thirteenth or early fourteenth century and is the work of three copyists; it in turn is a transcription of a manuscript of written in AD 1142. For a full discussion of its history see Díaz y Díaz [1974] 51-52. The

6 After this in a vast, deserted ravine far from this world, he built the monastery of Rufianum[26] in the bosom of the towering mountains, and hid himself in a small, narrow cell by the holy altar.[27] [While one night he lay prostrate in prayer, that envious foe, the Old Enemy, cast a huge stone through the window in order to strike him. Straightaway Fructuous reproved him fiercely, making the sign of the cross, and at once the devil was heard rushing into the depths of the mountains howling and screaming so that everyone knew that he had been put to flight, vanquished by the stratagems of the servant of God][28] When Fructuosus had passed some time in this place in quietness, the whole congregation of the monastery of Compludo sallied forth and this multitude of monks cast him out of his cloister there with pious violence and brought him back to his old home. Finally setting out from here, he founded the monastery of Visunia in the territory of Bierzo in the province of Gallaecia.[29]

---

passage's chronology is clearly awry in that it assumes that Fructuosus is an old man and has already founded many monasteries, neither of which is the case in the narrative of the life up to this point.

[26] The modern San Pedro de Los Montes (Astorga). The site is near the source of the river Oza in the Aguiana Mountains. Valerius of El Bierzo who stayed here describes the site as 'surrounded by high mountains like the Alps of Gaul', adding that as there was only one tortuous footpath leading to the monastery along which men had to walk in single file there was no need for the foundation to have a wall to keep out intruders. Near the monastery was a high rock with an oratory cut from the stone used by Fructuosus. See Valerius, *Residuum* 1. The path to the monastery appears to have been constructed by Fructuosus' servant Baldarius, see Valerius of El Bierzo, *De Coelestu Revelatione* = *PL* 87 435-6.

[27] An *ergastulum*, a word also used to mean a punishment cell, cf. *VPE* 2.5. These rooms were frequently found near the altar for meditative purposes and were often too narrow to allow the inmate to turn round in, see Pérez de Urbel [1944] t.2 67. This particular cell was later used by Valerius of El Bierzo, *Ordo* 7.169.

[28] Addition found in manuscript O.

[29] Gallaecia was one of the provinces of Late Roman Spain created out of the older and much larger province of *Hispania Tarraconensis* in AD 298. Its capital was Braga. Fructuosus' foundation is normally identified with the monastery dedicated to St Felix at San Fiz de Visuña in the province of Lugo; see López Valcárcel [1968]. Valerius of El Bierzo states that a church was established here after pagan shrines had been destroyed, which may indicate the lingering of pagan belief in this area of Spain, *Replicatio* 1. He further notes that Fructuosus used to pray on a rock below the monastery where later his disciple Saturninus built a church dedicated to the Holy Cross, St Pantaleon, and 'the other martyrs', *Replicatio* 9. The dangers of the area are well illustrated by the fact that

7 Afterwards he built the monastery of Peonense in the other part of Galicia by the sea [next to the Port of Foro.][30] [and with a lively desire to go on pilgrimage he embarked in the midst of the crashing waves on a ship which would take him to the land of the Franks and thence with the Lord's guidance to the East. Betrayed by his own servants, many Franks who were in the country carrying on their business were arrested by Dogila, the Duke of Lugo, and held as hostages until the man of God returned from the high sea to his monastery][31] While he was there, he conceived a great wish to sail on the sea and discovered a small island far out in the ocean.[32] He formed the idea of founding a monastery there with God's help. When they landed, the sailors on disembarking carelessly left the boat in which they had crossed over unmoored. Fructuosus prayed intensely with his disciples beneath a rock that fresh water might come forth.[33] On finishing their prayers, they wished to return to the mainland. They then saw their ship far off in the middle of the sea, cast about among the waves by blustering storms at the instigation of the Enemy. While all his disciples, made desperate by their peril, gave themselves up to great grief, Fructuosus prayed and then cast himself alone into the depths of the sea. His disciples cried out most pitiably in twofold lamentation: fearing for his danger and grieving over their own destruction. Because of the great distance, he was hidden from their eyes and they gave themselves up to renewed despair. Then,

---

one of Valerius' disciples, John, was beheaded by a local peasant while he lay prostrate before the altar at Visunia, *Replicatio* 14.

[30] The port of Foro is found in manuscript L of the life = National Library of Portugal, *ms.Alcobaça* 283/454 which dates from the late thirteenth century. For a full discussion see Díaz y Díaz [1974] 49-50. If 'Forensem' is a miscopying of 'farensem', *the port of the lighthouse*, the site of the monastery could be plausibly located at Corunna where a Roman Lighthouse has survived to the present day, incorporated into the 'Tower of Hercules'. However, no remains of a monastic foundation have been found in or near the town. The monastery has been traditionally identified with San Pedro de Calago near San Juan de Poyo close to Pontevedra; see, for example, Nock [1946]. Puertas Tricas [1975] is somewhat sceptical of this identification.

[31] Addition found in manuscript O. It has been misplaced from chapter 17.

[32] The phrase 'far out in the ocean' is difficult to interpret as the hagiographer also uses 'ocean' to mean 'river' -see chapter 13. The island remains unidentified: possible candidates are one of the Cies islands at the mouth of the river Vigo or Tambo, an island in the river Pontevedra.

[33] In order to make the island inhabitable. cf *Exodus* 17.6.

after many hours had gone by, looking out into the distance, they saw their ship slowly coming towards them. When it had drawn nearer, they saw Fructuosus sitting in it, full of joy. Welcoming him with great rejoicing, they crossed back to the mainland in exultation. Finally returning to the same island where the envious and evil Enemy had tried to stop him beginning his holy work, he built the promised holy monastery with God's aid and dedicating it according to his customary practice left it well fortified.[34]

8 As talk of his outstanding holiness grew ever greater, many distinguished and noble men, even some from the Royal Household,[35] left the service of the king and came thirsting for his most holy ministry. Many of them ascended with the guidance of the Lord to the office of bishop amongst whom one, steeped in wisdom and learning, Teudisclus, built, with God's aid and that of most blessed Fructuosus, a famous monastery in a secluded wilderness at the place called the Camp of the Lion and remained there to the end of his life.[36] And so the blessed Fructuosus showed himself very dear to the Lord from his birth. After this, finally spurning the temptations of this world, he gave all his extensive patrimony to holy churches, his freedmen, and the poor. Then taking himself off to the wilderness he founded very many monasteries where he dedicated the souls of many monks to the Lord through the religious life and holy discipline. When he had established a rule of right living for all who were following the monastic life and had lived there for a time, to avoid the flocks of people he took himself off to the remotest wilderness, and endeavoured to hide himself in the thick-leaved, secret woods, sometimes lying concealed in the high places, sometimes in the thickest forests, at others amid crags where only mountain goats can go, so that he might be seen by divine not human eyes.[37]

---

[34] This is probably a metaphorical reference, though, given the dangerous nature of North West Spain in this period, the comment may also be intended literally.

[35] The *Palatini*, composed of the Dukes, Counts, and *Gardingi*.

[36] Castrum Leonis. The site of this monastery remains unknown. Castraveón has been held out as a possible site, however there is no guarantee that Theudisclus was active in the same region of the peninsula as his master.

[37] cf Gregory the Great, *Dial.* 2.3. The majority of this chapter is a recapitulation of what has gone before.

9 While, with the Lord as his helper, the holy man was leading an irreproachable life as a hermit, many men often came and painstaking sought him out, but did not find him. However he was betrayed by some small black birds, called *gragulae* by the common people, which he used to keep in the monastery.[38] Diligently flying over all the woods until they found him, they betrayed his holy hideout with their chattering voices to all those looking for him, making its location plain to everyone. Then all the crowd rushed to the man in great joy. Finally, as we have said, he often worked many miracles with God's help and shone forth by his glorious practice of virtue. Of which holy virtue we shall now, with God as our helper, speak a little.

10 One day, it is said, a crowd of huntsmen were chasing a doe with their dogs. The little creature which was already overcome by the length of the chase, saw its death was nigh on the plains which extended far and wide in all directions. It was about to be taken by the hounds and torn limb from limb by their savage bites, when the man of God passed by unaware of the hunters. The little animal, knowing that it had no place to flee, as soon as it saw the holy man asked for his protection and straightaway, as if begging that its life be saved, went under the man of God's cloak.[39] He at once defended it from all persecution by these unjust men,[40] ordered them to call off their dogs, and led it back with him of its own freewill to the monastery. The creature, so it is said, became so tame that from this day on wherever he went he was never able to separate it from his steps. If he even left it for but a short time, it would endlessly bleat and call out until it saw him once more. It was so tame that it would often come into his dormitory and lie at his feet. He frequently ordered it to be set loose in the wood next to the monastery, but it did not forget the great favour he had done it, and,

---

[38] Jackdaws - the Spanish 'grajo'. Elijah was obeyed by ravens, *I Kings* 16.6 as was St Benedict, Gregory the Great, *Dial.* 2.8.

[39] See Sulpicius Severus, *Dialogues* 2.9 for a very similar incident involving St Martin and a hare. Martin however is not befriended by the hare after saving it. A further parallel is provided by Gregory of Tours' account (*VP* 2) of St Aemilian of Pionsat's rescue of a boar from the attentions of a huntsman.

[40] cf *Psalm* 91. Hunting held a somewhat ambiguous moral position in Visigothic Spain. The pastime was too popular to be condemned entirely, but it was prohibited to Clerics at *Agade* (AD 506).

spurning the pleasant woods which had reared it, swiftly returned to the presence of its liberator.[41] This continued to such a degree that if he set off for anywhere at all it would follow his tracks for the all the length of the journey until it found him. When this had been going on for a long time, the fame of the great wonder which was occurring in this place began to spread far and wide.[42] But the old Enemy when he sees good men striving towards glory then in his envy carries the wicked off to punishment.[43] A certain youth filled with the sprit of madness, or rather inflamed with the fire of envy, killed the little beast by feeding it to the dogs while the holy man was away.[44] When after a few days the holy man had returned to the monastery, concerned he asked why his doe had not come to him in its accustomed manner. He was then told that when it had gone out and was grazing in the woods, this boy

---

[41] Justinian, *Institutes* 2.1.5 contains a reference to stags which were tame enough to come from the woods to 'visit' humans and then return. However the bond between Fructuosus and the doe seems much closer than what is envisaged there.

[42] Fructuosus' befriending of the doe is a sharp contrast to the lions and other ferocious animals subdued by the Desert Fathers of the East. The animal was notoriously timid; see, e.g., Virgil, *Ecl.*8.28 and Apuleius, *Met.*8.4. Isidore, *Etym.*12.1.22, derives its name 'dammula' from its tendency to flee from man. The creature here demonstrates the goodness and purity of the saint who is able to win the trust of such a creature (cf the role of unicorns in medieval literature). It could be argued that a degree of pagan syncretism is present. Sertorius was given a pet hind by his troops which was given a semi-divine aura by him (Plutarch, *Sert.*11). In the late antique period we have a series of documents denouncing the Cervolus - a ceremony held at the beginning of the year when people dressed as stags, see Pacian (*fl.*360 AD), *Paraenesis* ch.1 (= *PL* 13 1081-2), and his (now lost) *Cervalus*; Ps.Augustine, *Serm* 123 (probably written by Caesarius of Arles; *Auxerre* (between 573-603 AD); *Dict.Abbat.Primin* (c.700 AD) ch.22. However the connection is tenucus. There seems little direct relation between the stags of the Cervolus (in fact occasionally the rite appears to have involved heifers and been called the betulus) and Fructuosus' hind, and 700 years separate Fructuosus and Sertorius, a period which would make the persistence of even folk religion seem unlikely. The story is utterly Christian in its message so even if there are pagan antecedents it would be better to speak of the pagan symbolism being absorbed into a Christian context rather than of syncretism.

[43] This sentence is taken from Gregory the Great, *Dial.* 3.15. This tells the story of Florentius of Nursia who was befriended by a bear. This bear was then killed out of jealousy by four monks who in their turn died of leprosy after Florentius cursed them for what they had done. Florentius, we are told, regretted what he had done for the rest of his life.

[44] Whose dogs these were is not clear. The remainder of the chapter suggests they were hunting dogs, not ones belonging to the monastery.

had come and killed it. On hearing this, he fell on his knees in great grief in the presence of the Lord, prostrating himself upon the flags. But it was God's will not to delay in inflicting the punishment of the most severe vengeance of divine majesty. The youth was seized at once by a grave fever, and soon began to beg Fructuosus through intermediaries to pray to God on his behalf in order that he should not be struck down by divine vengeance and so bring his life to a cruel close because of his wicked temerity. Fructuosus came to him at once, implored the Lord for mercy, laid his hand upon him and straightaway not only restored his body to its previous state of health, but at the same time cured the sicknesses of his soul through his holy prayer.

11 We learnt of another miracle of his great endurance from a reliable man who told us this story about our blessed subject. One day when along with the rest of his fellow travellers he was passing through the lands near the city of Idanha-a-Velha[45] while making for the glorious city of Merida in the province of Lusitania through his love of the famed virgin Eulalia - so that there he could might fulfil the holy vows of his mind with the most sacred devotions of his heart - in order that when he had poured out his sweet-flowing prayers in the sight of God and received the results of his petition through the bounteous piety of the Lord Jesus Christ, he might quickly reach, with the Lord's assistance, the island which lies in the territory of Cadiz.[46] But, as we have said, when he was on that part of his journey which passed through the lands of Idanha-a-Velha, it happened that all the companions of the blessed man went ahead of him a little way,[47] while he stopped in a secluded place in the woods, hidden away in the thick forests, and prayed a short while. While he lay prostrate in prayer, the Ancient Enemy, ever envious of all good men, swiftly brought a boorish countryman possessed by madness to the place where the man of God

---

[45] Ancient Egitania.

[46] In fact Fructuosus seems to have gone on a pilgrimage taking in the two provincial capitals of Merida and Seville before moving on to Cadiz. The island in question is probably the town of Cadiz itself, now connected to the mainland by a sand bar. Others, however, believe it to be the Isla de León.

[47] From the following chapter, where we hear of Fructuosus' refusal to travel other than on foot, this was probably a normal occurrence. Fructuosus' companions may also have kept unsuitable individuals from meeting the holy man, cf Nanctus' entourage in VPE 3.3.

was praying. When he had seen the man of God from afar, catching sight of him alone amongst the trees, dressed in poor clothes with unshod, naked feet, as he had a peasant's mind he despised him for his poor clothing and because of his mad rashness drew closer. Thinking Fructuosus a runaway slave, the peasant abused him with shameless words and did not delay to insult him with all kinds of vile expressions.[48] But when the man of God replied to him with a tranquil mind, 'I am clearly not a runaway', the peasant, thinking on the contrary that he certainly was one, goaded by the impulse of the devil, struck him a blow with the staff he was carrying in his hands. The man of God bore this patiently, but the other did not cease from striking him, so soon he made the sign of the cross to him. At once the demon left the woodsman and passed into the earth,[49] dashing him prostrate before the feet of the holy man and wounding him to such a degree in its fury that after cruelly lacerating him it left him lying in a pool of his own blood.[50] However, the man of God at once prayed and restored him to his previous state of health without any difficulty.

12 Now, therefore, we have learnt in truth from the account of the presbyter Benenatus, a venerable man, of new not ancient wonders, not of old, but new miracles, not ones worked in idle fables, but ones which can be proved by the Truth. For this reason we shall try to note them down briefly in this collection of pages just as they were told to us, paying every attention to accuracy. This most holy man spoke as follows: 'While I was journeying from the province of Lusitania to the province of Baetica[51] with the most holy Fructuosus, the wet weather brought forth, as is the custom in winter, great sheets of rain for many

---

[48] Part of the problem might have been Fructuosus' unkempt appearance. This probably involved growing his hair long, which was the sign of a slave - see *LV* 9.1.5 where it is made an offence to cut a fugitive slave's hair. There would have been a potential reward of at least a *tremiss* for the countryman had Fructuosus been an escaped slave, *LV* 9.1.14. The problem of runaways seems to have been a persistent feature of the Visigothic kingdom. Leovigild legislated on this matter (*LV* 9.1.3) as did many of his successors. See King [1972] 162 ff.

[49] cf the devil's flight into the depths of the mountains in ch.6 above.

[50] Demons characteristically injure their victims when forced from their bodies.

[51] The southernmost Roman province in the Iberian peninsula roughly comprising modern Andalusia and southern Extremadura.

days and the rivers had grown terribly swollen because of the amount of rain. It happened one day that a small boy while he was trying to wade across with the rest of his companions, fell along with the horse which was carrying the books of the man of God, into the deepest part of the river. For a long time he was swallowed up in the depths of the whirlpool along with the books. At last with the Lord's help, he escaped from the peril of the waters and reached the bank, soaked but safe. Fructuosus came a little behind them on foot, as it was always his custom not to use a carriage. When he reached his colleagues, he was told that all his books had fallen into the river. He, however, was not at all greatly perturbed, but with a serene and cheerful countenance and showing no sign of sorrow ordered that they be taken out of their bags and brought to him. He found them dry as if the river water had never touched them and had been unable to make them even slightly damp.[52]

13 I ought not to bury in silence another wondrous deed which I learned about from Benenatus. One day the blessed Fructuosus set out by boat from the city of Seville to the Basilica of St Gerontius in order to fulfill a vow.[53] When with the aid of the Lord he had fulfilled the vows of his

---

[52] We learn that Fructuosus was a great bibliophile from his correspondence with Braulio of Saragossa (Braulio *Ep*. 43-44) whom he asked for copies of the Lives of Sts Honoratus of Arles, German of Auxerre, and Aemilian, and part of Cassian's *Collationes*. An English translation of the letters can be found in Barlow [1969], the Latin text with Spanish translation in Riesco Terrero [1975]. Braulio died in 651 AD. For a similar miracles see Gregory of Tours, *GC* 22 for an incident which happened to Maximus of Chinon when he fell into the Saône, and Adamnan, *Vita Columbani* 2.9 for a book written by St Columban which was undamaged when it fell into a river in Leinster. A general discussion of such miracles can be found in Loomis [1948].

[53] Seville lies on the Guadalquivir, which was navigable as far upstream as Cordoba in the classical period (Strabo 3.2.3).

The St Gerontius mentioned here is probably the martyr-bishop of Italica for whom there is an office in the *Mozarabic Breviary* on the 26th August (*PL* 86 1198-1200, see also *PL* 85 835-836), this saint is also listed in ninth-century martyrology of Usuard, *PL* 124 397-398. Gerontius is described as active in the 'apostolic' period in the *Breviary*, but this appears to be the pious creation of a pedigree for the church at Italica. Several commentators have wished to amend the name of the saint concerned; Nock [1946] prefers Jerome, and Vives [1941] Sta Corona, the sister of St Victor. However, as the manuscript tradition is unanimous in recording Gerontius, there seems little cause to amend the reading. Italica itself lies some 6 miles upstream of Seville, which would fit the description of Fructuosus' journey found here. The identification is accepted by Gams

desire there, as evening was drawing on he was inclined to return whence he had come. The sailors who had navigated the boat over a great tract of the river[54] were tired from the voyage and not only said that they did not have the strength to manage the boat, but also began to complain that the day was already coming to an end. He said to them. 'I beg you take a little food as refreshment and since you are tired rest a little, while I finish my office of prayer. This I ask of you, take up the oars of the vessel and sleep a little while.'[55] They obeyed at once and, taking up the oars of the boat as he had instructed, slept. The holy man prayed and finished the office with his brothers and then with no man working the boat, but with it being guided solely by the hand of God, he swiftly returned to where he had set out. The sailors woke suddenly and began to hurl empty complaints at him, saying, 'Let us begin now, because we will not be able to sail safely in the darkness of the night.' He said to them in turn, 'Little children, do not weary yourselves for the Lord has already taken us whither we wish to be without your help'. When they roused themselves and saw that they were at the place from which they had set out, they were astounded and in their amazement wondered at what God had brought to pass.[56]

14 Now he told us another story which he insisted was altogether true, saying, 'One Sunday, when there was no end to the storms and rain, the holy man set out from the city of Seville to the island which lies in the territory of Cadiz. Many citizens of Seville, even the bishop, wished to keep him there[57] and wanted him to agree to stay at least until the end of the mass if not longer as it was Sunday and the weather was not good. He replied to them as follows: ' Do not, I beg of you, hold me back, for the Lord has marked out my journey. If you fear that I may come to harm and are worried about danger brought on by the rain, you can rest assured that there will be no more rain today after the second hour'.[58] And all those who were present saw this come to pass. For after

---

[1956] vol.1 280ff; Díaz y Díaz [1974] 103 is more sceptical.
[54] The word used here, 'pelagus', normally means 'ocean'.
[55] The oars were taken up to prevent the theft of the boat.
[56] cf Sulpicius Severus, Dial.3.9 & Gregory of Tours, Mir.Mar.4.29.
[57] Probably Bishop Antony (AD 641-655).
[58] The fears about what was merely river navigation are intriguing.

he had embarked on a ship at the second hour, the rain stopped at once and it did not rain again until after three days later when he arrived at his destination. During those three days, as he had said, the weather remained fine. From this we can see that it did not rain at all during the time that he was sailing towards the goal of his journey.'

When with the Lord's aid he reached the island of Cadiz that we have mentioned, he built, with the Lord's help, a holy monastery on that part of it opposite to where the Eastern sun casts its light upon Spain,[59] and created for it through his customary monastic rule the basis of a spiritual life.[60] Finally in a vast, hidden wilderness far from human habitation he founded with God's aid a glorious and outstanding religious house of remarkable size (which is called Nono as it is nine miles distant from the sea's shore).[61] I shall briefly relate a tale which I learned from the reliable testimony of that devout man, Julian the presbyter, who grew up in this monastery from his youth. The example of goodness of that most glorious and incomparable man shining forth with gleaming splendour so kindled the spirits of the people with love of the faith that the columns of converts coming in hordes from all over the land formed a vast chorus. And had not the dukes of the army of that province and the surrounding regions cried out to the king that there should be some restraints imposed - for if no bounds to permission to become a monk had been set, there would have been no one to fight in the army - a

---

[59] i.e. the Western side of the island.

[60] A major town in the pre-Roman and Roman period, Cadiz had fallen into decline by late antiquity, see the lament of Avienus (*fl.* AD 400) *Ora Maritima* 267-274. Castro [1858] records no legends about the town in this period, but merely notes that a hermitess named Servanda lived here in the time of Egica (AD 687-700). This is presumably a garbled reference to the abbess Servanda whose tomb (*ICERV* 286) dated to AD 630 was found at Medina Sidonia and Servandus who, along with Germanus, is one of the patron saints of the diocese of Cadiz: see Usuard's Martyrology, *PL* 123 609-610. Servandus and Germanus were said to have been martyred c. AD 300 by an official named Viator during the persecution of Diocletian in the village of Ursino which lay within the diocese of Cadiz. According to our account, Servandus was buried at Seville alongside the local martyrs Justa and Rufina and Germanus at Merida by the shrine of Eulalia. There is however no mention of Germanus in *VPE*. Cadiz was frequently used as a symbol of the end of the world in antiquity and it is difficult not to see Fructuosus' planting of a monastery here as, at least in part, a symbolic statement that Christianity had reached the ends of the earth.

[61] The monastery's location is unknown.

countless army of monks would have gathered together.[62] For not only
the minds of men, but even those of women had been set alight. Now,
as there was no place for women in that sacred congregation, I shall
relate in what way he established a congregation of women.[63]

15 A most holy maiden, Benedicta by name, sprung from noble stock
and betrothed to a *gardingus* of the king,[64] set on fire by her desire for
the faith and inflamed by the love of holy religion, secretly fled from
her parents. Alone she came to the wilderness and wandering through
pathless and unknown places finally with the Lord's guidance drew near
to the holy congregation of the monastery. Not daring to go up to them,
she remained far off in the wilderness and begged the holy man of God
through intermediaries that he should free a wandering sheep from the
jaws of wolves, show her the path of salvation, set her upon it, and
instruct with his spiritual teachings a soul seeking the Lord, in order that
she might obtain this gift from the Lord who once brought home a
sheep on his shoulders.[65] When he heard this, he gave manifold thanks
to almighty God and ordered a small dwelling place be built for her in
a wood in this same wilderness.[66] Benenatus told me, 'As none of the

---

[62] A play on this world and the world to come. Monks were exempted from military
service (*LV* 9.2.8, 9.2.9). Whether the flow of men did pose a potential threat to the size
of the provincial army is a moot point, as the host of maidens mentioned later is only 80
strong. cf The edict of the Emperor Maurice in 592 AD which forbade soldiers to become
monks (*edict* 110).

[63] The Fructuosian *Common Rule* English translation in Barlow [1969] p.176ff.) makes
it clear that Monks and Nuns should not live together, (ch.15).

[64] The *Gardingi* were members of the king's household or *palatini*. Unlike Dukes and
Counts who ranked higher than them, the *Gardingi* appear to have been assigned no
specific role in the Kingdom. They appear to have been a form of personal retinue such
as is found throughout the Germanic world and mentioned by Tacitus under the name of
comitatus (Tacitus, *Germania* 13ff).

Benedicta could have been either a Goth or a Hispano-Roman. Díaz y Díaz [1955]
asserts she was a Goth; however there is no firm evidence for such a view and Orlandis,
while initially of the same view [1966], is now [1992] inclined to think that she was a
Hispano-Roman.

[65] cf *Luke* 15.4-5. The parable here has become part of Christ's biography.

[66] In both the *Rule of Compludo* and the *Common Rule* aspirant monks are not to be
admitted to the monastery immediately but wait outside the gates for a period of time (3
days *Common Rule*, 10 days *Rule of Compludo*) to show their sincerity. Benedicta's stay
in the wilderness seems to be a variation on this principle.

older monks dared to go near her,[67] one of us younger ones took it in turn to take her letters and food.[68] She insisted firmly that no food be brought to her until the holy man had eaten at midnight and that it should not be brought unless he had blessed it.' She applied herself diligently to her spiritual studies and when news of her and her praise spread far and wide, so great a flame of desire inflamed the daughters of other men of all ranks that a glorious host of women swiftly gathered and in a short space of time the congregation was increased by eighty holy maidens for whom he built a monastery in his customary manner in a another solitary place. And so greatly did beneficent sanctity flourish amongst both sexes and the glorious fame of their perfections grow, that men along with their sons joined the congregation of monks and their wives along with their daughters entered the holy company of women.[69] But fiancé of the lady Benedicta, despatched by the Enemy's work of treacherous envy, weeping in great grief and sorrow, laid a petition against her before the king.[70] In this way he obtained a judge of the King's presence,[71] a Count called Argalate, who was to look into the truth of the matter between them and who arrived at the maidens'

---

[67] cf the attitude of Nanctus, *VPE* 3.3.

[68] The letters would have been tracts from Fructuosus.

[69] The problems caused by this are dealt with by the *Common Rule*, chapter 6. Parents and children are not to speak to one another without prior permission, though very young children are to be allowed to go to their parents when they wish to do so and both parents are to be involved in their upbringing. When the child can understand 'a little of the Rule' its family associations are to end. The women themselves are forbidden to speak to, or kiss (!) their former husbands, chapter 16.

[70] With good reason. Betrothal, *disponsatio*, in Visigothic Spain involved the payment or at least the pledge of a substantial bride-price which the *gardingus* now stood to lose (*LV* 3.4.2). Unilateral withdrawal from betrothal was forbidden by law (*LV* 3.1.3, 3.6.3). The only exceptions to this rule were if the woman was betrothed to a younger man, in fact such a marriage even if it came about would be invalid in the eyes of the law (*LV* 3.1.4.), or if death were imminent, when it was permitted to assume a religious life, (*LV* 3.6.3.). This latter exemption may lie at the bottom of the story of Benedicta. Though our hagiographer represents her as simply confounding her fiancé and winning the support of the judge, we are told that she died soon afterwards. It may be that the judge annulled the betrothal because Benedicta was already close to death. For a detailed discussion see King [1972] 224ff.

[71] Argalate would have been a *pacis Adsertor*, i.e. a judge appointed by the king to oversee a specific case, see *LV* 2.1.27.

monastery girt with the King's authority. The warden[72] of the maidens was compelled to separate Benedicta from the congregation and bring her before him to see how she would answer her fiancé's charges. When after a struggle she came out, lifting her eyes to the heavens, she absorbed herself in prayer so that she might not look on his face. When he pressed his case against her, by the grace of the Lord she was so filled with the Holy Spirit that she cut him short in a few words and he had nothing left to say to her. Then the judge said, 'Leave her to serve the Lord and look for another wife for yourself.' Soon after these events pious Godhead commanded this most holy woman to pass from this world.[73] And so it came about by the ineffable will of the Lord that she, who had preceded all the holy maidens in their conversion, went before them in her holy calling to the celestial glory of the heavenly kingdom through Him who lives and reigns for ever. Amen

16[74] When the blessed Fructuosus, shining forth with bright-flowing radiance, had brought light to all of Spain through his most glorious example of holiness, and, by establishing congregations of monks in diverse regions of the country on the model of his own innocent heart, had nourished the ranks of perfected disciples, with the result that to this day those who have just recently been converted, taking up in their turn their place among the saints who went before, make his example of olden days flower as if it happened today and so the fruit of his labour grows until the end of the world, his glorious memory is perpetually renewed, and in the kingdom of heaven the burgeoning ranks of his flock increases daily.

---

[72] The criteria for such a monk are dealt with in the *Common Rule*. They were to be 'few and perfect' and preferably old, having lived in a monastery for most of their lives and to live far away from the nuns' living quarters (chapter 16). *2 Seville* 11 (AD 619) had already legislated on these matters providing that only one monk should oversee a nunnery.

[73] This is quite possibly why the betrothal was annulled; see n.68 above. Another consideration is purely theological. In dying soon after conversion, Benedicta would not be able to imperil her soul by lapsing into sin, cf. the gluttonous monk of *VPE* 2.

[74] While the sense of this chapter is clear, its syntax is exceptionally convoluted and not complete in itself. It appears that it has been created by separating it from the following chapter. While this act in itself was a laudable attempt to make the account more readable, it has not been executed in the most workmanlike fashion.

17 after he brought all the devotion of his sacred work to the highest perfection through the aid of celestial virtue, a great fire of divine desire inflamed him to go to the East and make a new pilgrimage. When he had discussed this matter in secret with a few, select disciples and had prepared a boat for their voyage that he might embark with all haste[75] and cross to the East, he was apprehended through the treachery of one of his disciples and unable to gain permission for his journey.[76] What more is there to say? While the journey was being prepared, word came to the king of this world[77] and he, along with all his court advisers, fearing that such a light should abandon Spain, commanded that he should be arrested, though with no fear of harm being done to him, and brought to his presence. They say that one night, when they had brought him and were keeping guard over him in the utmost fear, they secured

---

[75] reading *festinatione* for *praedestinatione*

[76] Such travel was forbidden by Chindasvinth's treason law (*LV* 2.1.8) which notes the number of times that the state had been forced to go to war because of the activities of *refugae* or fugitives. See also the preface to *7 Toledo* of AD 646 where any cleric of any rank intending to travel abroad is to be instantly deprived of his rank, made a penitent in perpetuity, and only given communion at the end of his life. The terms are strong - any cleric who gave communion to one so punished was to share his fate even if the king had ordered him to allow the victim to communicate. In the context of his day Fructuosus was intending to travel to a foreign power which been in occupation of part of Visigothic territory until AD 624 and with whom relations had never been good. If we are to believe the interpolation found in manuscript O in chapter 7 but clearly relating to this incident, his journey was to take him East via Frankish Gaul, another area with which relations were perpetually poor. While most commentators have seen Fructuosus' motives as purely religious, it is easy to see why the King of the day may have been suspicious of such a journey - hence the need for both speed and secrecy in Fructuosus' preparations. Nor can politics be entirely excluded from the equation. The king of the day, either Chindasvinth or Reccesvinth, belonged to a family which had come to power supported by a faction hostile to the family of King Sisenand to whom Fructuosus may have been related. If Fructuosus' family was indeed based in Septimania a trip to Gaul would have looked even more suspicious as Sisenand had seized the throne with Frankish aid. Hence perhaps the violent action of Count Dogila recorded in the interpolation. Added to this is the fact that at the beginning of his reign in AD 653 Reccesvinth had been forced to put down a destructive rebellion led by Froia who with help from the Basques had even managed to lay siege to Saragossa. If this incident occurred soon after it is difficult to see how Reccesvinth could not have been suspicious of Fructuosus' motives.

[77] Most probably King Reccesvinth, joint King with his father Chindasvinth from AD 649 and sole king AD 653-672. He is described as 'amiable but debauched' by the continuator of *HG* ch.35.

the door of the chamber where he was staying with chains, hawsers, and other stout safeguards and in addition stood guard there themselves. When they woke in the still silence of the night, they saw from afar the bars cast aside and the doors lying wide open. Meanwhile Fructuosus, praying for the holy churches, safely meditated in prayer on the piety of the Lord.[78]

18 After these things, all unwillingly, he was ordained against his will bishop in the metropolitan seat by the gift of God.[79] He resisted fiercely, but was compelled to acquiesce through fear of inactivity.[80] On taking up so high an office he did not lay aside his old way of life, but keeping to his habit and customary rigorous practice of abstinence he spent the rest of his life dispensing alms and in the construction of monasteries.[81]

19 While bishop he built the outstanding monastery which lies between the city of Braga and the convent of Dumio on the crest of a small hill where his holy body is now buried.[82] I learnt how great was his

---

[78] cf *Acts* 12.

[79] cf *VSD* 3. Given the severity of the penalty for treason, Fructuosus must have been acquitted of the charges laid against him. The See referred to here is that of Braga; the absence of its name in the text is curious. Fructuosus' appointment is recorded by *10 Toledo* 1, giving us a firm date of December AD 656. He replaced the self-confessed fornicator Potamius. The canon also tells us that prior to this Fructuosus had been ordained bishop of Dumio. Our hagiographer makes no mention of this fact. The appointment cannot have been made prior to December AD 653, the date of *8 Toledo*, as Bishop Ricimir held the See at this date. It has been suggested that Fructuosus' appointment to the See of Dumio occurred early in AD 656 hence Potamius' demise meant that Fructuosus held this position for very little time, see Díaz y Díaz [1967].

[80] A royal threat probably lies behind this enigmatic phrase.

[81] cf *VSA* 12 & *VPE* 5.3.3. These monasteries are unknown. One may have been that of Samos which was restored by Ermefred, a contemporary of Fructuosus and as bishop of Lugo, one of his suffragan bishops; see González [1967].

[82] The Monastery of Montélios. The church involved is Sâo Fructuoso de Montélios. Its cruciform structure is almost unique in the Iberian peninsula and shows strong parallels with Byzantine architecture; its similarity to the mausoleum of Gallia Placidia at Ravenna is particularly striking. For a plan and detailed description see Fontaine [1978a] vol.1 163-167 & pl.s 46-7. The only similar structure may be the Church at Valdecebadar, Olivenza (Badajoz); however its remains are extremely fragmentary. Fructuosus' relics were kidnapped by Bishop Diego Gelmírez of Santiago in AD 1102, see Carro Otero [1968].

enthusiasm for the holy task of building churches from the account that man of God, the abbot Cassian, who was his first disciple. He told me that when Fructuosus had learnt that his holy death was upon him a good while before its occurrence, since he had undertaken the task of construction and as his life in this world was coming to its close, not only did he work unceasingly by day, but persevered in the same task by lamplight at night lest he should leave this world with his holy task unfinished. And so with divine help all that he had begun in faith he diligently brought to a conclusion and happily dedicated it to the Lord.

20 As his end drew on, he was seized by fever and when the violence of the disease had possessed him for several days, calculating the time from the day when he had been informed of his death, he discovered that the day upon which he was to pass from this world was nigh. He told this to those who were standing by him. While they all wept, he alone exulted because he knew without a shadow of doubt that he was hastening to heavenly and eternal glory. To those who asked him if he feared death he replied, 'Of course not. For I know that though a sinner I shall come into the presence of my Lord.'[83] After this, he asked to be taken to the church. When he had put all his affairs in order, he kept one slave, called Dicentius, who had served him well since he was a small boy. He ordered him to be summoned, and placing his hand upon him, and ordained him as abbot of the outstanding monastery of Toroño.[84] Finally having received the prescribed rites of penitence, he did not leave the church, but remained there lying prostrate before the holy altar all that day and for part of the night. A little before the light of dawn, stretching out his hands in prayer he commended his stainless and holy soul to the hands of the Lord who crowns his saints after their goodly life.[85]

---

[83] Perhaps the hagiographer intends his audience to think of *Matthew* 5.8 at this point.
[84] The form of ordination is highly irregular, cf Masona's freeing of church slaves at the end of his life. Both Díaz y Díaz [1974] and Orlandis [1968] believe that the monastery referred to is Montélios not Toroño. However this emendation has no evidence to support it.
[85] Traditionally Fructuosus' death day is 16 April 665. A lament for the saint by a contemporary anonymous disciple has survived = *PL* 87 1130-1132, poem 'C'.

Appendix

Signs of his virtue came to all who came to the most holy tomb of his blessed corpse and to this day the sick are cured there and demons put to flight, and whoever in his grief calls upon Fructuosus' indefatigable aid at once receives the full fruits of his petition from the Lord.

BIBLIOGRAPHY

Almagro, M.
1957   *Guía de la ciudad de Mérida y de sus monumentos* (Merida)
de Almeida, F.
1966   'Um palatium episcopal do Sec. VI em Idanha-a-Velha (Portugal)' in *Actas del IX Congreso nacional de Arqueología* (Valladolid)
1977   'As ruinas romanas e visigóticas de Idanha-a-Velha', *Anals* 24.2
Alonso Campos, J. I.
1986   'Sunna, Masona y Nepopis. Las luchas religiosas durante la dinastía de Leovigildo', *Semana* [1986]
Alvarez Martínez, J. M.
1983   *El Puente Romano de Mérida* (Badajoz)
Alvarez y Sáenz de Buruaga, J.
1970   'Epitafio del obispo emeritense Fidel (siglo VI)', *Habis* 1
1975   'El palacio del Duque de la Roca' in *Actas del V Congreso de Estudios Extremeños* (Badajoz)
Amador de Los Ríos, J.
1877   *Monumentos latino-bizantinos de Mérida* (Madrid)
Andrés Ordox, S.
1981   'La basílica hispanovisigoda de Alcuéscar (Cáceres)', *Norba* 2
Anglès, H.
1940   'Hispanic Musical Culture from the 6th to the 14th Century', *Musical Quarterly* 26.4
Arce, J.
1982   'Mérida Tardorromana', in *Homenaje a J Alvarez Sáenz de Buruaga* (Madrid)
1992   'Prudencio y Eulalia' in *Jornadas* [1992]
Auerbach, E.
1965   Literary Language and its Public Use in Late Latin Antiquity and in the Middle Ages (London)
Azkarate Garai-Olaun, A.
1988   *Arqueología cristiana de la antigüedad tardía en Alava, Guipuzcoa, y Vizcaya* (Vitoria)

1993   'Francos, Aquitanos, y Vascones al sur de Los Pirineos', *AeA* 66

Baker, D. (ed)
1978   *Medieval Women: essays dedicated and presented to Professor Rosalind M.T.Hill = Studies in Church History: Subsidia* 1 (Oxford)

Barbero, A. & Vigil, M.
1956   'Sobre los orígenes de la Reconquista: Cántabros y Vascones desde fines del imperio hasta la invasión musulmana', *BRAH* 156.2
1974   *Sobre los Orígenes Sociales de la Reconquista* (Barcelona)

Barlow, C. W.
1969   *Iberian Fathers, vol.2: Braulio of Saragossa, Fructuosus of Braga* (Washington)

Besga Marroquín, A.
1983   *La Situación política de los Pueblos del Norte de España en Época Visigoda* (Bilbao)

Bishko, C. J.
1951   'Gallegan Pactual Monasticism in the repopulation of Castille' in *Estudios dedicados a Menéndez Pidal* vol.1

Bishop, W. C.
1924   *The Mozarabic and Ambrosian Rites* (London)

Bowers, W. P.
1975   'Jewish Communities in Spain in the time of Paul the Apostle', *JThS* 26.2

Blume, C.
1897   *Analecta hymnica medii aevi* (Leipzig)

Brehaut, E.
1912   *An Encyclopaedist of the Dark Ages: Isidore of Seville* (New York)

Brody, S.
1974   *The Disease of the Soul* (Ithaca & London)

Caballero Zoreda, L. & Mateos Cruz, P.
1992   'Trabajos arqueológicos en la iglesia de Santa Eulalia de Mérida' in *Jornadas* [1992]
1993   *Santa Eulalia de Mérida* (Mérida)

Cairns, F. (ed)
1981   *Papers of the Liverpool Latin Seminar (3rd vol.) = Arca* 7

Campos, J.
1971   *Santos Padres españoles* 2 (Madrid)
Carro Otero, J.
1968   'Las reliquias de San Fructuoso y su culto en Compostela', *Bracara Augusta* 22
Castro, A.
1858   *Historia de Cádiz y su provincia* (Cádiz), reprinted Cádiz 1985.
Cerillo, E.
1978   *Las Construcciones basilicales en época paleocristiana y visigoda en la antigua Lusitania* (doctoral thesis, University of Salamanca)
Chadwick, H.
1976   *Priscillian of Avila* (Oxford)
Chaves, Ma. & R.
1988   *Cátalogo general de las monedas españolas II: Acuñaciones previsigodas y visigodas en Hispania (desde Honorio a Achilla II)* (Madrid)
Cheney, C. R.
1955   *Selected Letters of Pope Innocent III* (London)
Clark, F.
1986   'The authenticity of the Gregorian *Dialogues*: a re-opening of the question' in Fontaine [1986]
1987   *The Psuedo-Gregorian Dialogues* (Leiden)
Claude, D.
1972   *Adel, Kirche, und Königtum im Westgotenreich* (Sigmarigen)
1980   'Freedmen in the Visigothic Kingdom', in James [1980]
Codoñer Merino, C.
1972   *El <<De Viris Illustribus>> de Ildefonso de Toledo* (Salamanca)
1981   'The poetry of Eugenius of Toledo', in *Cairns* [1981]
1987   'Sobre la *Vita Fructuosi*', *Athlon: Satura gramatica in honorem FR Adrados* (Madrid)
Colgrave, B.
1968   *The Earliest Life of Gregory the Great* (Lawrence)
Collins, R.
1980   'Mérida and Toledo: 550-585' in James [1980]

1983   Early Medieval Spain (London)
1986   *The Basques* (Oxford)
1989   *The Arab Conquest of Spain 710-797* (Oxford)
1990   'Literacy and the Laity in Early Medieval Spain' in McKitterick [1990]
1991   '¿Dónde estaban los arrianos en el año 589?', *Concilio III de Toledo: XIV Centenario 589-1989* (Toledo), reprinted as 'King Leovigild and the Conversion of the Visigoths' in Collins [1992]
1992   *Law, Culture, and Regionalism in Early Medieval Spain* (Great Yarmouth)
Cuming, G. J. (ed)
1966   *Studies in Church History* 3 (Leiden)
Cronin, D.
1985   'New Heresy for Old', *Speculum* 60
Crusafont i Sabater, M.
1988   'The Copper Coinage of the Visigoths of Spain' in *Gómes Marques & Metcalf* [1988]
Cruz Villalón, M.
1982   *Mérida visigoda: la escultura arquitectónica y litúrgica* (Madrid)
De Bruyne, D.
1927   'Le plus ancien catalogue des reliques d'Oviedo', *AB* 45
De Smedt
1885   'Culto antiguo de San Masona, metropolitano de Mérida', *BRAH* 6
Di Berardino, A. (ed)
1992   *An Encyclopaedia of the Early Church* (Cambridge)
Díaz y Díaz, M. C.
1948   'Argia', *Emerita* 16
1953   'A próposito de la <<Vita Fructuosi>>, *Cuadernos de Estudios Gallegos* 8
1955   'El eremitismo en la España visigótica', *Revista Portuguesa de la Historia* 6
1955a   'Para una edición del poema astrónomico del rey Sisebuto', *Revista de Archivos, Bibliotecas, y Museos* 61.1
1957   'De Patrística española', *Revista española de Teología* 17
1958   *Anecdota Wisigothica 1 = Acta Salmanticensia* 12.2

1958a 'La cultura de España visigótica del siglo VII', *Settimane* 5

1961 (ed) *Isidoriana* (Léon)

1969 'Eremitical life in Visigothic Spain', *Classical Folia* 23 (reprinted in Díaz y Díaz 1992)

1974 *La Vida de San Fructuoso de Braga* (Braga)

1981 'Hagiographie du Haut Moyen Age Espagnol' in Patlagean and Riché [1981]

1992 *Vie chrétienne et culture dans l'Espagne du VIIe au XIe siècles* (Great Yarmouth)

1992a 'Fructuosiana' in Holtz & Foredouille [1992]

Díaz y Díaz, P. R.

1993 'Tres biografías latino medievales de san Desiderio de Viena (traducción y notas), *Fortunatae* 5

Dill, S.

1926 *Roman Society in Gaul in the Merovingian Age* (London)

Dutton, B.

1967 *La "Vida de San Millán de la Cogolla" de Gonzalo de Berceo* (London)

1992 'La Vida de San Millán de la Cogolla' in Uría Maqua [1992]

Étienne, R.

1982 'Merida, capitale du Vicariat des Espagnes' in *Homenaje a J Alvarez Sáenz de Buruaga* (Madrid)

Fábrega Grau, A.

1953 *Pasionario Hispánico 1* (Barcelona)

Fage, J. D.

1978 *The Cambridge History of Africa, vol.2* (Cambridge)

Fernández Alonso, J.

1955 *La cura pastoral en la España romanovisigoda* (Rome)

Férotin, M.

1902 'La Légende de Sainte Potamia', *AB* 21

1902a 'La légende de Sainte Potamia: notes additionelles', *AB* 21

1904 *Le Liber ordinum en usage dans l'église wisigothique y mozarabe d'Espagne du cinquième au onzième siècle = Monumenta Ecclesiae Liturgica* (ed F Carol & H leClercq) 5 (Paris)

1912   *Le Liber Mozarabicus Sacramentorum et les manuscrits mozarabes* = *Monumenta Ecclesiae Liturgica* (ed F.Carol & H leClercq) 6 (Paris)

Ferreiro, A.

1988   *The Visigoths in Gaul and Spain, A.D. 418-711: a bibliography* (Leiden and New York)

Fita, F.

1900   'Epigrafía cristiana de España', *BRAH* 37

Flórez Manjarín, F.

1967   'Compludo, primer monasterio de San Fructuoso', *Bracara Augusta* 21 & 22

Fontaine, J.

1948   'La culture poétique du roi wisigoth Sisebut', *Actes du Congrès de l'Association Guillaume Budé* (Grenoble)

1959   *Isidore de Séville et la culture classique dans l'Espagne Wisigothique* (Paris)

1960   *Isidore de Séville: Traité de la Nature* (Bordeaux)

1960a   'Théorie et Pratique de Style chez Isidore de Séville', *VC* 14.2

1966   'Culture et Conversion chez les Wisigoths d'Espagne', *Settimane* 14

1970   El <<De Viris Illustribus>> de San Ildefonso: tradición y originalidad', *Anales Toledanos* 3

1978   'Pénitence publique et Conversion personelle: l'apport d'Isidore de Séville à l'évolution médiévale de la pénitence', *Revue de droit canonique* 28. Reprinted in *Fontaine* [1988]

1978a   *L'Art Préromain Hispanique* (La Pierre-qui-vire)

1980'   King Sisebut's *Vita Desiderii* and the Political Function of Visigothic Hagiography' in James [1980]

1981   'Passionaires, Légendiers, et Compilations hagiographiques dans le Haut Moyen Âge espagnol', in Pataglean & Riché [1981]

1986 (ed) *Grégoire le Grand* (Paris)

Gaiffier, A.

1933   'La Controversie au sujet de la patrie de S.Émilien de la Cogolla', *AB* 51

1935   'Les reliques de l'abbaye de San Millan de La Cogolla au

XIIIᵉ siècle', *AB* 53

1941   'La Vie et Miracles de S.Turibius' *AB* 59

1949   'Les Oraisons de l'Office de S.Hippolyte dans le <<Libellus Orationum>> de Vérone', *Revue d'ascétique et de mystique* 25

1965   'La légende de S.Eugene de Tolède: martyr aʻ Deuil près de Paris', *AB* 83

1966   'Un <<presbyter Floharius>> est-il l'auteur de la *Passio S.Eugenii Toletani*?', *AB* 84

1966a   'Hispania et Lusitania 3', *AB* 84

Gams, P. F.

1956   *Die Kirchengeschicte von Spanien* (Graz)

García Moreno, L.

1970   *Prosopografía del reino visigodo de Toledo* (Salamanca)

1974   'Aspectos económico-sociales de la Mérida visigoda', *REE* 30

1977/8   'La cristianización de la topografía de las ciudades de la península ibérica durante la antigüedad tardía', *AeA* 50/51

1989   *Historia de España visigoda* (Madrid)

1993   *Los judíos de la España antigua* (Madrid)

García Rodríguez, C.

1966   El Culto de Los Santos en la España romana y visigoda (Madrid)

Gardner, R.

1982   'Miracles of healing in Anglo-Celtic Northumbria as recorded by the Venerable Bede and his contemporaries: a reappraisal in the light of twentieth century experience', *British Medical Journal* 287

Garvin, J.

1946   *The "Vitas Sanctorum Emeritensium"* (Washington)

Gil, J.

1974   *Miscelanea Wisigothica* (Sevilla)

Gilson, J. P.

1905   *The Mozarabic Psalter = Henry Bradshaw Society, vol.30* (London)

Glick, T.

1979   *Islamic and Christian Spain in the Early Middle Ages* (Princeton)

Goffart, W.
1957   'Byzantine policy in the West under Tiberius II and Maurice: the pretenders Hermenegild and Gundovald', *Traditio* 13
Gómes Marques, M. & Crusafont i Sabater (ed.s)
1986   *Problems in Medieval Coinage in the Iberian Area 2* (Aviles)
Gómes Marques, M. & Metcalf, D. M. (ed.s)
1988   *Problems in Medieval Coinage in the Iberian Area 3* (Santarem)
Gómez Moreno, M.
1919   *Iglesias mozárabes: arte español de los siglos IX a XI* (Madrid)
González, S.
1950   *La penitencia en la primitiva iglesia española* (Salamanca)
González, V.
1967   'San Fructuoso en la restauración de Samos por el obispo Ermefredo', *Bracara Augusta* 21
González Echegaray, J.
1976/7 'La "nota de Cantabria" del Códice Emilianense 39 y las citas medievales de Cantabria', *Altamira* 40
1986   *Cantabria Antigua* (Santander)
González y Gómez Soto, J.
1903   *La catedral metropolitana de Santa Jerusalem, hoy iglesia parroquial de Santa Maria* (Mérida)
1988   *Problems in medieval Coinage in the Iberian Area 3* (Santarem)
Görres, F.
1873   'Des Westgothenkönigs Leovigild Stellung zum Katholicismus und zur arianischer Staatskirche', *Zeitschrift für historische Theologie* 43
1873a   'Ueber den Aufstand und das Martyrium Hermanegilds', *Zeitschrift für historische Theologie* 43
Greenslade, S. L.
1966   'Reflections on Early Christian Topography' in Cumings [1966]
Guillermo Antolín, P.
1901   'San Hermanegildo ante la crítica histórica', *La Ciudad de*

Dios 56

Heather, P. & Matthews, J.
1991   The Goths in the Fourth Century (Liverpool)

Heine, G.
1848   Bibliotheca Anecdotorum (Leipzig)

Hillgarth, J. N.
1970   'Historiography in Visigothic Spain', Settimane 17
1985   'Coins and Chronicles: Propaganda in Sixth-Century Spain
       and the Byzantine Background' in Visigothic Spain,
       Byzantium and the Irish (London). An earlier version
       without an appendix can be found in Historia 15 (1966)

Horden, P.
1982   'Saints and Doctors in the early Byzantine Empire: the case
       of Theodore of Sykeon', in Shiels [1982]

Holtz, L. & Fredouille, J.
1992   De Tertullien aux Mozarabes: mélanges offerts à Jacques
       Fontaine (Paris)

Hubert, J.
1959   'Evolution de la topographie et l'aspect des villes de Gaule
       du Ve au Xe siècle' in La Città nell'Alto Medioevo
       (Spoleto)

Iñíguez Almech, F.
1955   'Algunos problemas de las viejas iglesias españoles',
       Cuadernos de Trabajos de la Escuela española de historia
       y arqueología en Roma 7

James, E. (ed.)
1980   Visigothic Spain: new approaches (Oxford)

Jiménez Duque, B.
1977   La Espiritualidad romano-visigoda y muzárabe (Madrid)

Jornadas
1992   Jornadas sobre Santa Eulalia de Mérida = Extremadura
       Arqueológica III (Badajoz)

Katz, S.
1937   The Jews in the Visigothic and Frankish Kingdoms of Spain
       and Gaul (Massachusetts)

King, P.
1972   Law and Society in the Visigothic Kingdom (Cambridge)
1980   'King Chindasvind and the First Territorial Law-code of the

Visigothic Kingdom' in James [1980]
Kurth, G.
1891   'La Reine Brunehaut', *Revue des Questions Historiques* 50, reprinted in Kurth [1919]
1919   *Études Franques* (Paris and Brussels)
Larrañaga Elorza, K.
1993   'El pasaje del psuedo-fredegario sobre el dux francio de Cantabria y otros indicios de naturaleza textual y onomástica sobre presencia franca tardo-antigua al sur de Los Pirineos', *AeA* 66
Levi Provençal, E.
1938   *La Péninsule ibérique au moyen age* (Leiden)
Linage Conde, A.
1973   *Los Orígenes del Monacato benedictino en la península ibérica* (Léon)
Linehan, P.
1992   *The History and Historians of Medieval Spain* (Oxford)
Loomis, C. G.
1948   *White Magic: an introduction to the folklore of Christian legend* (Cambridge, Mass)
López Valcárcel, A.
1968   'San Fructuoso de Braga y la Diócesis Lucense', *Bracara Augusta* 22
Lozano Sebastián, F-J.
1974   'La disciplina penitencial en tiempo de San Isidoro de Sevilla' *Revista de Teología* 34
1980   *La Penitencia Canónica en la España romano-visigoda* (Burgos)
Lynch, C. H.
1938   *Saint Braulio: Bishop of Saragossa* (Washington)
McKenna, S.
1938   *Paganism and Pagan Survivals in Spain up to the Fall of the Visigothic Kingdom* (Washington)
McKitterick, R. (ed)
1990   *The uses of Literacy in Early Mediaeval Europe* (Cambridge)
McNally, R. E.
1959   'Isidoriana', *Theological Studies* 20

McNamara, J-A. & Wemple, S.
1976   'Marriage and Divorce in the Frankish Kingdom' in Stuard
        [1976]
Madoz, P.
1846-50 Diccionario geográfico-estadístico-histórico de España y
         sus posesiones de Ultramar (Madrid)
Maloy, R.
1971   'The Sermonary of St.Ildephonsus of Toledo', Classical
        Folia 25.1- 2
Manuel de Estal, J.
1961   'El culto de Felipe II a San Hermanegildo', La Ciudad de
        Dios 174
Markus, R. A.
1966   'Religious dissent in North Africa in the Byzantine Period',
        in Cuming [1966]
1990   The End of Ancient Christianity (Cambridge)
Martínez Díez, G.
1968   'Algunos aspectos de la penitencia en la iglesia visigodo-
        mozárabe', Misceláneas Comillas 49
Martínez Hernández, F.
1970   'Escuelas de formación del clero el la España visigoda' in
        La Patrología Toledano-visigoda (Madrid)
Mateos Cruz, P.
1992   'El culto a Santa Eulalia y su influencia en el urbanismo
        emeritense' in Jornadas [1992]
Maya Sánchez, A.
1992   Vitas Sanctorum Patrum Emeretensium (=Corpus
        Christianorum 116) (Turnholt)
1994   'De Leovigildo perseguidor y Masona mártir', Emerita 62.1
Mélida, J. R.
1925   Catálogo monumental de España: Badajoz (Madrid)
Menéndez Pelayo, R.
1880   Historia de los heterodoxos españoles (Madrid)
Menéndez Pidal, R.
1906   El Ultimo Godo (Madrid)
1940   Historia de España, t3 La España visigoda (volume editor,
        M.Torres López)
1963   Historia de España, t3* La España visigoda (volume

editor, M.Torres López)

1991   *Historia de España, t3*** *La España visigoda* (volume editor, MC Díaz y Díaz)

de Mergelina, C.

1940   'La iglesia bizantina de Aljezares (Caceres)', *AeA* 40

Messenger, R. E.

1946   'Mozarabic Hymns and Contemporary Culture in Spain', *Traditio* 4

Messina, N.

1983   *Psuedo-Eugenio de Toledo: speculum per un nobile visigoto* (Santiago de Compostela)

Metcalf, D. M.

1986   'Some geographical aspects of Early Monetary Circulation in the Iberian peninsula', in Gómes Marques and Crusafont i Sabater [1986]

1988   'For what purposes were Suevic and Visigothic tremisses used?' in Gómes Marques & Metcalf [1988]

Meyvaert, P.

1988   'The Enigma of Gregory the Great's *Dialogues*: a response to Francis Clark', *Journal of Ecclesiastical History* 39.3

Miles, G. C.

1952   *The Coinage of the Visigoths of Spain* (New York)

Millás Vallicrosa, J. M.

1945   'Epigrafía hebraicoespañola', *Sefarad* 5

Moreno de Vargas, B.

1633   *Historia de la Ciudad de Mérida* (Madrid, reprinted Badajoz 1974)

Moret, P.

1655   *Investigaciones historicas de las antigüedades del reyno de Navarra* (Pamplona)

Nelson, J. L.

1978   'Queens as Jezebels:Brunhild and Bathild in Merovingian History' in Baker [1978] and reprinted in Nelson [1986]

1986   *Politics and Ritual in Early Medieval Europe (London and Ronceverte)*

Nicol, D. M.

1985   'Instabilitas loci: the wanderlust of late Byzantine Monks' in Shiels [1985]

Nock, F. C.
1946   The "Vita Sancti Fructuosi" (Washington)
Oihenart, A.
1638   Notitia utriusque Basconia ab Arnald Oihenarto (Paris)
Orlandis, J.
1966   'El elemento germánico en la iglesia española del siglo
        VII', Anuario de Estudios Medievales 3
1971   Estudios sobre institutiones monásticas medievales
        (Pamplona)
1992   Semblanzas visigodas (Madrid)
Oroz Reta, J. & Marcos Casquero, M.
1992   San Isidoro de Sevilla: Etimologías (Edición bilingüe)
        (Madrid)
Patlagean, E. & Riché, P. (eds)
1981   Hagiographie, Cultures, et Sociétés, IV°-XII° Siècles (Paris)
Pérez Bustamante, R.
1974   'Datos para la historia de la Montaña en los siglos VII y
        VIII', Altamira 38
Pérez Sánchez, D.
1989   El Ejército en la sociedad visigoda (Salamanca)
Pérez de Urbel, J.
1926   'Origen de los himnos mozárabes', Bulletin Hispanique 28
1944   Los Monjes españoles en la Edad media (Madrid)
Petersen, J. M.
1984   The Dialogues of Gregory the Great in their late antique
        cultural background (Wetteren)
Petruccione, J.
1990   'The Portrait of St Eulalia of Mérida in Prudentius'
        Peristephanon 3', AB 108
Pinell, J.
1972   Liber orationum Psalmographus (Barcelona & Madrid)
Prado, G.
1928   'Mozarabic Melodies', Speculum 3
Puech, H-C.
1949   'Le Cerf et le Serpent - Note sur le Symbolisme de la
        mosaïque découverte au bapistère de l'Henchir Messaouda',
        Cahiers archéologiques: fin de l'antiquité et Moyen Age 4

Puertas Tricas, R.

1975   *Iglesias hispánicas (siglos IV al VII): testimonios literarios*
        (Madrid)

Rabello, A. M.

1976   *A Tribute to Jean Juster - The Legal Condition of the Jews
        under the Visigoths* (no provenence, Jerusalem?)

Raby, F.

1927   *A History of Latin Christian Poetry* (Oxford)

Recio Veganzones, A.

1992   'La Mártir Eulalia de Mérida en Calendarios y
        Martirologios en la Devoción Popular y en su Iconografía
        (Siglos IV-VII)' in *Jornadas* [1992]

Riché, P.

1962   *Éducation et Culture dans l'Occident Barbare* (Paris)

Riesco Terrero, L.

1975   *Epistolario de San Braulio* (Sevilla)

Rivera Recio, J. F.

1948   '¿Cisma episcopal en la Iglesia toledanovisigoda?',
        Hispania Sacra 1

1955   'Encumbramiento de la sede toledana durante la
        dominación visigótica', *Hispania Sacra* 8

1963   *San Eugenio de Toledo y su culto* (Toledo)

1964   'Auténtica personalidad de San Eugenio 1 de Toledo',
        Anthologica annua 12

Robles, L.

1963   'Teología del episcopado en San Isidoro: problemas que
        plantea', *Teologia espiritual* 7

Rochel, R.

1902   'Sevilla: teatro de martirio de san Hermanegildo', *Razon y
        Fé* 4

1903   '¿Fue San Hermanegildo rebelde?', *Razón y Fe* 7

Rojo, C. & Prado, G.

1929   *El canto mozárabe* (Barcelona)

Roth, C.

1948   'The Judaeo-Latin Inscription of Merida', *Sefarad* 8

Rouche, M.

1986   'Brunehaut romaine ou wisigothe' in *Semana* [1986]

Rush, A. C.
1941   *Death and Burial in Christian Antiquity = Studies in Christian Antiquity* (ed. J Quasten) 1 (Washington)

Salisbury, J. E.
1985   *Iberian Popular Religion 600 BC to 700 AD* (New York & Toronto)

Sanabria Escudero, M.
1964   'La medicina emeritense en las épocas romana y visigoda', *REE* 20

Semana
1986   *Semana internacional de estudios visigoticos* 3 = *Los Visigodos, Cristianismo y Antigüedad* (Murcia)

Schlunk, H.
1945   'Esculturas visigodas de Ségobriga (Cabeza de Griego)', *AeA* 18
1945a   'Relaciones entre la peninsula ibérica y Bizancio durante le época visigoda', *AeA* 19

Serrano, L.
1930   Cartulario de San Millán de la Cogolla (Madrid)

Shaw, R. D.
1906   'The Fall of Visigothic Power in Spain', *English Historical Review* 21

Shiels, W. J. (ed)
1982   *The Church and Healing* (Oxford)
1985   *Monks, Hermits, and the Ascetic Tradition* (Padstow)

Straw, C.
1989   Review of Clark [1989], *Speculum* 64.2

Stuard, S. M.
1976   *Women in Medieval Society* (Pennsylvannia)

Thompson, E. A.
1957   'Two Notes on St Fructuosus of Braga', *Hermathena* 90
1969   *The Goths in Spain* (Oxford)

Ubieto Arteta, A.
1976   *Cartulario de San Millán de la Cogolla (759-1076)* (Valencia)

Uría Maqua, I.
1992   *Gonzalo de Berceo: obra completa* (Madrid)

Valázquez Soriano, I.
   1989   *Las Pizarras Visigodas* (Murcia)
Van Uytfanghe, M.
   1993   'L'Hagiographie: un <<genre>> chrétien ou antique tardif?',
          AB 111
Vázquez de Parga, L.
   1943   Vita S. Emiliani:edición crítica (Madrid)
Vega, A. C.
   1961   'Cuestiones críticas de las biografías isidorianas' in *Díaz y
          Díaz* [1961]
   1969   'De Patrología espanola en torno a la herencia literaria de
          Juan de Biclar', *BRAH* 164
   1969a 'De Patrología española: San Ildefonso de Toledo', *BRAH*
          165
Vives, J.
   1941   'Santoral visigodo en calendarios e inscripciones', *Analecta
          Sacra Tarraconensia* 14
   1946   *Oracional Visigótico* (Barcelona)
de Vogüé, A.
   1985   'La *Regula Cassiani*. Sa destination et ses rapports avec
          le monachisme fructuosien' , *Revue Bénédictine* 95
Vollmer, F.
   1905   *Monumenta   Germaniae   Historica: auctorum
          antiquissimorum, tomus XIV - Merobaudes, Dracontius,
          Eugenius Toletanus (Berlin)*
Walsh, J. K.
   1992   *Relic and Literature: St Turibius of Astorga and his Arca
          Sancta* (St Albans)
Ward, B.
   1986   *The Wisdom of the Desert Fathers* (Oxford)
Wolf, K. B.
   1990   *Conquerors and Chronicles of Early Medieval Spain*
          (Liverpool)

INDEX

Index of people and places in the text

MAP   167

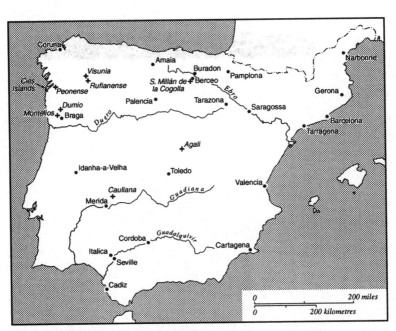

Map of Spain showing places mentioned in the text